# Beginning Android C++
# Game Development

Bruce Sutherland

**Beginning Android C++ Game Development**

ISBN-13 (pbk): 978-1-4302-5830-8

ISBN-13 (electronic): 978-1-4302-5831-5

President and Publisher: Paul Manning
Lead Editor: Steve Anglin
Developmental Editor: Matthew Moodie
Technical Reviewer: Onur Cinar
Editorial Board: Steve Anglin, Mark Beckner, Ewan Buckingham, Gary Cornell, Louise Corrigan, Morgan Ertel,
     Jonathan Gennick, Jonathan Hassell, Robert Hutchinson, Michelle Lowman, James Markham,
     Matthew Moodie, Jeff Olson, Jeffrey Pepper, Douglas Pundick, Ben Renow-Clarke, Dominic Shakeshaft,
     Gwenan Spearing, Matt Wade, Tom Welsh
Coordinating Editor: Jill Balzano
Copy Editor: Brendan Frost
Compositor: SPi Global
Indexer: SPi Global
Artist: SPi Global
Cover Designer: Anna Ishchenko

Distributed to the book trade worldwide by Springer Science+Business Media New York, 233 Spring Street, 6th Floor, New York, NY 10013. Phone 1-800-SPRINGER, fax (201) 348-4505, e-mail orders-ny@springer-sbm.com, or visit www.springeronline.com. Apress Media, LLC is a California LLC and the sole member (owner) is Springer Science + Business Media Finance Inc (SSBM Finance Inc). SSBM Finance Inc is a Delaware corporation.

For information on translations, please e-mail rights@apress.com, or visit www.apress.com.

Apress and friends of ED books may be purchased in bulk for academic, corporate, or promotional use. eBook versions and licenses are also available for most titles. For more information, reference our Special Bulk Sales–eBook Licensing web page at www.apress.com/bulk-sales.

Any source code or other supplementary materials referenced by the author in this text is available to readers at www.apress.com. For detailed information about how to locate your book's source code, go to www.apress.com/source-code/.

# Contents at a Glance

# Contents

# About the Author

**Bruce Sutherland** is a video game developer from Dundee, Scotland. He graduated from the University of Abertay, Dundee's Computer Games Technology degree program in 2005. He began work at 4J Studios the same year where he worked on several titles including *The Elder Scrolls IV: Oblivion* for the PS3. After leaving Dundee in 2008, he moved to Melbourne and began work at Visceral Games, where he was part of the development team on *Dead Space*, *The Godfather II*, and *Dead Space 3*. Most recently, Bruce has been working on the Android version of *Real Racing* 3 for Firemonkey Studios.

# About the Technical Reviewer

**Onur Cinar** is the author of *Android Apps* with Eclipse, and *Pro Android C++* with the NDK books from Apress. He has over 17 years of experience in design, development, and management of large-scale complex software projects, primarily in mobile and telecommunication space. His expertise spans VoIP, video communication, mobile applications, grid computing, and networking technologies on diverse platforms. He has been actively working with the Android platform since its beginning. He has a B.S. degree in Computer Science from Drexel University in Philadelphia, PA. He is currently working at the Skype division of Microsoft as the Principal Development Manager for the Skype client on Android platform.

# Acknowledgments

I'd like to thank the team at Apress for their help and support during the process of writing this book. To Steve Anglin for being easy to work with during the initial pitch process. To Matthew Moodie, Dhaneesh Kumar, Onur Cinar, and the editing team at Apress for providing valuable feedback on my writing; as a new author it was greatly appreciated.

A special thanks to Jill Balzano at Apress. Jill has had to help me through the entire process of writing the book, from forgetting passwords to reminding me of when chapters were due to be finished. Thank you Jill.

I'd also like to thank my wife, Claire. Claire has been exceptionally supportive as I invested a lot of time into both working and writing. This book would not have been possible without that support.

# Introduction

Over the last few years, game development has become more open to bedroom programmers. In the 1980s and early 1990s, this was a common route into game development. In the late 1990s and early 2000s, game development budgets, schedules, and technical requirements meant that it was very uncommon to find game programmers creating games in their own right.

This all changed with the release of mobile phones and more recently tablets with 3D graphics capabilities which surpass consoles such as the Playstation 2 and Sega Dreamcast.

This book will introduce the reader to the world of game development on the Android platform. The reader will learn how to plan, begin, and execute a game development project from beginning to end.

I hope you enjoy it.

# Chapter 1

# An Introduction to Game Development

Video games have become an important part of our culture in a relatively short period of time. The industry is also developing into a major pillar of many modern economies, with game development tax schemes being introduced into many developed countries. These are coinciding with a period of time where it has never been easier to release a game into the commercial market. For the last two decades, game development teams have required financial backing and a level of expertise to pass stringent tests by platform holders to be allowed access to their development hardware. Today, anyone with a mobile phone or a tablet and a computer, even a laptop, can build a game and have it for sale with a minimum of time and financial backing. This does not mean that every game is successful: it is still essential to have a good understanding of the technical aspects involved in making games and the considerations involved in designing games which people will want to play. Sometimes the best way to develop this knowledge is to begin at the very beginning, so we'll look at some video game history.

## A Brief History of Video Games

One of the first video games is widely acknowledged to be *Spacewar!*. *Spacewar!* was created by Stephen Russell at MIT and released in 1962 as a demonstration of the power of the recently released PDP-1 computer system. Games such as *Spacewar!*, however, did not reach a mass critical appeal.

The era of commercially successful video games arguably began when a student of Russell's at Stanford, Nolan Bushnell, along with his partner Ted Dabney, formed Atari in 1972. Atari was responsible for releasing massively popular and commercially successful games such as *Pong*, *Asteroids*, and *Breakout*. Atari would remain one of the biggest players in the video game business until the entry of two major competitors.

Nintendo and Sega both entered the video game business in 1983 with the Nintendo Entertainment System and Sega SG-1000 (and later the Master System). These companies would become the major players in the video game business through to the late nineties and would spawn the creation of massive gaming franchises such as *Mario*, *Legend of Zelda*, *Sonic the Hedgehog*, and *Sega Rally*.

Almost as importantly, Nintendo and Sega would popularize the concept of handheld gaming. Through their platforms such as the Game Boy, Game Gear through to the Nintendo 3DS, and current competition from Sony's Playstation Vita, Nintendo and Sega proved that there was an appetite for people to play games on the move.

This branch of gaming has been converging with the mobile phone platforms ever since phones begun to have processors and graphics capabilities to run programs which we can recognize as games. Nokia handsets in the late nineties were released with a version of the game *Snake*, which was very popular. Qualcomm released the BREW (Binary Runtime Environment for Wireless) platform in 2001. Nokia tried to develop a dedicated mobile phone–based gaming platform called NGage and released this in 2003. Both of these platforms showed what a mobile phone platform could eventually be capable of.

The first breakout success in mobile phone gaming came from Apple in 2008, when they released their App Store onto the iPhone 3GS in 2008. This was followed shortly after by Google's Android Market (currently Google Play), which launched in September 2008. These stores democratized console game development by, for the first time, allowing any company or individual to register as a developer and release games for sale directly to the public. Video game consoles up to this point required a developer to be registered and pay considerable sums to gain access to development versions of the hardware which they were targeting. Now anyone could make apps and games with their home computer and their own mobile phone.

The App Store and Google Play have gone from strength to strength as the hardware in mobile phones has improved rapidly. In the last four years, the mobile platforms have moved from single-core processors with no hardware floating point support to multi-core setups, which are arguably as capable as low-end desktop CPUs. Similarly, the GPUs available have gone from fixed-pipeline OpenGL ES 1.1–capable parts to modern chips with at least OpenGL ES 2.0 support as well as some of the most modern GPUs supporting version 3.0.

Some of those terms still sound daunting for a complete newcomer to the game development scene, and this can create a barrier to entry. Many people can be put off at this point, so it's important to dispel these feelings and take a look at who can and should make games.

# Who Makes Games?

As I touched on in the previous section, with the modern app platforms on mobile phones, the traditional model of well-established companies signing publishing deals with massive game publishing houses is no longer the most common method for releasing video games.

There are currently all manner of developers on these mobile platforms. Some of the biggest remain the traditional companies such as Electronic Arts, who make very popular and successful games. However, there is a growing community of independent developers who are creating meaningful game experiences which are also hitting some very large numbers of downloads and creating substantial revenues. A great example of this is *Temple Run*. *Temple Run* is developed by Imangi Studios, a husband-and-wife team who added an extra member to create the art for their game.

I think Jesse Schell put it best in his book, *The Art of Game Design*, when discussing who can be a games designer. In his very first chapter he addresses how to become a game designer by asking the question:

> *"How do you become a game designer?"*

His response is:

> *"Design games. Start now! Don't wait! Don't even finish this conversation!*
> *Just start designing! Go! Now!"*

By the time you finish this book, you'll have made a game from scratch and will be ready to move on to developing your own games from your own designs.

It's also worth noting that games don't always have to be video games. Many of the most popular games throughout history have been board games, and examples such as chess and Monopoly spring instantly to mind. So what is it that makes video games different?

# The Difference between Computer Games and Board Games

Traditional games have been around for thousands of years, yet there is an appeal to modern video games which sets them apart from those games. Traditional games have a formal structure. They usually have a set of rules, an element of randomness, a conflicting goal for players to achieve, and a win condition.

An example would be Monopoly. The goal of the game for each player is to be the last with money remaining. You can reduce the amount of money others have by developing property squares which you own, and the rules of the game dictate how and when you can carry out this development. There is an element of randomness added to the game by way of having dice to roll, which determine which property squares your piece lands on.

Despite the endless variations which can occur when playing a game such as Monopoly, the rules and actions are still fairly limited in scope. These games still rely on the players to remember how to play the game for it to be successful. Video games have an advantage in the sense that the computer can simulate a game without the need for the player to remember the state of the game.

Video games can therefore be much more complicated systems than traditional games. Today's console and PC games are perfect examples of this complexity. Games such as Microsoft's *Halo 4* have an enormous set of rules which are all executed in real time. Each weapon has different characteristics; there are vehicles and enemies which each have a unique tuning in their AI to represent differing personalities. To many on the surface, it might seem much like many other first-person shooter games, but the interplay among the different game rules is what separates video games from traditional games and also separates the good games from the great ones. Great games almost seamlessly blend complicated rules, AI, and player interaction into a believable world and story.

Now that we've looked at the differences between board games and console games, we'll take a look at what makes games designed for mobile devices different from games designed for a home console.

# Comparing Mobile Phones to Game Consoles

This may come as a surprise, but there is actually very little difference between current Android mobile phones and the traditional game platforms such as the Microsoft Xbox 360, the Sony Playstation 3, and Nintendo's Wii U.

Each system has its own trade-offs and potentially unique controller interfaces, but under the surface each system conforms to a few set standards.

- They all have a CPU which executes the game code.
- Each has a GPU which renders the game geometry.
- Each has a display of varying resolution and aspect ratio.
- They all output sound.
- They all take user input.

The major differentiating factor from a user's perspective is the aspect of input. Traditionally, PC games have been played with a keyboard and mouse, console games with a controller, and modern mobile games with a touch screen. This requires that the games be designed differently to best suit the input device of the system being targeted.

From a development perspective, mobile phones are currently weaker than the consoles and much weaker than PCs. Despite supporting modern features such as vertex and fragment shaders, the number of vertices which can be processed and the number of pixels which can be drawn is limited on a phone compared to a PC or console. There are also stricter limits to the memory bandwidth between the phone's memory and the GPU, making it important to send only relevant information which the GPU can use to render the current frame.

These restrictions can impact a game at the lowest level of its implementation, and game programmers have become adept at designing their technology to accommodate these differences. Many of the challenges will be common to all mobile games, and sharing the advances made from one project will only help to benefit games which follow. To that end, game engines have become a fundamental part of developing games on console and ever more increasingly on mobile platforms also.

# An Overview of Game Engines

In the 1980s, it was not uncommon for every individual game to be written from scratch, with very little code reuse between projects. This began to change with the emergence of game engines in the early to mid-1990s. With the advent of 3D accelerators, the complexity of game code was increasing rapidly. It was quickly becoming necessary to understand a large number of topics related to game development, such as audio, physics, AI, and graphics programming. As the complexity increased, so did the sizes of teams necessary to create games and also the money required. It wasn't long before there was a dual track developing within game development. There were technical teams writing the systems which games run upon and there were the game programming teams developing the games themselves.

From this was born the concept of a game engine. The low-level systems were written in an abstract manner so that games could be developed over the top. A key player in the engine market at this time was Id Software, which licensed its Id Tech engines to other developers. A notable franchise which was born on Id's game engines was *Half-Life*, which was created using the *Quake* engine. Id's own *Quake 3*, released in 1999, was their largest release at the time and was developed on their Id Tech 3 engine. This engine was also licensed, and the most notable example was the use of the engine by Infinity Ward to create *Call of Duty*.

Since then, Unreal has become a massively successful engine licensed by many game teams from the United States, Europe, and Japan to create some of the largest console games of the current generation, and the Unity engine is currently used in a wide range of titles on both Android and iOS.

From an individual perspective, it's important to realize the core concept of what makes a game engine an attractive prospect, whether it's through licensing another developer's technology or writing your own code in an engine-like manner. Using this technique allows you to reuse large sections of code between projects. This reduces the financial cost of developing titles as you move forward and increases your productivity by allowing you to spend more and more time on game features and less time on the engine. In reality, it's never quite that simple, but it is important to try to separate engine code from game logic code as much and as often as possible. This is something which we will be trying to achieve as we move through this book: from the beginning to the end, we'll be sure to look at the separation of reusable engine code and game logic which is specific to an individual app.

# Summary

That concludes a whirlwind introduction to video game development, from its roots all the way through to the current state of modern development. Each of these topics could be covered in depth in volumes of their own, but the grounding we have established here should stand us in good stead for the rest of this book.

We're going to walk through the development of a game, from setting up a game project in Eclipse, designing a small game, and implementing a game engine, all the way through to publishing our first title in Google Play.

Let's get started.

# Chapter 2

# An Introduction to the Android Game Development Ecosystem

After our brief introduction to the history of video games, we'll look at taking our first steps into defining their future. The Android platform provides us with easier access to cross-platform development tools and 3D graphics hardware than has ever been available before. This makes it an ideal candidate platform for an introduction to game development. All you need is a computer, so let's get started.

## Java and the Dalvik Virtual Machine

The Java programming language was released in 1995 by Sun Microsystems and is currently maintained by Oracle. The syntax for the language was based on C and was therefore familiar to many programmers who were already well practiced in C and C++. The major differences between C++ and Java are that Java is a managed language and the code is executed on the Java Virtual Machine.

Java was the only language option available for app developers when Android was launched. The Android developers did not use the Java Virtual Machine and wrote their own implementation, which they named Dalvik. Dalvik originally did not have many of the features which were associated with other mature Java Virtual Machines. One particularly notable omission was just-in-time (JIT) compilation. As Java is a managed language which runs in a virtual machine, the code is not compiled directly into native CPU instructions but rather into bytecode which can be consumed by the virtual machine. With JIT, the virtual machine can compile blocks of bytecode into machine code ahead of it being needed by the program and therefore can provide a speed boost to the running program. These compiled units can also be cached for future speed improvements. Android did not have this feature until version 2.2.

Many of the low-level APIs relevant to game programming are also still implemented in C on the Android platform, such as Open GL. Java on Android supports these APIs by using the Java Native Interface (JNI). The JNI provides a mechanism to support the passing of parameters to function calls of native libraries from the Java Virtual Machine and also for the native libraries to return values to the Java Virtual Machine.

This creates suboptimal conditions for game developers. The managed nature of the Java language means that the developer is not responsible for the game's memory management during its lifetime. While there are many arguments for why this may be a good thing for normal apps, games which require execution in real time cannot afford to hand control of memory allocation and garbage collection exclusively to an external system, which also adds hidden costs to calling certain functions in Java.

A good example of a hidden cost is found when using iterators on collections. As with many other Java objects, iterators are immutable. This means that once you have an iterator, it cannot be changed. When moving from the current iterator to the next position in a collection, Java allocates a new iterator and returns it in the new position to the caller while marking the old iterator for deletion. Eventually, Dalvik will call the garbage collector to free all of the orphaned iterators, and this will cause a noticeable drop in framerate and even cause your game to stall. This leads us to C++ and the NDK.

# C++ and the NDK

Google released the Android Native Development Kit (NDK) to provide developers with another option for developing their apps on Android. The first version was released for Android 1.5 but did not contain essential support for SDKs such as OpenGL ES. The Revision 5 release of the NDK is the version which I would consider to be the first viable version of the NDK for game programming. This revision added the ability to support `NativeActivity` and the native app glue library, which allows developers to write Android apps entirely in C++ without any need for Java. This is possible because this revision of the NDK also added support for audio through OpenGL ES, native audio support, native access to the system's sensors such as the accelerometers and gyroscope, and also native access to files stores within the app APK package.

There are a number of benefits to being able to write Android apps in C++. Existing developers can add support for the platform to their existing C++ codebases without requiring the expense of maintaining Java code as well as C++ code for the system, and new developers can begin writing apps for Android, which can then be ported to other platforms or developed for multiple platforms simultaneously.

Developing games in C++ doesn't come without challenges. As C++ is compiled to native code and Android supports multiple CPU instruction sets, it becomes important to ensure that the code written compiles and executes without error and as expected on all of these. Android to date supports the following:

- ARM
- ARM v7a
- MIPS
- x86

There are devices on the market which support each of these instruction sets. As Java compiles to bytecode and runs on a virtual machine, this is transparent to the Java developer. The NDK toolset at the time of writing is also not as mature as the Java toolset, and the integration with the Eclipse IDE is a little more complicated and troublesome, especially with regard to code completion, building, and debugging functionality.

Despite the troubles and drawbacks, the performance benefits to developing on Android in C++ still outweigh the downsides to working with the NDK toolsets, and hopefully the maturity and functionality of these tools will only improve over time. Now that you can see the advantages of C++ over Java for game development, it's important to take a look at some of the issues which are common to both languages in the Android ecosystem. These sets of problems are not entirely new and have been encountered, tackled, and solved for many years in PC development in both the OpenGL and DirectX space; however, these considerations are new to many mobile phone developers. These problems have been grouped together, and the term "fragmentation" has been coined to encompass them all.

# Fragmentation and the Android Ecosystem

There are many opinions and varying definitions of what fragmentation on the Android platform means to different people. I will look at the problem purely from a game development perspective.

## Android Versions

The first issue from a development perspective is to choose a version of Android which we would like to target as the minimum. As I discussed in the previous section, many essential features of the NDK were added only with Revision 5. NDK r5 supports Android API level 9 and, at the time of writing, the Android Developers Dashboard shows that 86.6% of Android devices which accessed Google Play in the proceeding 14 days supported this version; 13.4% may be a considerable chunk of the market which you may not be willing to forego from your potential customer base. For ease of development, I have decided that it is acceptable to not support this ever-decreasing percentage of Android versions. So, to be clear, this book will target Android API level 9.

## Screen Resolution and Aspect Ratio

The next often discussed aspect of fragmentation is screen resolution and aspect ratio. This is one aspect of the argument which I have never fully understood. Games have been written for the last couple of decades to support multiple resolutions and aspect ratios. This is a common requirement on PC, Xbox 360, and PS3 as well as for developers who previously developed cross-platform titles. It is less convenient that the early versions of iOS devices supported the same resolutions or a multiple of those and maintained the same aspect ratio, but that is also no longer the case. We will be developing our games with multiple screen resolutions and aspect ratios in mind.

## Input Device Support

Another area of fragmentation is with input device support. Some Android devices support single touch, some varying levels of multi-touch. Some have accurate sensors; some don't have those sensors at all. The best approach is to design the game you would like to make which supports an acceptable number of devices. If your design doesn't require multi-touch support, you will reach a wider audience, but if the game would be noticeably better with that support it may not be worth diminishing the quality of your work and damaging the sales by supporting devices which don't allow for the best experience. Another option is to offer multiple control schemes if and where possible and choosing which to use at runtime.

## GPUs

The last major area of fragmentation is with GPUs. There are four major players in the Android GPU space, and more advanced graphics programming techniques will run into issues where some are not optimal for certain GPUs or not supported at all. Each has different support for texture compression formats, for instance, but mostly these issues are outside the scope of this book.

## HelloDroid – Our First Android Game

After digesting all of the information so far on games, development, and the Android platform, now would be a great time to look at a small game example. The game is a basic *Breakout* clone. You can control the paddle using the left and right arrows on the screen. Figure 2-1 is a screenshot from the game running on a Galaxy Nexus.

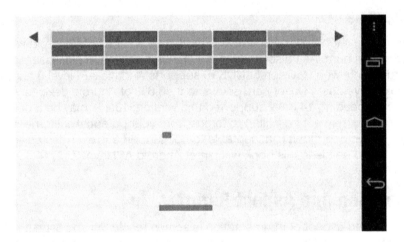

*Figure 2-1. HelloDroid, a Breakout clone*

Parts of the code are quite complex and will be the subject of discussion in later chapters; some of this code involves setting up Open GL, polling for Android system events, and handling user input. *Breakout* is a great first attempt at writing our own game, as it incorporates several key concepts from larger games.

- First, there is a player entity which is controlled by the user, the paddle.
- There is a basic UI in the buttons to control the paddle.
- There are basic nonplayer entities in the ball and blocks, which also cause us to have to consider real-time collision detection and response.

Despite the relatively primitive graphics and simple gameplay mechanics, it's a good exercise in creating a fully formed game experience, and it really wasn't all that long ago when games weren't much more than what we're about to create in the next few sections.

To achieve our goals, you're going to run through the steps required to organize, write, and build the game for Android. You'll organize your game into a project using Eclipse, write your code using the NDK, and build your game using the NDK build process.

## Creating a New Eclipse Project

Eclipse is the IDE of choice for Android development. The Android team at Google provides a version of Eclipse with most of the Android tools bundled for all platforms. The latest information on how to obtain this IDE can be obtained from `http://developer.android.com/sdk/index.html`.

The NDK is a separate download which is updated frequently. For the best installation instructions, please visit `http://developer.android.com/tools/sdk/ndk/index.html`.

Once you have these downloaded, installed, and configured for your chosen platform, it's time to begin your first Android game. The first step in this process is to create a new project.

1.  Ensure that the Eclipse IDE is aware of the location of the NDK on your computer by setting the option in Preferences. You can find the option by opening Window ➤ Preferences, then navigating to Android ➤ NDK and setting the appropriate path into NDK Location.

2.  Start the New Project wizard (see Figure 2-2) from the File ➤ New ➤ Project menu.

*Figure 2-2.* The New Project Dialog

3.  From here, select the **Android Application Project** and click **Next**. The New
    Android Application box as shown in Figure 2-3 should be shown.

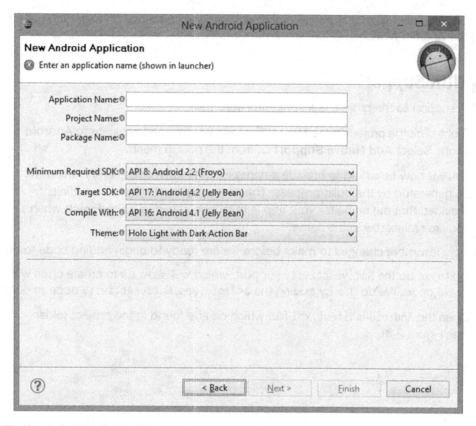

*Figure 2-3. The New Android Application Dialog*

4.  On the New Android Application Dialog, enter the application name for your app; I have chosen HelloDroid. The project name will be automatically filled out as you enter the application name and is the name used by Eclipse to identify the project in the Project Explorer.

5.  The package name is a unique identifier to be used by the Android ecosystem. It is usually broken up into separate sections which are delimited by a period. The first section is usually com and identifies the developer of the app as a company. The next entry is usually a derivative of a company name, a personal name, or a project name. For my example, I have used beginndkgamecode. The last entry is generally the name of the project. My final package name was com.beginndkgamecode.hellodroid.

6.  Changing the **Minimum Required SDK** to **API 9: Android 2.3 (Gingerbread)** is the other change to be made to these options.

7.  Once those options are set, click **Next**.

8.  On the next screen, uncheck **Create custom launcher icon** and **Create activity**. If you are happy with the path for the project, click **Finish**.

Your project should now exist in the Project Explorer and we can move on to setting the project up to support the Android NDK.

## Adding NDK Support

Adding NDK support to the project is a straightforward task.

1. Right-click the project in the Project Explorer window and navigate to **Android Tools**. Select **Add Native Support ...** from the popup menu.

2. You will now be asked to provide a name for the native code library which will be generated by the build process. The name provided should be sufficient provided that the name for your app is reasonably unique. Click **Finish** when you are satisfied with the name.

We now have a few more changes to make before we are ready to begin adding code to our project.

First we need to set up the `NativeActivity` support, which will allow us to create apps without adding any Java code. We do this by adding the `android.app.NativeActivity` node to our manifest.

1. Open the `AndroidManifest.xml` file, which can be found in the project folder (see Figure 2-4).

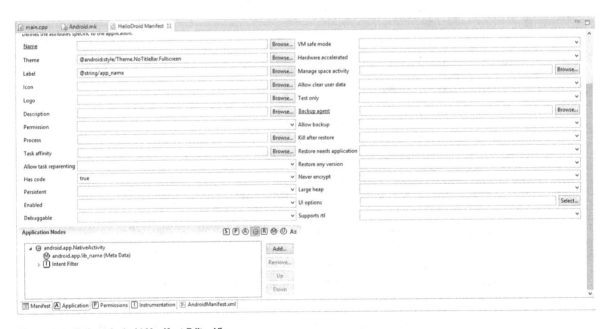

*Figure 2-4.  Eclipse Android Manifest Editor View*

2.   The options we need to access can be found on the **Application** tab, so click that now (see the bottom of Figure 2-4).

3.   Click **Browse** beside the **Theme** selection box and select **Theme.NoTitleBar.Fullscreen** from the options provided. This option informs our app to run in full screen and also hides the Android status bar.

4.   Set **HasCode** to true. This is necessary to ensure that our app builds properly.

5.   Click the **Add** button, which can be found beside the **Application Nodes** window. Select **Activity** and click **OK**.

6.   Click **Browse** beside the **Name** entry in the **Attributes for Activity** section. Untick **Display classes from sources of project '<project name>' only** and type **NativeActivity** into the filter box. Select the NativeActivity class and click **OK**.

7.   For **label**, enter @string/app_name.

8.   Select **landscape** for the **screen orientation** to ensure that our game will always run in landscape mode.

9.   Click the **NativeActivity** node in the **Application Nodes** window and click **Add** once more. Enter the **Name** as android.app.lib_name and the **Value** as the LOCAL_MODULE name, which can be found in the Android.mk file in the project's jni folder.

10.  Select the **NativeActivity** node in the **Application Nodes** window (this is the last time, phew!) and **Add** an **Intent Filter**. **Add** an **Action** and a **Category** to the **Intent Filter** by selecting it and using the **Add** menu.

11.  Set the name of the **Action** to android.intent.action.MAIN and the name of the **Category** to android.intent.category.LAUNCHER.

Your project setup is now complete. We can now move on to the NDK build process.

# A Look at the NDK Build System

The NDK provides a build process called ndk-build. This process reads Android-specific makefiles which contain all the information needed to build a native library.

> **Note**   The Android NDK contains a build system which is based on Make. Make is a popular program-building utility, especially within Linux-based operating systems, which can specify the parameters for building programs in files known as makefiles. The Android NDK has a modified version of these files which we will look at during various chapters in this book.

The default Android.mk file, which can be found in the jni folder, will contain the following text:

```
LOCAL_PATH := $(call my-dir)

include $(CLEAR_VARS)

LOCAL_MODULE    := hellodroid
LOCAL_SRC_FILES := hellodroid.cpp

include $(BUILD_SHARED_LIBRARY)
```

This basic makefile carries out only a few steps.

1. It sets the local build path for the makefile which allows it to find other files relative to its own path.

2. It then calls an external command which clears the previously set build variables.

3. It defines the name of the library to be built in the LOCAL_MODULE variable and the source files to be compiled in the LOCAL_SRC_FILES variable.

4. To wrap the file up, it calls the command which causes the build system to execute the build process and compiles and then links the code.

## Modifying the Build File

We need to modify this file to add the external libraries necessary for building games using the NDK, which requires these features. More information on the available libraries can be found in the STABLE-APIS.html file included in the docs folder in the NDK.

First, we define the external libraries which our app will need to load by using LOCAL_LDLIBS.

```
LOCAL_LDLIBS := -llog -landroid -lEGL -lGLESv2
```

This line tells the build system that we would like our app to be able to use Android's existing log, android, EGL, and GLESv2 (Open GL ES 2.0) libraries. As these are common to many apps and the Android OS itself, they are linked in dynamically.

We will also require a static NDK library to be linked in with our app. This static library is called android_native_app_glue and provides the functionality which we require to enable us to write our app in C++ without using any Java. We include this as a static library by using the following line:

```
LOCAL_STATIC_LIBRARIES := android_native_app_glue
```

We have one last line to add to our makefile. This line tells the build system to import the static library into our app.

```
$(call import-module, android/native_app_glue)
```

The final Android.mk file will look like this:

```
LOCAL_PATH := $(call my-dir)

include $(CLEAR_VARS)

LOCAL_MODULE    := hellodroid
LOCAL_SRC_FILES := hellodroid.cpp
LOCAL_LDLIBS := -llog -landroid -lEGL -lGLESv2
LOCAL_STATIC_LIBRARIES := android_native_app_glue

include $(BUILD_SHARED_LIBRARY)

$(call import-module, android/native_app_glue)
```

## Adding Application-Level Build Options

There are also application-level build options which we need to have set. These are added to a file named Application.mk. This file is not created as part of the default project setup in Eclipse, so you will have to create this one yourself. You can right-click the jni folder and select **New ➤ File** from the menu. Name the new file Application.mk and enter the following line:

```
APP_PLATFORM := android-9
```

This line informs the NDK that we are using API level 9 of its libraries. That's all we need for now, but we'll be adding more to these files further down the track.

At this point, you should be able to right-click the project name and select **Build Project**. This should output text in the output console and hopefully be error free. If you do encounter any errors at this point, try to tackle the first error in the list and then retry. Many errors cause cascading effects, and often fixing the first then fixes all subsequent errors. If the errors are proving to be stubborn, you should go back over everything from the beginning and try to look for differences between the code, makefiles and projects which you have, and the sample provided for this chapter. Once you find differences which fix the errors in question, try to have a play around with the configuration or code to become familiar with the errors, how to spot them, and, importantly, how to fix them. Game developers are not infallible, and learning how to decipher errors created by our tools, such as the compiler, is an important skill to develop and one you will likely need to use often.

## Enabling Debugging

Setting up the build for debugging support is the next task which we must complete.

1.  Right-click the project, mouse over **Build Configurations**, and select **Manage**.

2.  Select **New** in the window which appears. Name the new configuration **Debug** and copy the settings from **Default**; click **OK**. Click **OK** again in the **Manage Configurations** window.

3. Right-click the project once more and select **Properties**. Navigate to the **C/C++ Build** menu and switch to the Debug configuration. Untick **Use default build command** and change the entered line to the following:

```
ndk-build NDK_DEBUG=1
```

> **Note**   If you have a multi-core machine and would like to utilize the extra processors in your system, you can also add the option -jX, where X is the number of jobs to be created. I use the option -j8 on my quad-core system with Hyper-Threading support.

Now you can switch between a debuggable and an optimized build via the **Build Configurations ➤ Set Active** menu.

Our project setup is complete and ready to go; now we can add some code to make a game.

# Running the Game

The source code for the game can be found in the file Chapter2.cpp included with this book or available from the book's website at http://www.apress.com/9781430258308.

You can copy the contents of this file directly into the cpp file in your project, and build and run the game on your device.

The core game functionality lives in the following function:

```
static void enigine_update_frame(struct engine* engine)
{
        if (engine->touchIsDown)
        {
                if (engine->touchX < 0.15f && engine->touchY < 0.2f)
                {
                        engine->playerX -= 0.015f;
                        if (engine->playerX < PADDLE_LEFT_BOUND)
                        {
                                engine->playerX = PADDLE_LEFT_BOUND;
                        }
                }
                else if (engine->touchX > 0.85f && engine->touchY < 0.2f)
                {
                        engine->playerX += 0.015f;
                        if (engine->playerX > PADDLE_RIGHT_BOUND)
                        {
                                engine->playerX = PADDLE_RIGHT_BOUND;
                        }
                }
        }
}
```

```
engine->ballX += engine->ballVelocityX;
if (engine->ballX < BALL_LEFT_BOUND || engine->ballX > BALL_RIGHT_BOUND)
{
        engine->ballVelocityX = -engine->ballVelocityX;
}

engine->ballY += engine->ballVelocityY;
if (engine->ballY > BALL_TOP_BOUND)
{
        engine->ballVelocityY = -engine->ballVelocityY;
}

if (engine->ballY < BALL_BOTTOM_BOUND)
{
        // reset the ball
        if (engine->ballVelocityY < 0.0f)
        {
                engine->ballVelocityY = -engine->ballVelocityY;
        }

        engine->ballX = BALL_START_X;
        engine->ballY = BALL_START_Y;

        engine_init_blocks(engine);
}

float ballXPlusVelocity = engine->ballX + engine->ballVelocityX;
float ballYPlusVelocity = engine->ballY + engine->ballVelocityY;

const float ballLeft = ballXPlusVelocity - BALL_HALF_WIDTH;
const float ballRight = ballXPlusVelocity + BALL_HALF_WIDTH;
const float ballTop = ballYPlusVelocity + BALL_HALF_HEIGHT;
const float ballBottom = ballYPlusVelocity - BALL_HALF_HEIGHT;
const float paddleLeft = engine->playerX - PADDLE_HALF_WIDTH;
const float paddleRight = engine->playerX + PADDLE_HALF_WIDTH;
const float paddleTop = engine->playerY + PADDLE_HALF_HEIGHT;
const float paddleBottom = engine->playerY - PADDLE_HALF_HEIGHT;
if (!((ballRight < paddleLeft) ||
                (ballLeft > paddleRight) ||
                (ballBottom > paddleTop) ||
                (ballTop < paddleBottom)))
{
        if (engine->ballVelocityY < 0.0f)
        {
                engine->ballVelocityY = -engine->ballVelocityY;
        }
}
)
bool anyBlockActive = false;
for (int32_t i=0; i<NUM_BLOCKS; ++i)
```

```
        {
                block& currentBlock = engine->blocks[i];
                if (currentBlock.isActive)
                {
                        const float blockLeft = currentBlock.x - BLOCK_HALF_WIDTH;
                        const float blockRight = currentBlock.x + BLOCK_HALF_WIDTH;
                        const float blockTop = currentBlock.y + BLOCK_HALF_HEIGHT;
                        const float blockBottom = currentBlock.y - BLOCK_HALF_HEIGHT;
                        if (!((ballRight < blockLeft) ||
                                        (ballLeft > blockRight) ||
                                        (ballTop < blockBottom) ||
                                        (ballBottom > blockTop)))
                        {
                                engine->ballVelocityY = -engine->ballVelocityY;

                                if (ballLeft < blockLeft ||
                                                ballRight > blockRight)
                                {
                                        engine->ballVelocityX = -engine->ballVelocityX;
                                }

                                currentBlock.isActive = false;
                        }
                        anyBlockActive = true;
                }
        }

        if (!anyBlockActive)
        {
                engine_init_blocks(engine);
        }
})
```

The lack of comments in the code reflects the fact that code should be fairly self-documenting in its simplicity. The first section of this function is concerned with updating the paddle position if the player is pressing on the top left or right corner of the screen.

touchIsDown is set to true in the function engine_handle_input when Android informs the app that the user has put their finger on the screen; it is set to false again when Android informs us that the finger has been lifted.

```
if (engine->touchIsDown)
{
```

The touch coordinates start from 0,0 in the top left corner and go to 1,1 in the bottom right corner. The if check below tells the app if the player is touching the top left corner; if so, we move the player's position to the left. Once the player is as far to the left as we would like to allow, we clamp their position at that point.

```
        if (engine->touchX < 0.15f && engine->touchY < 0.2f)
        {
engine->playerX -= 0.015f;
if (engine->playerX < PADDLE_LEFT_BOUND)
{
        engine->playerX = PADDLE_LEFT_BOUND;
}
}
```

This next test is doing exactly the same, except that it is checking the top right corner for touch and is moving the player to the right.

```
        else if (engine->touchX > 0.85f && engine->touchY < 0.2f)
        {
                engine->playerX += 0.015f;
                if (engine->playerX > PADDLE_RIGHT_BOUND)
                {
                        engine->playerX = PADDLE_RIGHT_BOUND;
                }
        }
}
```

The next section updates the ball's position.

The first line moves the ball horizontally by its horizontal velocity.

```
engine->ballX += engine->ballVelocityX;
```

This test reverses the direction of travel for the ball if it moves off the left or right of the screen.

```
if (engine->ballX < BALL_LEFT_BOUND || engine->ballX > BALL_RIGHT_BOUND)
{
        engine->ballVelocityX = -engine->ballVelocityX;
}
```

This code does the same but for the vertical direction and tests against the top of the screen only.

```
engine->ballY += engine->ballVelocityY;
if (engine->ballY > BALL_TOP_BOUND)
{
        engine->ballVelocityY = -engine->ballVelocityY;
}
```

This code checks if the player has allowed the ball to drop off of the bottom of the screen. If the ball has gone off the bottom, we reset the ball to its starting positing, ensure it is travelling up the screen, and re-enable all of the blocks.

```
if (engine->ballY < BALL_BOTTOM_BOUND)
{
        // reset the ball
        if (engine->ballVelocityY < 0.0f)
```

```
        {
                engine->ballVelocityY = -engine->ballVelocityY;
        }

        engine->ballX = BALL_START_X;
        engine->ballY = BALL_START_Y;

        engine_init_blocks(engine);
}
```

The next piece of code is checking if the player has successfully hit the ball by carrying out an overlap test on the two rectangles.

First we get the ball x and y coordinates plus the current velocity. This allows us to determine if there will be a collision next frame and allows us to react accordingly.

```
float ballXPlusVelocity = engine->ballX + engine->ballVelocityX;
float ballYPlusVelocity = engine->ballY + engine->ballVelocityY;
```

We then calculate the positions of the edges of the ball's bounding rectangle.

```
const float ballLeft = ballXPlusVelocity - BALL_HALF_WIDTH;
const float ballRight = ballXPlusVelocity + BALL_HALF_WIDTH;
const float ballTop = ballYPlusVelocity + BALL_HALF_HEIGHT;
const float ballBottom = ballYPlusVelocity - BALL_HALF_HEIGHT;
```

And do the same for the paddle:

```
const float paddleLeft = engine->playerX - PADDLE_HALF_WIDTH;
const float paddleRight = engine->playerX + PADDLE_HALF_WIDTH;
const float paddleTop = engine->playerY + PADDLE_HALF_HEIGHT;
const float paddleBottom = engine->playerY - PADDLE_HALF_HEIGHT;
```

We then use if tests to determine if the two are overlapping. A plain-English example of the test would be as follows:

- If the right edge of the ball is to the left of the paddle's left edge, then we are not overlapping.
- Or if the ball's left edge is further right than the paddle's right edge, then we are not overlapping.
- Or if the ball's bottom edge is higher than the paddle's top edge, then we are not overlapping.
- Or if the ball's top edge is lower than the paddle's bottom edge, then we are not overlapping.
- If none of those tests are true, then we are overlapping.

```
        if (!((ballRight < paddleLeft) ||
                (ballLeft > paddleRight) ||
                (ballBottom > paddleTop) ||
```

```
                        (ballTop < paddleBottom)))
        {
                if (engine->ballVelocityY < 0.0f)
                {
                        engine->ballVelocityY = -engine->ballVelocityY;
                }
        }
}
```

This overlapping-rectangles algorithm can be quite confusing, and while illustrations at this point may help make this clear, I'd advocate sitting down with a pen and paper or cutting out two rectangles and working through the different scenarios until it makes sense. You can also edit the code to slow down the ball velocity and try to work out the mechanics with the running game. A firm grasp of collisions and visualizing geometry will come in handy during a game development career.

We then loop over all of the blocks and carry out the same test between the ball and each of the blocks individually.

The first bool is used to track whether we have any blocks remaining. We initially set this to false.

```
bool anyBlockActive = false;
```

We then loop over the blocks.

```
for (int32_t i=0; i<NUM_BLOCKS; ++i)
{
        block& currentBlock = engine->blocks[i];
```

We check if the block is still active:

```
if (currentBlock.isActive)
{
```

And then calculate the bounding edges of the rectangle

```
const float blockLeft = currentBlock.x - BLOCK_HALF_WIDTH;
const float blockRight = currentBlock.x + BLOCK_HALF_WIDTH;
const float blockTop = currentBlock.y + BLOCK_HALF_HEIGHT;
const float blockBottom = currentBlock.y - BLOCK_HALF_HEIGHT;
```

And if the ball and block are overlapping.

```
if (!((ballRight < blockLeft) ||
                (ballLeft > blockRight) ||
                (ballTop < blockBottom) ||
                (ballBottom > blockTop)))
{
```

We reverse the vertical direction of the ball.

```
engine->ballVelocityY = -engine->ballVelocityY;
```

This test determines if the ball has hit the block on the left or right edges. If the left edge of the ball is further left than the left edge of the block, the ball must have come from the left side. We can work out whether the ball hit from the right with a similar condition.

```
if (ballLeft < blockLeft ||
              ballRight > blockRight)
{
```

If the ball hit from the side, we reverse its horizontal velocity.

```
      engine->ballVelocityX = -engine->ballVelocityX;
}
```

We set this block to inactive.

```
      currentBlock.isActive = false;
}
```

We set anyBlockActive to true if the block was active this frame.

```
        anyBlockActive = true;
      }
}
```

Once all of the blocks have been destroyed, we reset them all and carry on playing.

```
if (!anyBlockActive)
{
      engine_init_blocks(engine);
}
```

# Summary

Congratulations: at this point, you can set up, build, and run your very first Android NDK game app. It may be missing many of the polished features of a professional title but it still covers all of the basics. We have initialized the graphics library, polled for Android events, handled input, and created a game loop which updates and renders the state of the game frame by frame.

Now we can move on to build a commercial-quality title from the ground up.

# Chapter 3

# Game Design for Beginners: Droid Runner

Developing a video game is generally a collaborative effort among a group of people. There are usually artists, designers, programmers, and production staff involved from the beginning of the game development cycle right through to the end. It's also possible that you will be pitching your ideas to a third party, possibly a platform holder or a publisher, to acquire funding or marketing support for your title.

In all of these scenarios, it is vitally important that you have good lines of communication among staff members to ensure that production of your title goes to plan. The central focus of this communication in the initial stages of development is the game design document.

As the document is such a key pillar in the development of a game, we will dive into looking at how we can write our own before we look at writing our code.

## An Introduction to Design Documents

Design documents serve a few different purposes. First and foremost, they contain a functional specification of the game. This functional specification details the game world, mechanics, and gameplay systems from the point of view of the user. It helps determine how the game will play and how different parts of the game come together to create the user experience.

The second purpose of the design document is the technical specification. The technical design section will describe in more detail how certain aspects of the game will be implemented. This will be useful when it comes to implementing the game as it can provide a high-level overview of how the different systems will interface with each other. It's also essential to have at least a rough spec to help with scheduling development. An attempt at creating an accurate schedule is vitally important if you're developing your game in a commercial environment with a limited amount of time and budget.

It's not uncommon for there to be multiple documents containing different aspects of the design but for our small game, a single document will be good enough. The first required section is the overview.

# Creating a World, Telling a Story, and Setting the Scene

Every game needs to tell a story. This story, however detailed, helps to create a sense of urgency and empathy within the player and can turn a collection of mechanics into a compelling experience. Even the earliest successful games managed to tell a story: *Donkey Kong* was released by Nintendo in 1981 and told the story of Jumpman trying to save the Princess from the giant ape. *Pac-Man*'s story is in the relationship between the player and the AI. Each of the four ghosts try to catch Pac-Man in their own way up until the point where the player collects a power pellet, the tables are turned, and the ghosts then run away from Pac-Man. The power of storytelling is evident in the fact that the developers even gave the ghosts unique names: Blinky, Pinky, Inky and Clyde.

Modern games are becoming more and more story driven as the technology used to play games advances. Home console and PC games are now commonly written by writers who have been involved with Hollywood movies. Games for mobile platforms such as Android have already been written and developed in a similar fashion at the larger game publishers, and while this is out of the reach of most small developers, a sense of story and journey is still important.

Our back story will be covered in the overview, and we don't really need to add any more for our simple game. What we should do is keep our story in mind and ensure that everything we add to the game is in keeping with the narrow theme we wish to portray. For our game, that's a theme of trying to escape from a place where we're held captive and have little power.

# The *Droid Runner* Design Overview

In the following sections, we'll cover the different sections of our game design document. This example covers the minimum number of sections which we need to fully describe our game to others. There is not a hard set of rules which you can follow when laying out your game design. This makes some sense, as each game is different and no two documents could possibly contain the same information and also describe completely different designs for games. We'll begin by looking at the game overview.

## Section 1 - Game Overview

> *Droid Runner is a side scrolling game where the player automatically moves from left to right on the screen. The main character in the game is Droid, a green android who is trying to escape from an environment where he is utilized as a tool. The red security droids patrolling the environment will prevent Droid from leaving if they manage to catch him. The environment contains different obstacles which Droid must overcome to reach the exit.*

The short overview above sets the basic scene for *Droid Runner*. It helps lay out who the player is and the antagonists who are trying to prevent the player from achieving their goal. As we're creating our first game using a new platform, this is an adequate overview of the game we will be aiming to create. The following sections will cover the details of the gameplay.

# Defining the Gameplay and Mechanics

The gameplay section of the design document should cover a description of the actions which the player will be carrying out during the game. This section is split between a high-level overview of the gameplay structure as well as a more detailed analysis of the game mechanics which will be used to create the high-level experience. More complicated games will have a description of different levels in which the game will take place, and for games with role-playing elements, a description of the skill system would also be found here.

## Section 2 - Gameplay and Mechanics

## Section 2.1 - Gameplay

*A level will progress from left to right and have no vertical movement. As the camera moves along, the player will be exposed to enemy characters as well as obstacles which he must avoid. The core fun experience of the game will be created by designing levels which position enemies and obstacles in a manner which presents the player with a challenge which increases in difficulty as the player progresses through the level.*

*The player will complete the level by reaching the goal area at the far right extremity of the level.*

*The game over scenario will be triggered by the player coming into contact with an obstacle or an enemy droid.*

## Section 2.2 - Mechanics

## Section 2.2.1 - Movement

*The player will move automatically from left to right. The speed at which the player moves will be tuned to an appropriate velocity to ensure that a challenge is presented by the positioning of obstacles and enemies which is neither too easy nor too difficult.*

*The player will be able to jump at a height which represents 33% of the height of the level. The upward and downward velocity will be symmetrical as to provide a consistent and predictable jumping behavior. There will be no delay between landing a jump and starting another as the gameplay relies on responsive controls and timing to create a sense of tension and fun. The velocity of the jump should slow around the peak to create an area of floating to allow the player some ability to preemptively jump over obstacles and utilize timing to their advantage.*

### Section 2.2.2 - Obstacles

*Crates - The level will contain stacked crates which the player must jump over or onto. Crates will be square, and obstacles will be created by placing crates side by side or one on top of another. All crates will have equal dimensions with the sides being equal to 25% of the height of the screen. This will allow the player to be able to comfortably clear the crates with their 33% jump height.*

*Enemies - The level will contain enemy droids which will be following a set path between two points. These paths will be linear, either vertically or horizontally. Horizontal paths should cover no more than 75% of the visible width of the screen at 720p. Vertical paths can cover the entire height of the level. Enemies will move at a speed which is slightly slower than the player's horizontal velocity. This will allow the player to move past enemies and only be concerned with new enemies coming from the right.*

### Section 2.2.3 - Pickups

*The player will be able to pick up an invincibility pickup which allows them to pass through obstacles and enemy players without triggering the game-over scenario.*

# Level Design

A lot of developers who are new to making games look for a perfect set of rules on how to construct levels. From my experience, such a set of rules doesn't exist. If such a set of rules did exist, we may end up in a situation where the levels of different games become very similar as they are designed from the same formula but those levels may not fit in with the game which is being developed. This is the crux of why I feel there are no hard-and-fast rules on level design: every game strives to have slightly different mechanics and therefore slightly different design considerations. What do exist are some tenets of level design which can be considered when designing a level for a game.

## Pacing

The first tenet of level design, I believe, is pacing. When constructing a full game across multiple levels, it's important to consider how often you introduce new gameplay mechanics and then build the use of these mechanics into the world.

The *Legend of Zelda* games provide a classic blueprint of ramping difficulty through their games using pacing. A new weapon is introduced and there will be a small task which is required to be completed with the new ability provided by the weapon to instruct the player on how it can be used. There will then be a boss encounter which requires the new ability to complete the dungeon and advance in the story. The player will then be able to access new areas of the map in the outer world which were previously inaccessible and, more often than not, more difficult than the areas which had come before.

Games can also use pacing of intensity to create engagement for the player. High intensity levels for sustained periods of time may cause players to become stressed. If this stress is perceived as difficulty then many players will feel overwhelmed and decide to stop playing the game. What you should strive for is variations in the pacing to create a sense of interest. Periods of high intensity with lots happening and high levels of engagement for the player should be followed by relative calm. This will give the player a chance to recover and regain some composure. In the beginning, a game can have longer periods of calm with short bursts of high intensity, and the opposite closer to the end once the player is experienced and requires a higher level of challenge.

We will attempt to use the complexity of the obstacles and placement of the AI characters in our level to alternate between periods in which the player will be required to tap on the screen in rapid succession to clear areas and periods of lower levels of input, which will denote calm. Towards the end of the level, the periods of relative calm may be as intense as the areas of high intensity from earlier in the level, but the player should be more experienced and therefore less stressed by the level of these areas towards the end of the level.

## Aesthetics

The aesthetics of a level are vitally important in conveying the setting and theme to the player. If an area of a game is to feel intense for a player, depending on the type of game, the aesthetics will help to convey that sense of intensity if they are done properly.

Aesthetics can also be used to lead a player through a level. Generally, the path the designer wants a player to take through the level will be lit using bright lights at key points. If you ever find yourself lost in a first-person shooter such as *Halo 4*, take a while to stand still and look around for any path openings or doors which look like they may be lit more brightly or with different colors to the rest; there's a reasonable chance that this is the way you should go. Placing secrets in darker areas also makes them less likely to be found by players who are subconsciously following the directed path and therefore warrant the reward offered to those exploring off the beaten track.

## Scale

The scale of a level is important in determining how long it will take to build. Everyone would like a game of unlimited scope. RPGs such as *Skyrim* are heralded for their scale. Scale does not come for free and the scope of your game will be intrinsically linked to the scale of your levels and vice versa.

Larger levels generally require a large number of game mechanics to ensure that they remain compelling to play. A large level will quickly become repetitive and boring to a player if it requires them to repeat the exact same challenges over and over. Levels which are also small for the number of available mechanics may also mean that the player may not get to use some of the most compelling features which they are being offered, damaging the perceived quality of the title.

The scale of the level is also impacted by the target hardware which the game is intended for. A PC game can make use of several gigabytes of RAM and can store very large data sets for levels in memory all at once. A Playstation 3, on the other hand has only 256MB of system memory and can therefore store data only for much smaller levels and the objects contained within. Issues such as these will be reliant upon the technical requirements we look at in the next section.

# Technical Requirements

The technical requirements document details the engineering specs of the low-level systems which will be used to create the game. This documentation will rarely contain implementation details but will instead give an overview of how such a system should work, algorithms to be used, and the interfaces which will allow different systems to communicate.

There are a couple of important reasons for writing a requirements document. This first is for team communication, which is relevant even if you're developing a game on your own to communicate with your future self about how you envisioned the system integrates with other systems in the framework.

Another is for scheduling. With experience, you'll begin to learn how much effort will be required to implement a given system while writing the requirements document. This in turn will lead to better budgeting and planning, an important aspect of building games which are commercially successful.

The technical requirements of a given system should define the interface which the system will expose to the outside world. Taking the time to design the interface will allow you to understand how data will flow into and out of the system and will help identify any areas of high coupling and low cohesion. Identifying areas where these properties exist at design time can help to avoid costly refactoring once development has already begun.

The Unified Modeling Language was created in the 1990s to help technical writers visualize their object-oriented designs. Some software has been written to aid in the construction of the models of your system, and the example in Figure 3-1 was created using ArgoUML. The design is for the Kernel and Task system, which we will be using to create our game loop a little later in the book.

Framework

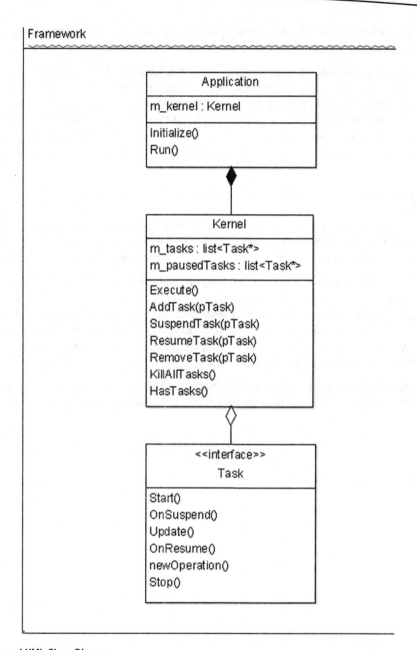

*Figure 3-1.  The Kernel UML Class Diagram*

The technical documentation can contain as much or as little documentation as you feel is necessary; however, it is important to note that it is generally accepted that the more time spent planning means less time spent implementing. Implementing systems is usually the process in software development which takes the most time and costs the most money, so anything which can help reduce this period is welcome. It isn't necessary to write all of the documentation before beginning any development. Using a development methodology such as Agile can mean that the documentation is filled out as you go; however, it is still a good idea to plan some work in advance to be sure that system interfaces will be adequate for the job at hand.

Writing good documentation comes with experience and at this point we have little experience with the Android system. It would be a good exercise for you to write some tech docs for the systems which we will be implementing as we move through the following chapters. Writing technical documentation can be a daunting prospect and a difficult task to undertake. A selection of example documents is available via the web site along with the source code for the samples used throughout this book.

# Summary

This chapter has taken a look at the design document which is produced during what is commonly referred to as pre-production. This is the stage of development where prototypes are created, brainstorming sessions take place, and the look and feel of the game are thrashed out.

We've seen that it's useful to split the design into two discrete sections; one covering the gameplay, logic, and story and another covering the technology which will be used to create the vision. The remainder of this book will look at both of these sections simultaneously moving forward. We'll do this by looking at building games from the ground up, starting with creating a game loop, communicating with the Android OS, then initializing OpenGL before moving onto more game logic–focused code from Section 2 onwards.

We will begin in the next chapter by tackling the creation of a task-based game loop and encapsulating the Android native app glue event polling into a task.

# Chapter 4

# Building a Game Engine

Productivity in modern game companies is primarily driven by the reuse of code and tools from one project to the next. By reusing code, companies and individuals can free up more time to developing actual game titles rather than reimplementing technology which, while necessary, will not have a visible impact on the finished product.

The sample game we looked at in Chapter 2 did not have any code which could be reused from one project to the next in an easy manner. That may be acceptable for a small example but for someone who would like to make more than one game or has hopes to start a business in the game development field, this approach would not be particularly beneficial.

We are going to begin the development of our own game engine in this chapter. The engine itself will be light-years away from the complexity of the commercial engines such as Unreal or Unity, but it will help us develop an understanding of why engines are a good idea and how we can approach the separation of game code and framework code. We'll begin by looking at a reusable game loop, communicating with the Android OS, and learning how to time our frames.

Let's start by looking at our application object.

## Creating an Application Object

One of the first lessons in object-oriented design is to create classes which represent the nouns in your application design. The very first noun we encounter when creating a game for Android is the word **app**. It makes sense for us to create a class to encapsulate our app, and it also makes sense for this to be our first class which we write to be a reusable object; this means that no code specific to the app you are building should be contained within the class itself. Fortunately, C++ provides us with a mechanism through inheritance where this is not an issue, but to begin we will just look at creating the class itself, which is shown in Listing 4-1.

*Listing 4-1.  The Application Class: Application.h*

```
namespace Framework
{
        class Application
        {
        private:

        public:
                Application(android_app* state);
                virtual ~Application();

                bool        Initialize();
                void        Run();
        };
}
```

This is the class definition for the application. At the moment, there isn't anything particularly interesting about this code, but we will be adding objects to the application as we move forward. You can think of Application as being the root object in your app. We will use it from main as shown in Listing 4-2.

*Listing 4-2.  android_main, the App Entry Point: Chapter4.cpp*

```
void android_main(struct android_app* state)
{
        app_dummy();

        Framework::Application app(state);

        if (app.Initialize())
        {
                app.Run();
        }
}
```

Here you can see that the contents of main are relatively simple in comparison to the basic game we created earlier. This is good as we've managed to create an interface which will allow us to hide a lot of the more complex operations from this level and should give us code which is easier to read and to work with.

The definitions of the Initialize and Run methods are similarly basic and empty at the moment, as you can see in Listing 4-3.

*Listing 4-3.  Application's Initialize and Run Methods: Application.h*

```
bool Application::Initialize()
{
        bool ret = true;
        return ret;
}
```

```
void Application::Run()
{
}
```

All real-time games run in what is known as the **game loop**. In the next section, we'll look at an object which we will use to create this loop.

# Creating the Game Loop Using a Kernel and Tasks

The object which will encapsulate our game loop is called the kernel. The basic design for this object was proposed by Richard Fine in his Enginuity series, which can be found at www.gamedev.net. The kernel works by maintaining a list of tasks. The tasks are added to the list in priority order and the kernel updates the tasks sequentially, once per frame.

## Starting the Kernel Class

Again, the Kernel class has been declared within the Framework namespace but for brevity I'm going to omit this line from the text; you can see the important code in Listing 4-4. You can see how the classes are written with their relevant includes, etc., in the sample code for this chapter.

*Listing 4-4. The Kernel Class: Kernel.h*

```
class Kernel
{
        private:
                typedef std::list<Task*>                TaskList;
                typedef std::list<Task*>::iterator      TaskListIterator;

                TaskList        m_tasks;
                TaskList        m_pausedTasks;

                void            PriorityAdd(Task* pTask);

        public:
                Kernel();
                virtual ~Kernel();

                void        Execute();

                bool        AddTask(Task* pTask);
                void        SuspendTask(Task* task);
                void        ResumeTask(Task* task);
                void        RemoveTask(Task* task);
                void        KillAllTasks();

                bool        HasTasks()        { return m_tasks.size(); }
};
```

The definition for the Kernel class is fairly self-explanatory. As I noted earlier, we have a list which contains pointers to Task objects. We also declare public methods which allow us to add and remove as well as suspend and resume individual tasks. There is also a KillAllTasks method which will allow us to kill all of the current tasks, and we can also check if the Kernel has any current running tasks using the HasTasks method.

There is also a member which we hadn't discussed previously, and that's the list of paused tasks (m_pausedTasks). We'll look at what that is used for when we come to looking at the SuspendTask and ResumeTask methods.

## Defining the Task Interface

First we'll take a look at the Task interface, shown in Listing 4-5.

*Listing 4-5. The Task Interface: Task.h*

```
class Task
{
private:
        unsigned int        m_priority;
        bool                m_canKill;

public:
        explicit Task(const unsigned int priority);
        virtual ~Task();

        virtual bool        Start()             = 0;
        virtual void        OnSuspend()         = 0;
        virtual void        Update()            = 0;
        virtual void        OnResume()          = 0;
        virtual void        Stop()              = 0;

        void                SetCanKill(const bool canKill);
        bool                CanKill() const;
        unsigned int        Priority() const;
};
```

This interface is the base class which all future Task classes will inherit. We can see that each Task will have a priority and a flag to tell whether it can be killed (m_canKill).

The pure virtual methods are also the interface which the kernel uses to interact with Tasks. Each child of Task will override these to provide the specific functionality for the given Task. We'll be looking at those more in detail when we come to implement actual Tasks but for now we can take a look at Kernel's methods and see how it uses the Task interface.

## Examining the Kernel Methods

Listing 4-6 shows the PriorityAdd and AddTask methods. In PriorityAdd, we get an iterator to the task list and loop through the list until the current task's priority is greater than the new task's priority. This means that zero will be the highest priority in our system as the Task::m_priority field is unsigned. The task is then inserted into the list at that point. As you can see, this means that our priority determines the order in which our tasks are updated.

We can see that Kernel::AddTask calls Task::Start in its very first line. This is important as it means that we are adding tasks to the kernel only if they have been successfully started. If the task was started, we call PriorityAdd.

*Listing 4-6. Kernel's PriorityAdd and AddTask: Kernel.cpp*

```cpp
void Kernel::PriorityAdd(Task* pTask)
{
        TaskListIterator iter;
        for (iter = m_tasks.begin(); iter != m_tasks.end(); ++iter)
        {
                Task* pCurrentTask = (*iter);
                if (pCurrentTask->Priority() > pTask->Priority())
                {
                        break;
                }
        }
        m_tasks.insert(iter, pTask);
}

bool Kernel::AddTask(Task* pTask)
{
        bool started = pTask->Start();

        if (started)
        {
                PriorityAdd(pTask);
        }
        return started;
}
```

RemoveTask is straightforward; we find the task in the list and set it to be killable, as shown in Listing 4-7.

*Listing 4-7. Kernel's RemoveTask: Kernel.cpp*

```cpp
void Kernel::RemoveTask(Task* pTask)
{
        if (std::find(m_tasks.begin(), m_tasks.end(), pTask) != m_tasks.end())
        {
                pTask->SetCanKill(true);
        }
}
```

SuspendTask finds the task if it is currently running and calls OnSuspend on the task. It then removes the task from the running tasks list and adds it to the paused tasks list. Listing 4-8 shows the SuspendTask method.

*Listing 4-8. Kernel's SuspendTask: Kernel.cpp*

```
void Kernel::SuspendTask(Task* pTask)
{
        if (std::find(m_tasks.begin(), m_tasks.end(), pTask) != m_tasks.end())
        {
                pTask->OnSuspend();
                m_tasks.remove(pTask);
                m_pausedTasks.push_back(pTask);
        }
}
```

ResumeTask checks if the task is currently paused (see Listing 4-9). Next, it calls Task::OnResume, removes it from the paused list, and then adds the task back into the running list at the correct priority.

*Listing 4-9. Kernel's ResumeTask: Kernel.cpp*

```
void Kernel::ResumeTask(Task* pTask)
{
        if (std::find(m_pausedTasks.begin(), m_pausedTasks.end(), pTask) != m_pausedTasks.end())
        {
                pTask->OnResume();
                m_pausedTasks.remove(pTask);

                PriorityAdd(pTask);
        }
}
```

KillAllTasks is another straightforward method (see Listing 4-10). It simply loops over all of the running tasks and sets their can-kill flag to true.

*Listing 4-10. Kernel's KillAllTasks: Kernel.cpp*

```
void Kernel::KillAllTasks()
{
        for (TaskListIterator iter = m_tasks.begin(); iter != m_tasks.end(); ++iter)
        {
                (*iter)->SetCanKill(true);
        }
}
```

The Execute method is where our game loop resides and is shown in Listing 4-11. This method loops over the tasks and calls Task::Update on each one.

*Listing 4-11. Kernel's Execute, the Game Loop: Kernel.cpp*

```
void Kernel::Execute()
{
        while (m_tasks.size())
            {
                    if (Android::IsClosing())
```

```
        {
                KillAllTasks();
        }

    TaskListIterator iter;
        for (iter = m_tasks.begin(); iter != m_tasks.end(); ++iter)
        {
                Task* pTask = (*iter);
                if (!pTask->CanKill())
                {
                        pTask->Update();
                }
        }

        for (iter = m_tasks.begin(); iter != m_tasks.end();)
        {
                Task* pTask = (*iter);
                ++iter;
                if (pTask->CanKill())
                {
                        pTask->Stop();
                    m_tasks.remove(pTask);
                    pTask = 0;
                }
        }
    }

    Android::ClearClosing();
}
```

Here we can see that Execute will run in a while loop for as long as it has tasks to execute.

If the system is closing the app, we call KillAllTasks to make them aware that the game will be closing. Execute then iterates over the list of tasks and calls Task::Update on any which have not been flagged for destruction. This is important, as we cannot guarantee that any tasks which expect to be removed still have valid data. A second loop is run to remove any tasks which are flagged for destruction from the running loop.

At this point, you will have noticed the reference to a class named Android. This class is used to poll the Android event system; we'll look at that in the next section.

# Android's Native App Glue

The Android NDK provides a framework which provides an interface to the OS without needing to implement the basic app structure using the Java programming language. This interface is the NativeActivity. Despite this, programmers would still have to implement a lot of glue code to get the lifecycle updates from NativeActivity into a usable format in their own app. Fortunately, the Android NDK developers also provided this layer in their Native App Glue code.

First and foremost, this glue code provides us with easy access to an interface to the Android app lifecycle, which will be the focus of this section. In later chapters, we'll also be looking at the other interfaces which this framework provides such as input and sensor information.

The Android class will require to be updated every frame to get the latest events from the Android OS. This makes it a perfect candidate to be our first task; see Listing 4-12 for details of the Android class.

*Listing 4-12. An Android Task: Android.h*

```
class Android
        :       public Task
{
private:
        static bool     m_bClosing;
        static bool     m_bPaused;
        android_app*     m_pState;

public:
        Android(android_app* pState, const unsigned int priority);
        virtual ~Android();

        android_app*    GetAppState() { return m_pState; }

        virtual bool    Start();
        virtual void    OnSuspend();
        virtual void    Update();
        virtual void    OnResume();
        virtual void    Stop();

        static void ClearClosing()                      { m_bClosing = false; }
        static bool IsClosing()                          { return m_bClosing; }
        static void SetPaused(const bool paused)     { m_bPaused = paused; }
        static bool IsPaused()                          { return m_bPaused; }
};
```

Here we can see that the Android class inherits from Task. We have used static variables for the closing and paused flags for convenience. The kernel needs to know if the app is closing or not, but it does not necessarily need access to the Android object to do so. We also override the methods from Task and we'll take a look at these now.

OnSuspend, OnResume, and Stop are all empty methods. At the moment, there is nothing which we would need to put into those. Similarly, Start does nothing but return true. We do not have any initialization code which we need to run to allow the Android system to execute, so there is no need to prevent our task from being added to the kernel's running list. That leaves us with Update, shown in Listing 4-13.

*Listing 4-13. Android's Update: Android.cpp*

```cpp
void Android::Update()
{
        int events;
        struct android_poll_source* pSource;
        int ident = ALooper_pollAll(0, 0, &events, (void**)&pSource);
        if (ident >= 0)
        {
                if (pSource)
                {
                        pSource->process(m_pState, pSource);
                }

                if (m_pState->destroyRequested)
                {
                        m_bClosing = true;
                }
        }
}
```

The Update method is fairly straightforward. The ALooper_pollAll method is called and retrieves any current events for our app from the Android OS.

- The first parameter passed is a timeout value. As we are running in a real-time loop, we do not want this call to remain blocked for longer than a certain time. We tell the method to return immediately without waiting for events by passing zero as the first parameter.

- The second parameter can be used to get a pointer to a file descriptor in certain circumstances. We are not concerned with this and pass zero.

- We are also not interested in the third parameter, but we are required to pass an address of an int to retrieve its value.

- The fourth parameter retrieves the source structure for the event. We call process on this structure and pass it the state object for our app.

We can look at where the state object is initialized now, as shown in Listing 4-14.

*Listing 4-14. Android's Constructor and Event Processor: Android.cpp*

```cpp
static void android_handle_cmd(struct android_app* app, int32_t cmd)
{
        switch (cmd)
        {
        case APP_CMD_RESUME:
                {
                        Android::SetPaused(false);
                }
                break;
```

```
            case APP_CMD_PAUSE:
                {
                        Android::SetPaused(true);
                }
                break;
        }
}

Android::Android(android_app* pState, unsigned int priority)
        :          Task(priority)
{
        m_pState = pState;
        m_pState->onAppCmd = android_handle_cmd;
}
```

Android provides a callback mechanism for dealing with system events. The callback signature returns void and is passed an android_app struct pointer and an integer which contains the value of the event to be processed. For Win32 programmers, this setup is not all that dissimilar to WndProc.

We do not yet have any need to handle any Android OS events, but for the sake of example I've added a switch statement which handles the APP_CMD_RESUME and APP_CMD_PAUSE cases.

We can see from the Android constructor that we have stored the android_app pointer which we have been provided and set the onAppCmd function pointer to the address of the static command handler method. This method will be called during the process call on the event structure we were supplied by ALooper_pollAll.

The only thing left to do with the Android class is to instantiate an instance and add it to our kernel, as shown in Listing 4-15.

*Listing 4-15. Instantiating the Android Task: Application.h, Task.h, and Application.cpp*

```
class Application
{
private:
        Kernel          m_kernel;
        Android          m_androidTask;

public:
        Application(android_app* state);
        virtual ~Application();

        bool          Initialize();
        void          Run();
};

class Task
{
private:
        unsigned int          m_priority;
        bool                  m_canKill;
```

```
public:
        explicit Task(const unsigned int priority);
        virtual ~Task();

        virtual bool      Start()                = 0;
        virtual void      OnSuspend()            = 0;
        virtual void      Update()               = 0;
        virtual void      OnResume()             = 0;
        virtual void      Stop()                 = 0;

        void              SetCanKill(const bool canKill);
        bool              CanKill() const;
        unsigned int      Priority() const;

        static const unsigned int PLATFORM_PRIORITY = 1000;
};

Application::Application(android_app* state)
        :         m_androidTask(state, Task::PLATFORM_PRIORITY)
{
}

bool Application::Initialize()
{
        bool ret = true;

        m_kernel.AddTask(&m_androidTask);

        return ret;
}

void Application::Run()
{
        m_kernel.Execute();
}
```

Those are the changes required to instantiate the Android object and add it to the kernel. You can see that we added the Kernel and Android objects as private members to the application. The Android constructor is called in the Application constructor initialization list and is passed the android_app struct and its priority. The Android object is added to the kernel in the Initialize method and we call Kernel::Execute in Application::Run.

We now have a working game loop which properly interfaces with the Android OS. We still have a lot of low-level plumbing to be done before we are in a position to begin writing game code. Next up is frame timing.

# Timekeeping

One of the more important benchmarks in gaming through the years has been the fps or frames per second. For the current generation of games consoles, 30fps has been the standard achieved by most games. A few companies such as id still aim for 60fps and the benefits to responsiveness that provides through reduced latency.

Whichever frame rate you wish to target, timekeeping in game is going to be important. An accurate frame time is necessary for moving objects around in the game in a consistent manner. In the early 1990s, it was common on the SNES and Sega Genesis for games to run at different speeds in different countries. This was due to games being written with characters moving at consistent speeds per frame. The issue was that TVs updated at a rate of 50 times per second in Europe but at 60 in North America. The effect was that games appeared to be noticeably slower for European players.

The situation could have been avoided altogether if the developers had written their games to update with respect to time rather than frame rate. We achieve that by storing how long the last frame took to process and moving objects relative to that time. We'll consider that's done in Chapter 6, but for now we'll look at how to store the time for the previous frame, as shown in Listing 4-16.

*Listing 4-16. The Timer Task: Timer.h*

```
class Timer
        :       public Task
{
public:
        typedef long long       TimeUnits;

private:
        TimeUnits nanoTime();

        TimeUnits               m_timeLastFrame;
        float                   m_frameDt;
        float                   m_simDt;
        float                   m_simMultiplier;

public:
        Timer(const unsigned int priority);
        ~Timer();

        float                   GetTimeFrame() const;
        float                   GetTimeSim() const;
        void                    SetSimMultiplier(const float simMultiplier);

        virtual bool            Start();
        virtual void            OnSuspend();
        virtual void            Update();
        virtual void            OnResume();
        virtual void            Stop();
};
```

Unsurprisingly, we are using a Task to update the Timer each frame. The Timer will be given a priority of zero and will be the first task to be updated each frame.

We have two notions of time in our Timer. We have the frame time, which is the actual time taken to complete the last frame, and we have **sim time**. Sim time is the time we will use in the gameplay sections of our code. The sim time will be modified by a multiplier. This multiplier will allow us to modify the speed at which our game updates. We might be able to use this for gameplay purposes, but it will also be useful for debugging purposes. If we have a bug to reproduce which happens at the end of a sequence of events, we can speed up the reproduction process by increasing the time multiplier and making everything in game occur more quickly. Listing 4-17 shows the method for calculating the current system time.

*Listing 4-17. Timer, nanoTime: Timer.cpp*

```
Timer::TimeUnits Timer::nanoTime()
{
        timespec now;
        int err = clock_gettime(CLOCK_MONOTONIC, &now);
        return now.tv_sec*1000000000L + now.tv_nsec;
}
```

As Android is a Linux-based OS, we have access to many of the Linux methods from the C++ environment. One example of this is clock_gettime. clock_gettime is included in the time.h header file and provides us with an interface to the system clock in the computer we are running on. We are specifically using the monotonic clock, which gives us an arbitrary time since a past event. We don't know when that event was, but since we are comparing our own frame time, we are not overly concerned.

The timespec structure contains two members:

- The first is time in seconds;
- The second is nanoseconds.

The value we return is in nanoseconds; we multiply the seconds by 1,000,000,000 to convert them to nanoseconds and we add the nanosecond value.

The Timer task has its initial value set in Start, as shown in Listing 4-18.

*Listing 4-18. Starting and Restarting the Timer: Timer.cpp*

```
bool Timer::Start()
{
        m_timeLastFrame = nanoTime();
        return true;
}

void Timer::OnResume()
{
        m_timeLastFrame = nanoTime();
}
```

Setting the initial value here is necessary, as we always need a previous value to compare to. If we didn't initialize this value when starting our timer, our initial frame time would be completely unreliable. By initializing the previous time here, we are limiting our worst case to an initial frame time of zero, which isn't disastrous. We do the same in OnResume, although I can't imagine a case where the Timer would ever be paused under normal running.

The last method of importance for the Timer class is Update, which is shown in Listing 4-19.

*Listing 4-19. Timer's Update: Timer.cpp*

```
void Timer::Update()
{
        // Get the delta between the last frame and this
        TimeUnits currentTime = nanoTime();
        const float MULTIPLIER = 0.000000001f;
        m_frameDt = (currentTime-m_timeLastFrame) * MULTIPLIER;
        m_timeLastFrame = currentTime;
        m_simDt = m_frameDt * m_simMultiplier;
}
```

In this method, you can see that we are getting the delta time between the last frame and the current frame. We start by getting the latest nanoTime value from the system clock. We then calculate the frame time by subtracting the previous nanoTime from the current nanoTime. During this step, we also convert the time into a float which contains the frame time in seconds. This format is the simplest way to deal with times in gameplay code, as we can deal with all movement speeds in terms of per-second values and use the time as a multiplier.

The currentTime is then stored into the last frame time member for calculating the time in the next processed frame, and finally, we calculate the sim time as the result of the frame time multiplied by the sim multiplier.

# Summary

We've covered a lot of groundwork for our engine in this chapter. We have created a reusable task and kernel system and populated it with an Android task, which communicates with the OS, and a Timer task which can work out how long our frames are taking to process. Now that these tasks have been written, we will hopefully never have to write them again. This is the beginning of a game engine, and we'll extend this framework in the next chapter by looking at our OpenGL Renderer.

As with all of the chapters in this book, full sample source code can be obtained from the Apress web site.

# Chapter 5

# Writing a Renderer

One of the key tasks carried out by a game engine is to feed geometry data to the graphics processing unit (GPU). A GPU is a highly specialized piece of hardware which operates on streams of data in parallel. This parallelization of processing is what makes GPUs essential in modern real-time graphics applications and is the reason why they were dubbed hardware accelerators.

A renderer's job is to feed the geometry to the GPU as efficiently as possible. In a game engine there will be a distinct split between processing the game updates, that is, moving game objects, AI, physics, etc., and rendering the scene.

It is entirely possible to write a software renderer which operates on the CPU, but this would be a futile task on a mobile phone, where CPU processing power is at a premium. The best solution is to use the GPU. In this chapter, we're going to look at a basic renderer.

## Initializing the Window and OpenGL Using EGL

That heading throws into the mix a few acronyms and concepts with which new programmers may not be familiar. Operating systems have used a window-based system for the last couple of decades, and most people will be aware of the concept of a window. You might however be surprised to see the window concept in relation to mobile operating systems, which generally do not have repositionable windows. Android still uses a window system under the hood to describe the abstract object which we use to access the screen on our device.

OpenGL is a graphics library which has been around since 1992. OpenGL was initially developed by SGI and is currently maintained by the Khronos Group. It is one of the two main graphics APIs which are primarily used in games development. The other is DirectX, which was developed by Microsoft and is exclusive to Windows-based operating systems. OpenGL therefore has been the API of choice on Linux and mobile-based operating systems for a long time.

EGL (the Embedded-System Graphics Library) is a library provided by Khronos, which is a not-for-profit consortium in control of several industry standard APIs such as OpenGL, OpenCL, and many others. EGL is an interface API which provides an easy method for developers to communicate between the operating system's window architecture and the OpenGL API. This library allows us to initialize and use OpenGL with only a few lines of code, and anyone who developed applications using graphics APIs ten or more years ago will appreciate its brevity.

To get started with our renderer, we will create a new class named Renderer which will inherit from the Task class which we created in the previous chapter. The class definition in Listing 5-1 shows the Renderer interface.

*Listing 5-1. The Renderer Class*

```
class Renderer
        :        public Task
{
private:
        android_app*        m_pState;
        EGLDisplay          m_display;
        EGLContext          m_context;
        EGLSurface          m_surface;
        int                 m_width;
        int                 m_height;
        bool                m_initialized;

public:
        explicit Renderer(android_app* pState, const unsigned int priority);
        virtual ~Renderer();

        void Init();
        void Destroy();

        // From Task
        virtual bool        Start();
        virtual void        OnSuspend();
        virtual void        Update();
        virtual void        OnResume();
        virtual void        Stop();

        bool IsInitialized() { return m_initialized; }
};
```

The usual Task methods are in place: we'll take a look at those now (see Listing 5-2).

*Listing 5-2. Renderer's Overridden Task Methods*

```
bool Renderer::Start()
{
        return true;
}

void Renderer::OnSuspend()
{

}
```

```
void Renderer::Update()
{

}

void Renderer::OnResume()
{

}

void Renderer::Stop()
{

}
```

For now, the Renderer class doesn't do very much. We'll fill it out as we move through this chapter. The next method of interest is Init (see Listing 5-3).

*Listing 5-3. Initializing OpenGL Using EGL*

```
void Renderer::Init()
{
    // initialize OpenGL ES and EGL

    /* Here, specify the attributes of the desired configuration. In the following code, we select
an EGLConfig with at least eight bits per color component, compatible with on-screen windows. */
    const EGLint attribs[] =
    {
        EGL_RENDERABLE_TYPE, EGL_OPENGL_ES2_BIT,
        EGL_SURFACE_TYPE, EGL_WINDOW_BIT,
        EGL_BLUE_SIZE, 8,
        EGL_GREEN_SIZE, 8,
        EGL_RED_SIZE, 8,
        EGL_NONE
    };

    EGLint      format;
    EGLint      numConfigs;
    EGLConfig   config;

    m_display = eglGetDisplay(EGL_DEFAULT_DISPLAY);

    eglInitialize(m_display, NULL, NULL);

    /* Here, the application chooses the configuration it desires. In this sample, we have a very
simplified selection process, where we pick the first EGLConfig that matches our criteria. */
    eglChooseConfig(m_display, attribs, &config, 1, &numConfigs);

    /* EGL_NATIVE_VISUAL_ID is an attribute of the EGLConfig that is guaranteed to be accepted by
ANativeWindow_setBuffersGeometry(). As soon as we pick a EGLConfig, we can safely reconfigure the
ANativeWindow buffers to match, using EGL_NATIVE_VISUAL_ID. */
    eglGetConfigAttrib(m_display, config, EGL_NATIVE_VISUAL_ID, &format);
```

```
      ANativeWindow_setBuffersGeometry(m_pState->window, 0, 0, format);

      m_surface = eglCreateWindowSurface(m_display, config, m_pState->window, NULL);

      EGLint contextAttribs[] =
      {
              EGL_CONTEXT_CLIENT_VERSION, 2,
              EGL_NONE
      };
      m_context = eglCreateContext(m_display, config, NULL, contextAttribs);

      eglMakeCurrent(m_display, m_surface, m_surface, m_context);

      eglQuerySurface(m_display, m_surface, EGL_WIDTH, &m_width);
      eglQuerySurface(m_display, m_surface, EGL_HEIGHT, &m_height);

      m_initialized = true;
}
```

This code is essentially a copy of the code which is provided in the sample app. There are many
other things which can be achieved with different configurations and combinations of settings, some
of which are more advanced than we would like for now, so we'll stick with this basic setup until we
are up and running.

From a quick glance through Listing 5-3, you can see that we are setting up a rendering surface
using OpenGL ES 2.0 which can store eight-bit values for red, green, and blue.

We then set up EGL through subsequent calls to eglInitialize, eglChooseConfig, and
eglGetConfigAttrib (the EGL documentation can be found at www.khronos.org/registry/egl/).
The information obtained via these methods is then used to tell the Android OS how we would like
the window to be configured for displaying our game. Last but not least, we set our display, surface,
and context to be the current objects with EGL and get the width and height of the screen.

Everything we need to be able to draw graphics onto the screen is now set up and working. The next
step is to look at how to clean up after ourselves properly (see Listing 5-4).

*Listing 5-4. Destroying OpenGL*

```
void Renderer::Destroy()
{
      m_initialized = false;

      if (m_display != EGL_NO_DISPLAY)
      {
              eglMakeCurrent(m_display, EGL_NO_SURFACE, EGL_NO_SURFACE, EGL_NO_CONTEXT);
              if (m_context != EGL_NO_CONTEXT)
              {
                      eglDestroyContext(m_display, m_context);
              }
```

```
            if (m_surface != EGL_NO_SURFACE)
            {
                    eglDestroySurface(m_display, m_surface);
            }
            eglTerminate(m_display);
    }
    m_display = EGL_NO_DISPLAY;
    m_context = EGL_NO_CONTEXT;
    m_surface = EGL_NO_SURFACE;
}
```

As you can see from Listing 5-4, tearing down OpenGL is an easy process. This is necessary to properly hand back resources to the operating system in a timely fashion and to ensure that our game stands the best chance possible of properly resuming when the user restarts their session. By setting no surface and context to be present for the current display, we can ensure that there are no other resources which can successfully request to use these at a later point and cause issues. We then also destroy the context and surface to free their resources. Lastly, we terminate EGL to finalize the shutdown. Simple, straightforward, and a good step toward creating a well-behaved app.

With our renderer set up and ready to go, now would be a good time to look at how a programmable GPU operates with vertex and fragment shaders.

# An Introduction to Shaders

When consumer hardware 3D accelerators first appeared in the mid-1990s, they contained fixed-function pipelines. This meant that each accelerator operated in exactly the same way, as the algorithms they carried out were built into the chips created for these specific purposes.

The first generation of cards from all manufacturers carried out hardware-accelerated rasterizing of polygons; for example, the algorithms to take a texture and to apply it to a polygon were the first specific tasks carried out by these cards.

Vertices were still being transformed and lit in software on the CPU at this point in time. The first consumer graphics card to implement what was known as hardware transform and lighting (T&L) was the Nvidea GeForce 256. This shift from software to hardware-accelerated vertex processing had a slow adoption rate as it took quite a while for drivers and APIs to catch up with the hardware. Eventually, hardware T&L became more widely adopted and this resulted in the demise of almost all GPU manufacturers outside of Nvidia and ATI, who had moved quickly into producing budget cards with T&L support which outperformed much more expensive cards which did not feature this hardware.

The next big shift in consumer GPU hardware again came from Nvidia with the release of the GeForce 3. Released in 2001, it was the first GPU to incorporate programmable pixel and vertex shaders. It coincided with the release of the DirectX 8.0 API, which included support for writing shaders using assembly language.

Assembly language shader support in OpenGL was added through extensions in OpenGL 1.5. Full shader support would not come until the release of OpenGL 2.0 in 2004. A major paradigm shift also occurred at this time with assembly language shaders being replaced by the OpenGL shading language, GLSL. The introduction of a programming language for shaders opened up the feature set to more people as the language was much more intuitive than assembly programming.

This history leads us right up to modern-day Android. Mobile graphics processors were generally designed to run on small battery-operated devices and as such forego some features which are found in desktop systems to preserve battery life. This led to the development of a mobile-specific version of OpenGL, called OpenGL for Embedded Systems (OpenGL ES). Version 1.0 of OpenGL ES did not support vertex and pixel shaders; however, these were introduced with the release of OpenGL ES 2.0, which was incorporated into the Android operating system and made available via the SDK from version 2.0 onwards.

With this book, I have decided to look at OpenGL ES 2.0 only, as the previous version is being phased out and very few new devices which support only this version of the API are being released. This means that we need to have some knowledge of how to write and use vertex and pixel shaders in our games. The next section will introduce us to vertex shaders.

# An Introduction to Vertex Shaders in OpenGL ES 2.0

The purpose of a vertex shader is to transform vertices from their local space, the space in which they were modeled in the modeling package, into the canonical view volume. This volume is a cube which goes from 1,1,1 to −1,−1,−1 and it is necessary to get our vertices into this cube for the next step in the pipeline to ensure that they are not discarded by the GPU before the fragment-shading stage. A look at the pipeline can be seen in Figure 5-1. The clipping stage removes sections of the polygons which will not be rendered to prevent these fragments being sent through the expensive rasterizing stage.

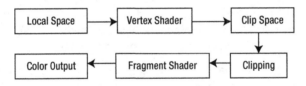

*Figure 5-1. The graphics pipeline*

Vertex data is fed to the GPU in streams, and there are two ways to construct these data streams. The common terms to describe these constructs are

- The array of structures;
- The structure of arrays.

We will be looking only at examples of an array of structures. The reason for this is that an array of structures interleaves the vertex data in the stream, which makes the data contiguous in memory. Modern processors work best when the data they require can be prefetched into a cache, and this works by grabbing data from memory in blocks. If the next set of data required by the processor is already in the block, we save a copy from memory, which could stall the GPU.

Listing 5-5 shows our array of structures for a quad which will be transformed with the vertex shader. It consists of an array of floats where we have three floats which describe the position of the vertex and then four floats describing the color of the vertex. We then repeat this same format for each vertex we require to render our object, in the case of a quad that's four.

*Listing 5-5. The Quad Vertex Specification*

```
float verts[] =
{
        -0.5f, 0.5f, 0.0f,           // Position 1 x, y, z

        1.0f, 0.0f, 0.0f, 1.0f,      // Color 1 r, g, b, a
        0.5f, 0.5f, 0.0f,            // Position 2 x, y, z
        0.0f, 1.0f, 0.0f, 1.0f,      // Color 2 r, g, b, a
        -0.5f, -0.5f, 0.0f,          // Position 3 x, y, z
        0.0f, 0.0f, 1.0f, 1.0f,      // Color 3 r, g, b, a
        0.5f, -0.5f, 0.0f,           // Position 4 x, y, z
        1.0f, 1.0f, 1.0f, 1.0f,      // Color 4 r, g, b, a
};
```

GPUs render triangles and therefore to be able to render our quad, we need to supply some additional information. We could supply six vertices in order; however, at seven floats totaling 28 bytes, we would need to send duplicate vertices of that size, which wastes some memory and bandwidth when we transfer these to the GPU. Instead, we send a stream of indices describing the order in which the GPU should use the vertices we supplied to render our triangles. Our indices can be seen in Listing 5-6.

*Listing 5-6. Quad Indices*

```
unsigned short indices[] =
{
        0,      2,      1,      2,      3,      1
};
```

With our indices, you can see that we're uploading only two bytes per vertex, and therefore even in our simple example, we are making a considerable saving over specifying duplicates. Now we'll take a look at the code for our vertex shader in Listing 5-7.

*Listing 5-7. A Basic Vertex Shader*

```
attribute vec4 a_vPosition;
attribute vec4 a_vColor;
varying vec4 v_vColor;
void main()
{
        gl_Position = a_vPosition;
        v_vColor = a_vColor;
}
```

The preceding listing shows a very basic vertex shader written in GLSL. The first two lines specify attributes of the shader. Our attributes are the data which comes from the data stream which we supply. Despite specifying only the x, y, and z elements of the position values in our array in Listing 5-1, we use a four-element vector here (vec4). The graphics driver can fill in this additional information when we set up our data. As you can see, we specify one attribute for the position and one for the color of our vertex. The next line specifies a varying. A varying is an output variable which we wish to pass from this vertex into our pixel shader. It has an important property in that it interpolates the value from one vertex to the next.

The gl_Position variable is a special variable within GLSL which is specifically designed to store the output vertex position from the vertex shader. It's necessary to use this, as it indicates the data which is required to be passed through the subsequent pipeline stages such as clipping. We can see from the first line in main() that we're simply passing the input vertex position out to this variable. We also similarly pass the input color out to our varying color variable.

That's all we have for now with a simple vertex shader program. The next major step is to look at a basic fragment shader and see how we access the output from our vertex shaders in the fragment shader stage.

# An Introduction to Fragment Shaders in OpenGL ES 2.0

Listing 5-8 shows the code of a basic fragment shader written in GLSL.

*Listing 5-8. A Basic Fragment Shader*

```
varying vec4 v_vColor;
void main()
{
        gl_FragColor = v_vColor;
}
```

A vertex shader and a fragment shader are bundled together into a program object. For a program to be valid, any varying objects from the vertex shader must be matched by a varying of identical type and name in the fragment shader. Here we can see that we have a varying called v_vColor which is of type vec4. The purpose of a fragment shader is to provide the color for the pixel being processed, and GLSL provides the gl_FragColor variable to store this output result; as you can see, we are storing the value of the varying v_vColor into this variable.

That's all we need to create an exceptionally basic fragment shader. Combined with the preceding vertex shader, we have a basic shader program which can render a colored primitive. The benefit of this structure is that it scales exceptionally well; GPUs achieve the high levels of performance that they do compared to general CPUs because they combine multiple vertex and shader processors in parallel and execute the shaders of multiple vertices and fragments simultaneously. Modern desktop GPUs have unified shader processors which can execute vertex and fragment shaders and implement load balancers to spread the load based on the demand at any given time. I'm sure this is a development which we will see in mobile architectures in the not-too-distant future.

Now that we know about vertex and pixel shaders, we'll take a look at what we need to do in code to build these into shader programs.

# Creating a Shader Program

As our engine will only support OpenGL ES 2.0, all of our rendering operations will use shaders. This gives us a clear design goal, as our renderer will have to set up a shader for use before it can execute a draw call. We also know that we are likely to want to specify different shader operations for different objects. Some of our shaders may be complex and carry out operations to give key objects high-quality lighting and material properties. A mobile GPU is not capable of carrying out these complex shaders too often in a single frame, so we're going to have to support switching out our shaders to support more basic operations for simpler objects to achieve a real-time frame rate. To achieve this, we will specify an interface for a shader, as shown in Listing 5-9.

*Listing 5-9. A Shader Interface*

```
class Shader
{
private:
        void LoadShader(GLenum shaderType, std::string& shaderCode);

protected:
        GLuint                  m_vertexShaderId;
        GLuint                  m_fragmentShaderId;
        GLint                   m_programId;

        std::string             m_vertexShaderCode;
        std::string             m_fragmentShaderCode;

        bool                    m_isLinked;

public:
        Shader();
        virtual ~Shader();


        virtual void Link();
        virtual void Setup(Renderable& renderable);

        bool IsLinked()         { return m_isLinked; }
};
```

Listing 5-9 shows the class definition of the Shader. It contains identifiers for the vertex and fragment shaders as well as for the program object. It also has member variables to contain the source code for the vertex and fragment shaders and a Boolean to track whether the shader has been linked.

The LoadShader method is used to load, compile, and attach the shader code for the vertex and fragment shaders to the program object. It is specified in Listing 5-10.

*Listing 5-10. Shader's LoadShader Method*

```
void Shader::LoadShader(GLuint id, std::string& shaderCode)
{
        static const uint32_t NUM_SHADERS = 1;

        const GLchar* pCode = shaderCode.c_str();
        GLint length = shaderCode.length();

        glShaderSource(id, NUM_SHADERS, &pCode, &length);

        glCompileShader(id);

        glAttachShader(m_programId, id);
}
```

LoadShader begins by getting a pointer to the source code and the length of the source. We then call glShaderSource to set the source code into the GL context at the specified shader ID. glCompileShader is called to compile the source, and glAttachShader attaches the compiled shader object to the program. Listing 5-11 shows how the LoadShader method fits into the context of the program as a whole.

*Listing 5-11. Shader's Link Method*

```
void Shader::Link()
{
        m_programId = glCreateProgram();

        m_vertexShaderId = glCreateShader(GL_VERTEX_SHADER);
        LoadShader(m_vertexShaderId, m_vertexShaderCode);

        m_fragmentShaderId = glCreateShader(GL_FRAGMENT_SHADER);
        LoadShader(m_fragmentShaderId, m_fragmentShaderCode);

        glLinkProgram(m_programId);

        m_isLinked = true;
}
```

Here we can see that Link begins by calling glCreateProgram, which requests the GL context to create a new shader program object. We are not given access to the object but instead are returned an identifier which we use when calling subsequent shader methods. We then ask OpenGL to create a VERTEX_SHADER object for us and call LoadShader with the vertex shader id and code as parameters. We then repeat this process for a FRAGMENT_SHADER object. Finally, we call glLinkProgram to finalize the shader object.

Our Setup method will be used to tell the OpenGL context which shader is the active shader for the next draw call. The base Shader class has a very basic task at this point and calls glUseProgram, as shown in Listing 5-12.

*Listing 5-12. Shader::Setup()*

```
void Shader::Setup(Renderable& renderable)
{
        glUseProgram(m_programId);
}
```

# Rendering a Quad with OpenGL

It's finally time for us to render our first triangles to the screen. This is an important point in creating a game system, as all graphics which we render from this point on will be extensions to this simple task. All complex models and effects in games are born from the ability to render a list of triangles which are created with an array of vertices and an array of indices. This simple example will show you how to render a quad using two triangles made from the four vertices and six indices which we looked at in Listings 5-5 and 5-6 earlier in this chapter.

# Representing Geometry

Representing vertices and indices is something which we are likely to want to do repeatedly throughout our games, and therefore it makes sense to encapsulate their representation within a class. We'll do this in our Geometry class, as shown in Listing 5-13.

*Listing 5-13. The Geometry Class*

```cpp
class Geometry
{

private:
        static const unsigned int NAME_MAX_LENGTH = 16;

        char            m_name[NAME_MAX_LENGTH];
        int             m_numVertices;
        int             m_numIndices;
        void*           m_pVertices;
        void*           m_pIndices;

        int             m_numVertexPositionElements;
        int             m_numColorElements;
        int             m_numTexCoordElements;
        int             m_vertexStride;

public:
        Geometry();
        virtual ~Geometry();

        void SetName(const char* name)                    { strcpy(m_name, name); }
        void SetNumVertices(const int numVertices)        { m_numVertices = numVertices; }
        void SetNumIndices(const int numIndices)          { m_numIndices = numIndices; }

        const char* GetName() const                       { return m_name; }

        const int GetNumVertices() const                  { return m_numVertices; }
        const int GetNumIndices() const                   { return m_numIndices; }

        void* GetVertexBuffer() const                     { return m_pVertices; }
        void* GetIndexBuffer() const                      { return m_pIndices; }

        void SetVertexBuffer(void* pVertices)             { m_pVertices = pVertices; }
        void SetIndexBuffer(void* pIndices)               { m_pIndices = pIndices; }

        void SetNumVertexPositionElements(const int numVertexPositionElements);
        int  GetNumVertexPositionElements() const         { return m_numVertexPositionElements; }

        void SetNumColorElements(const int numColorElements);
        int  GetNumColorElements() const                  { return m_numColorElements; }

        void SetNumTexCoordElements(const int numTexCoordElements);
        int  GetNumTexCoordElements() const               { return m_numTexCoordElements; }
```

```
      void SetVertexStride(const int vertexStride)    { m_vertexStride = vertexStride; }
      int  GetVertexStride() const                    { return m_vertexStride; }
            };

      inline void Geometry::SetNumVertexPositionElements(const int numVertexPositionElements)
      {
            m_numVertexPositionElements = numVertexPositionElements;
      }

      inline void Geometry::SetNumTexCoordElements(const int numTexCoordElements)
      {
            m_numTexCoordElements = numTexCoordElements;
      }

      inline void Geometry::SetNumColorElements(const int numColorElements)
      {
            m_numColorElements = numColorElements;
      }
```

Listing 5-13 gives the definition of the Geometry class. As well as storing pointers to the vertices and indices, the class contains fields which are used to describe how the vertex data is stored in the array. These members include the number of vertices and indices but also the number of position elements in the position data, the number of color elements, and the number of texture coordinate elements per vertex. We then also have a field which stores the stride of a vertex. The stride is the number of bytes which we jump from the beginning of one vertex to the next and is required when we describe the data to OpenGL, which we'll look at shortly.

First, we'll take a look at creating an object which the renderer can consume.

# Creating a Renderable

We know that the job of the Renderer will be to feed Geometry to the OpenGL API to be drawn to the screen. Therefore, it makes sense for us to be able to describe the objects which the Renderer should consider in a consistent manner. Listing 5-14 shows the class which we will use to send Renderable objects to the renderer for drawing.

*Listing 5-14. Defining a Renderable*

```
class Renderable
{
private:
      Geometry*           m_pGeometry;
      Shader*             m_pShader;

public:
      Renderable();
      ~Renderable();

      void                SetGeometry(Geometry* pGeometry);
      Geometry*           GetGeometry();
```

```
        void                    SetShader(Shader* pShader);
        Shader*                 GetShader();
};

inline Renderable::Renderable()
        :       m_pGeometry(NULL)
        ,       m_pShader(NULL)
{
}

inline Renderable::~Renderable()
{
}

inline void Renderable::SetGeometry(Geometry* pGeometry)
{
        m_pGeometry = pGeometry;
}

inline Geometry* Renderable::GetGeometry()
{
        return m_pGeometry;
}

inline void Renderable::SetShader(Shader* pShader)
{
        m_pShader = pShader;
}

inline Shader* Renderable::GetShader()
{
        return m_pShader;
}
```

This is a straightforward class at the moment, as it simply contains a pointer to a Geometry object and a Shader object. This is another class which will develop as we move forward.

We also need to augment the Renderer class to handle these Renderable objects. Listing 5-15 shows how the Renderer handles the objects which we have added to be drawn.

*Listing 5-15. Updating the Renderer*

```
class Renderer
{
private:
        typedef std::vector<Renderable*>                RenderableVector;
        typedef RenderableVector::iterator              RenderableVectorIterator;

        RenderableVector                m_renderables;

        void Draw(Renderable* pRenderable);
```

```cpp
public:
        void AddRenderable(Renderable* pRenderable);
        void RemoveRenderable(Renderable* pRenderable);
}

void Renderer::AddRenderable(Renderable* pRenderable)
{
        m_renderables.push_back(pRenderable);
}

void Renderer::RemoveRenderable(Renderable* pRenderable)
{
        for (RenderableVectorIterator iter = m_renderables.begin();
            iter != m_renderables.end();
            ++iter)
        {
            Renderable* pCurrent = *iter;
            if (pCurrent == pRenderable)
            {
                    m_renderables.erase(iter);
                    break;
            }
        }
}

void Renderer::Update()
{
        if (m_initialized)
        {
            glClearColor(0.95f, 0.95f, 0.95f, 1);
            glClear(GL_COLOR_BUFFER_BIT);

            for (RenderableVectorIterator iter = m_renderables.begin();
                iter != m_renderables.end();
                ++iter)
            {
                Renderable* pRenderable = *iter;
                if (pRenderable)
                {
                        Draw(pRenderable);
                }
            }

            eglSwapBuffers(m_display, m_surface);
        }
}
```

We store the Renderable objects in a vector and loop over these during the call to Update. Each Renderable is then passed to the private Draw method, which we describe in Listing 5-16.

*Listing 5-16. Renderer's Draw Method*

```
void Renderer::Draw(Renderable* pRenderable)
{
        assert(pRenderable);
        if (pRenderable)
        {
                Geometry* pGeometry = pRenderable->GetGeometry();
                Shader* pShader = pRenderable->GetShader();
                assert(pShader && pGeometry);

                pShader->Setup(*pRenderable);

                glDrawElements(
                        GL_TRIANGLES,
                        pGeometry->GetNumIndices(),
                        GL_UNSIGNED_SHORT,
                        pGeometry->GetIndexBuffer());
        }
}
```

Our Draw method shows that we carry out only two tasks per object. After verifying that we have a valid Renderable pointer and that our Renderable contains valid Geometry and Shader pointers, we call Shader::Setup() and then glDrawElements. glDrawElements is passed parameters which let the context know that we would like to render triangles, how many indices we are passing it, the format of our indices, and the index buffer itself.

One thing you may notice is that we do not pass any information about the vertices to the draw call. This is because this information is part of the shader setup stage and is passed as a data stream to the shader. We'll look at how we handle passing data to the shader now.

# Creating the Basic Shader

Earlier, we looked at a base class for representing shaders in our framework; now we'll take a look at a specific implementation. To create a shader which we can use on the GPU, we'll begin by deriving a new class from the Shader class. Listing 5-17 shows the BasicShader class.

*Listing 5-17. The BasicShader Class*

```
class BasicShader
        :       public Shader
{
private:
        GLint           m_positionAttributeHandle;

public:
        BasicShader();
        virtual ~BasicShader();

        virtual void Link();
        virtual void Setup(Renderable& renderable);
};
```

As you can see from Listing 5-17, we inherit from Shader and overload its public methods. We also have added a field to store the index of the position attribute in the GL context. For simplicity, this shader will render the color directly from the fragment shader and will forego the color values in the stream which we looked at previously. Listing 5-18 shows the BasicShader class constructor which contains the shader source code.

*Listing 5-18. The BasicShader Constructor*

```
BasicShader::BasicShader()
{
        m_vertexShaderCode =
                "attribute vec4 a_vPosition; \n"
                "void main(){\n"
                "    gl_Position = a_vPosition; \n"
                "} \n";

        m_fragmentShaderCode =
                "precision highp float; \n"
                "void main(){\n"
                "    gl_FragColor = vec4(0.2, 0.2, 0.2, 1.0); \n"
                "} \n";
}
```

> **Note** The first line of the fragment shader source code sets the precision of floating point variables for the shader. Variable precision is an advanced topic which we will not cover here. The minimum which you need to know for beginning is that in OpenGL ES 2.0, your fragment shaders must declare the default precision for floats to be valid. In this text, we will always use the value highp.

As you can see, our basic shader simply sets the output position to match the input vertex position, and our fragment shader sets the color to be a dark gray. We'll now look at the methods which we need to override. The first is shown in Listing 5-19.

*Listing 5-19. BasicShader's Link Method*

```
void BasicShader::Link()
{
        Shader::Link();

        m_positionAtributeHandle = glGetAttribLocation(m_programId, "a_vPosition");
}
```

Here you can see that we first need to call our parent class' Link method. This ensures that the shaders have been compiled and linked into our program object. We then call glGetAttribLocation; this method returns to us with the index of the a_vPosition attribute which we will use in the next method, Setup, as shown in Listing 5-20.

> **Note**   It is possible to use the attribute name each time you wish to set the vertex stream for the position attribute, but it's good practice to query for the location as it's much faster than looking up the position by name each time you call.

*Listing 5-20. BasicShader::Setup()*

```
void BasicShader::Setup(Renderable& renderable)
{
        Shader::Setup(renderable);

        Geometry* pGeometry = renderable.GetGeometry();
        assert(pGeometry);

        glVertexAttribPointer(
                m_positionAttributeHandle,
                pGeometry->GetNumVertexPositionElements(),
                GL_FLOAT,
                GL_FALSE,
                pGeometry->GetVertexStride(),
                pGeometry->GetVertexBuffer());
        glEnableVertexAttribArray(m_positionAttributeHandle);
}
```

In this method, we again call our parent class to ensure that any operations required on the base have been completed and that our shader is ready to be used.

We then call the `glVertexAttribPointer` OpenGL method to specify the vertex stream. `glVertexAttribPointer`'s arguments are as follows:

- The first parameter is the location of the attribute in the shader which we are describing. In this case, we have data only for the position of the vertex.

- The second parameter tells OpenGL how many elements are contained per vertex. This value can be one, two, three, or four. In our case, it will be three, as we are specifying the x, y, and z coordinates of the vertex.

- The third parameter specifies the type of data that this location uses.

- The fourth determines whether we would like the values to be normalized.

- We then pass a parameter which tells OpenGL how many bytes to jump from the beginning of the data for this vertex to the next, called the stride. Zero is a valid value when there is no data between vertices, or they are tightly packed, as it is known. We will look at the stride in more detail when we look at vertex data which requires it to be nonzero.

- Last but not least, we pass a pointer to the address in memory, where the vertex data for the object can be found.

Before we can use the shader, we are then required to call `glEnableVertexAttribArray` to ensure that the OpenGL context is aware that the data is ready for use.

Now that we have a shader which can be instantiated and used within our program as well as `Geometry` and `Renderable` classes, let's create an app which can use these to draw a quad to the screen.

## Creating an App-Specific Application and Task

Each app that we create is likely to contain different functionality. We'll want to have different menus, different levels, and different gameplay. To differentiate functionality between apps, we can inherit our `Framework Application` class into an app-specific implementation and contain a `Task` inside it, as shown in Listing 5-21.

*Listing 5-21. The Chapter5Task*

```
class Chapter5Task
        :       public Framework::Task
{
private:
        State                           m_state;

        Framework::Renderer*            m_pRenderer;
                Framework::Geometry     m_geometry;
                Framework::BasicShader  m_basicShader;
                Framework::Renderable   m_renderable;

public:
        Chapter5Task(Framework::Renderer* pRenderer, const unsigned int priority);
        virtual ~Chapter5Task();

        // From Task
        virtual bool            Start();
        virtual void            OnSuspend();
        virtual void            Update();
        virtual void            OnResume();


        virtual void            Stop();
};
```

Listing 5-21 shows our `Task` for this app. It contains a pointer to the `Renderer` and members to represent `Geometry`, a `BasicShader`, and a `Renderable`. Using these is fairly straightforward.

Listing 5-22 shows the basic setup required in the constructor.

*Listing 5-22. Chapter5Task Constructor*

```
Chapter5Task::Chapter5Task(Framework::Renderer* pRenderer, const unsigned int priority)
        :       m_pRenderer(pRenderer)
        ,       Framework::Task(priority)
```

```
{
        m_renderable.SetGeometry(&m_geometry);
        m_renderable.SetShader(&m_basicShader);
}
```

Here we set `m_pRenderer` to be the passed in `Renderer` and we call through to the `Task` constructor with the priority which we have assigned.

We also call `SetGeometry` and `SetShader` on `m_renderable` with the addresses of the member variables for the corresponding parameters.

In Listing 5-23, we look at what needs to happen when the `Task` is started on being added to the kernel.

*Listing 5-23. Chapter5Task Start*

```
namespace
{
        float verts[] =
        {
                -0.5f, 0.5f, 0.0f,
                0.5f, 0.5f, 0.0f,
                -0.5f, -0.5f, 0.0f,
                0.5f, -0.5f, 0.0f,
        };

        unsigned short indices[] =
        {
                0,      2,      1,      2,      3,      1
        };
}

bool Chapter5Task::Start()
{
        Framework::Geometry* pGeometry = m_renderable.GetGeometry();
        pGeometry ->SetVertexBuffer(verts);
        pGeometry ->SetNumVertices(4);
        pGeometry ->SetIndexBuffer(indices);
        pGeometry ->SetNumIndices(6);
        pGeometry ->SetName("quad");

        pGeometry ->SetNumVertexPositionElements(3);
        pGeometry ->SetVertexStride(0);

        m_pRenderer->AddRenderable(&m_renderable);

        return true;
}
```

Here we are specifying the vertex and index data in a local anonymous namespace before the method declaration. In the future, we will be loading this data from a file.

The Start method gets the valid pointer from the Renderable object and then sets all of the relevant data. The vertex and index buffers and sizes are set, we give the object a name, and we set the number of position elements per vertex to be three and the stride to be zero.

We then add m_renderable to the Renderer for drawing.

The Stop method (Listing 5-24) has a simple task, and that is to remove the renderable object from the renderer. The destructor should do the same.

*Listing 5-24. Chapter5Task Stop*

```
void Chapter5Task::Stop()
{
        m_pRenderer->RemoveRenderable(&m_renderable);
}
```

We'll now look at how to add Chapter5Task to the Kernel, as shown in Listing 5-25.

*Listing 5-25. Chapter5App*

```
class Chapter5App
        :       public Framework::Application
{
private:
        Chapter5Task            m_chapter5Task;

public:
        Chapter5App(android_app* pState);
        virtual ~Chapter5App();

        virtual bool Initialize();
};
```

Creating the Chapter5App class is as simple as inheriting from Application. We override the Initialize method and add a member of type Chapter5Task.

The methods for Chapter5App are very simple, as shown in Listing 5-26.

*Listing 5-26. Chapter5App Methods*

```
Chapter5App::Chapter5App(android_app* pState)
        :       Framework::Application(pState)
        ,       m_chapter5Task(&m_rendererTask, Framework::Task::GAME_PRIORITY)
{
}

bool Chapter5App::Initialize()
{
        bool success = Framework::Application::Initialize();
```

```
   if (success)
   {
         m_kernel.AddTask(&m_chapter5Task);
   }

   return success;
}
```

The simplicity you see here is a result of us hiding all of the tasks which will be shared between future apps into the Framework layer of the code. We are well on our way to creating a reusable base, and hopefully the benefits you are beginning to see will be even more evident in the next section. Our simple constructor has the easy task of calling its parent and initializing the Chapter5Task object.

Initialize simply calls its parent and then adds the Chapter5Task object to the Kernel if all is well.

We're doing well so far, but the code we have looked at to now will render only a blank quad onto the screen, and that isn't particularly interesting. A screenshot of the output is shown in Figure 5-2.

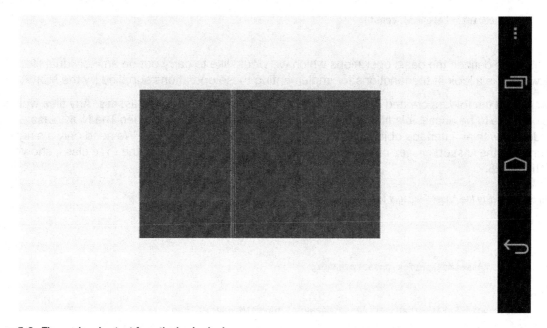

*Figure 5-2. The rendered output from the basic shaders*

Let's quickly move on to look at how we can render a textured quad instead.

# Applying Textures to Geometry

Specifying geometry and vertices in the code was a straightforward task. Representing texture data in the same way would be a much more difficult proposition. I could supply you with a preset texture in a code format; however, now seems like as good a time as any to look at loading files with the Android NDK.

# Loading a File

The word "file" is quite obviously a noun, and basic object oriented-design tells us that nouns make for great candidates to be turned into classes, so that's where we will begin. The interface for the File class is shown in Listing 5-27.

*Listing 5-27. The File Class Interface*

```
class File
{
public:
        explicit File(std::string name);
        virtual ~File();

        bool            Open();
        void            Read(void* pBuffer, const unsigned int bytesToRead, size_t& bytesRead);
        void            Close();

        unsigned int  Length() const;
};
```

The interface defines the basic operations which we would like to carry out on an individual file. Now we'll take a look at the functions for implementing these operations supplied by the NDK.

If you look at the folders created in your project, you should see one called assets. Any files which we would like to be accessible from within our app will be added to this folder. The NDK class provides us with an interface object to this folder called the AAssetManager. We need only a single reference to the AAssetManager object, so we create a static pointer to it in the File class, shown in Listing 5-28.

*Listing 5-28. Adding the AAssetManager to File*

```
class File
{
private:
        static AAssetManager* m_pAssetmanager;

public:
        static void SetAssetManager(AAssetManager* pAssetManager)
        {
                m_pAssetManager = pAssetmanager;
        }
};
```

To ensure this is set before creating an instance of File, it's a good idea to assert on the pointer not being NULL in the constructor, as shown in Listing 5-29.

*Listing 5-29. File Constructor*

```
File::File(std::string name)
{
        assert(m_pAssetManager != NULL);
}
```

The first operation carried out on a file is to open it. We do this via a call to AAssetManager_open, which is shown in Listing 5-30.

*Listing 5-30. File Open*

```
bool File::Open()
{
        m_pAsset = AAssetManager_open(m_pAssetManager, m_filename.c_str(), AASSET_MODE_UNKNOWN);
        return !!m_pAsset;
}
```

As you can see, this is relatively straightforward. You will need to add an AAsset pointer and a string for the filename to the class definition to represent m_pAsset and m_filename. m_filename can be initialized with the string passed into File's constructor.

At this point, we can ask the NDK how long the file is in bytes, as shown in Listing 5-31.

*Listing 5-31. File Length*

```
unsigned int File::Length() const
{
        return AAsset_getLength(m_pAsset);
}
```

We can also close the file when we are finished with it, as shown in Listing 5-32.

*Listing 5-32. File Close*

```
void File::Close()
{
        if (m_pAsset)
        {
                AAsset_close(m_pAsset);
                m_pAsset = NULL;
        }
}
```

It's good practice to ensure that all files are closed before shutting down a program; therefore, I'd also advise calling Close from File's destructor (Listing 5-33).

*Listing 5-33. ~File*

```
File::~File()
{
        Close();
}
```

Now for the real workhorse of the File class, the Read method, as shown in Listing 5-34.

*Listing 5-34. File's Read Method*

```
void File::Read(void* pBuffer, const unsigned int bytesToRead, size_t& bytesRead)
{
        bytesRead = AAsset_read(m_pAsset, pBuffer, bytesToRead);
}
```

Hardly complicated, but there's a good reason for that. Many file types have headers which the program may wish to read without having to read the entire contents of a large file. This is especially true of files which are collections of other files.

As it would be impossible for the File class itself to know the intentions of the code which is calling it, we do not encumber it with any unwarranted code. We'll look at how we can handle a texture file next.

# Loading a TGA File

TGA files are widely used within game development. There is a simple reason for their widespread adoption: they are very easy to read and write and they support all of the information which a game requires, which includes an alpha channel. There is also a developer area specified in the TGA format which devs can use for whatever purposes they wish, which makes the format very flexible. For now, we'll deal with a basic TGA file. Listing 5-35 shows the exact byte pattern of a TGA file's header.

*Listing 5-35. TGAHeader*

```
struct TGAHeader
{
        unsigned char           m_idSize;
        unsigned char           m_colorMapType;
        unsigned char           m_imageType;

        unsigned short          m_paletteStart;
        unsigned short          m_paletteLength;
        unsigned char           m_paletteBits;

        unsigned short          m_xOrigin;
        unsigned short          m_yOrigin;
        unsigned short          m_width;
        unsigned short          m_height;
        unsigned char           m_bpp;
        unsigned char           m_descriptor;
} __attribute__ ((packed));
```

This 18-byte section exists at the beginning of every valid TGA file and always in the same format. A lot of the data is unnecessary for us to consider at the moment. Initially, we will be dealing with uncompressed bitmap data. While TGA files can support compression and palettized textures, they are not in a format which is supported by OpenGL, and as such we will avoid creating textures in this format. In the case where we have a normal bitmap file, the only fields of interest in the header are width, height, and bpp. bpp represents the bytes per pixel, a value of one would indicate that we are dealing with a grayscale image, three would indicate RGB, and four would indicate RGBA. We can work out the size of the image data which follows on from the header by calculating m_width * m_height * m_bpp.

Unfortunately, we have to cover a relatively advanced concept at this time. When we load our file data, we will load the entire 18 bytes of the header, or the entire file, from memory. We can then cast the pointer addressing the data loaded from the file into a TGAHeader pointer; using a cast in this manner prevents us from having to copy the loaded data into a structure and is commonly referred to as memory mapping. The __attribute__ ((packed)) directive is essential when doing this. Its job is to ensure that the compiler does not add any padding between the members in the structure. For instance, the first three fields, m_idSize, m_colorMapType, and m_imageType, are represented within three bytes. Most processors are more efficient at copying and accessing data from a memory address which is aligned on a boundary of a certain number of bytes. The compiler therefore can pad out the structure by skipping over the fourth byte and storing m_paletteStart on the next address which is divisible by four.

The problem this creates for us is that different compilers are free to pad whichever way they please for the processor they are targeting, while our files which we are loading from memory are guaranteed to not have any padding present; this means that compilers are likely to make the addresses of the fields of the structure not match the position of the data in the binary chunk. The __attribute__ ((packed)) line at the end of the struct definition prevents the compiler from adding padding which we do not want.

Sorry for the slight detour and bump in difficulty. If that last piece of information was a little complex, rest assured that you do not have to understand exactly what is happening at this point in time; you just need to know that it's needed in this instance. I've also added it everywhere else in this book where it is necessary, so you won't have to worry about getting it correct later.

Let's take a look at the TGAFile class as a whole (see Listing 5-36).

*Listing 5-36. TGAFile*

```
class TGAFile
{
public:
    struct TGAHeader
    {
        unsigned char      m_idSize;
        unsigned char      m_colorMapType;
        unsigned char      m_imageType;

        unsigned short     m_paletteStart;
        unsigned short     m_paletteLength;
        unsigned char      m_paletteBits;

        unsigned short     m_xOrigin;


        unsigned short     m_yOrigin;
        unsigned short     m_width;
        unsigned short     m_height;
```

```
                unsigned char        m_bpp;
                unsigned char        m_descriptor;
        } __attribute__ ((packed));

        TGAFile(void* pData);
        virtual ~TGAFile();

        unsigned short               GetWidth() const;
        unsigned short               GetHeight() const;
        void*                        GetImageData() const;

private:
        TGAHeader*                   m_pHeader;
        void*                        m_pImageData;
};

inline unsigned short TGAFile::GetWidth() const
{
        unsigned short width = m_pHeader
                ?        m_pHeader->m_width
                :        0;
        return width;
}

inline unsigned short TGAFile::GetHeight() const
{
        unsigned short height = m_pHeader
                ?        m_pHeader->m_height
                :        0;
        return height;
}

inline void* TGAFile::GetImageData() const
{
        return m_pImageData;
}
```

It's quite easy to understand for the most part. Now we can take a look at how we will represent a texture to the Renderer.

# Representing a GL Texture

Textures are used in computer graphics to give flat surfaces more detail than would otherwise be possible using geometry alone. The classic example is a brick wall. The bricks themselves have a rough surface, and the mortar between the bricks is usually a different color from the bricks.

Representing these surfaces using a purely geometric method would require many more vertices than we could possibly process at a real-time frame rate. We get around the processing limitation by faking the appearance of the surface by drawing an image over it. These images are textures.

Textures are now used for many purposes. They can be used in the traditional manner by defining the color of each pixel on a polygon. They are also now used for diverse applications such as to map normals and lighting data. These are known as normal maps and light maps, respectively. We'll stick with the traditional use at this beginner level and will take a look in this chapter at how we use texture maps. Listing 5-37 shows how we represent a texture map in code.

*Listing 5-37. Framework's Texture Class*

```
class Texture
{
public:
        struct Header
        {
                unsigned int                m_width;
                unsigned int                m_height;
                unsigned int                m_bytesPerPixel;
                unsigned int                m_dataSize;

                Header()
                        :       m_width(0)
                        ,       m_height(0)
                        ,       m_bytesPerPixel(0)
                        ,       m_dataSize(0)
                {
                }

                Header(const Header& header)
                {
                        m_width            = header.m_width;
                        m_height           = header.m_height;
                        m_bytesPerPixel    = header.m_bytesPerPixel;
                        m_dataSize         = header.m_dataSize;
                }
        };

private:
        GLuint      m_id;
        Header      m_header;
        void*       m_pImageData;

public:
        Texture();
        ~Texture();


        void SetData(Header& header, void* pImageData);

        GLuint GetId() const { return m_id; }

        void Init();
};
```

This class is another fairly straightforward affair and is mostly self-documenting. It takes some pointers and stores the information it needs to describe the texture data in a struct named Header. The one method worth taking a proper look at is Init, which we do in Listing 5-38.

*Listing 5-38. Texture's Init*

```
void Texture::Init()
{
        GLint   packBits                = 4;
        GLint   internalFormat          = GL_RGBA;
        GLenum  format                  = GL_RGBA;
        switch (m_header.m_bytesPerPixel)
        {
        case 1:
        {
                packBits                = 1;
                internalFormat          = GL_ALPHA;
                format                  = GL_ALPHA;
        }
        break;
        };

        glGenTextures(1, &m_id);

        glBindTexture(GL_TEXTURE_2D, m_id);

        glPixelStorei(GL_UNPACK_ALIGNMENT, packBits);

        glTexImage2D(
                GL_TEXTURE_2D,
                0,
                internalFormat,
                m_header.m_width,
                m_header.m_height,
                0,
                format,
                GL_UNSIGNED_BYTE,
                m_pImageData);
}
```

For now, Init is written to handle only GL_RGBA or GL_ALPHA textures. glGenTextures creates a new texture and returns an id through the parameter reference. It would be possible to create multiple textures at once, but for now we're happy with creating single textures at a time.

glBindTexture serves to attach the texture at the specified ID to the named texture unit and also locks the texture to that type. At the moment, we are interested only in traditional two-dimensional textures, so we have specified that in the first parameter.

glPixelStorei informs OpenGL how many bytes are in each pixel. For grayscale, we have one byte per pixel and for RGBA textures, we have four. Specifically, this function tells OpenGL how it should read the texture into its own memory.

We then use glTexImage2D. This function has the OpenGL context copy the image data from our source array into its own usable memory space. The parameters are as follows:

- target - the texture unit to read into, in our case GL_TEXTURE_2D.

- level - the mip level to read into; for now we are interested only in level zero.

- internalFormat - the format of the texture to copy into. This can be different from format but we are not using this functionality.

- width - the width of the texture in pixels.

- height - the height of the texture in pixels.

- border - this value must always be zero.

- format - the format of the source pixel data. We are using GL_ALPHA or GL_RGBA and will match the value passed to internalFormat.

- type - the data type of the individual pixels. We are using unsigned bytes.

- data - the pointer to the first pixel in the image data.

Once this function has been successfully called, we will have a usable texture at the ID created.

## Creating TextureShader

We can write the shader which will be used to apply the texture to the geometry now that we know what a texture looks like to OpenGL. We start by again inheriting a new class from Shader in Listing 5-39.

*Listing 5-39. The TextureShader Class*

```
class TextureShader
        :       public Shader
{
private:
        Texture*        m_pTexture;
        GLint           m_positionAttributeHandle;
        GLint           m_texCoordAttributeHandle;
        GLint           m_samplerHandle;

public:
        TextureShader();
        virtual ~TextureShader();

        virtual void  Link();
        virtual void  Setup(Renderable& renderable);

        void          SetTexture(Texture* pTexture);
        Texture*      GetTexture();
};
```

The code is not all that much more complicated than the BasicShader which we created earlier. The standout differences are that we do not have an attribute handle for texture coordinates or one for something called a sampler, which I will explain more in the following text. Let's take a look at the constructor for TextureShader, as shown in Listing 5-40.

*Listing 5-40. The TextureShader Constructor*

```
TextureShader::TextureShader()
        :       m_pTexture(NULL)
{
     m_vertexShaderCode =
             "attribute vec4 a_vPosition;                          \n"
             "attribute vec2 a_texCoord;                           \n"
             "varying   vec2 v_texCoord;                           \n"
             "void main(){                                         \n"
             "    gl_Position = a_vPosition;                       \n"
             "    v_texCoord = a_texCoord;                         \n"
             "}                                                    \n";

     m_fragmentShaderCode =
             "precision highp float;                               \n"
             "varying vec2 v_texCoord;                             \n"
             "uniform sampler2D s_texture;                         \n"
             "void main(){                                         \n"
             "    gl_FragColor = texture2D(s_texture, v_texCoord); \n"
             "}                                                    \n";
}
```

The shader code should look a little familiar by now. We have attributes which will correspond to the data being passed in to the vertex shader, one to represent the position and another to represent the texture coordinates. We then also have a varying named v_textCoord which will be used to interpolate the current texture coordinate for processing in the fragment shader. You can see this varying being set up in the vertex shader, where we pass the texture coordinate attribute into the varying.

The fragment shader introduces a new concept, that of the **sampler**. Sampling is the process by which a GPU takes a texture coordinate and looks up the texel color. Note the change in terminology there: when talking about textures, we tend to talk about the individual elements as texels rather than pixels.

The coordinates themselves are also usually referred to as UV coordinates when they are used in discussion about looking up texels in a texture. U corresponds to the usual x axis and V to the y axis. The origin of UV coordinates is at position (0, 0) and is found in the top left-hand corner of the image. The coordinates are specified as numbers ranging from zero to one, where U at zero is the left-hand edge and one is the right-hand edge, the same applied for V from top to bottom.

The program gets access to the locations of the shader's variables in a familiar manner. As you can see in Listing 5-41, we gain access to the sampler's location by using glGetUniformPosition rather than glGetAttribLocation.

*Listing 5-41.  TextureShader Link*

```
void TextureShader::Link()
{
        Shader::Link();

        m_positionAttributeHandle    = glGetAttribLocation(m_programId, "a_vPosition");
        m_texCoordAttributeHandle    = glGetAttribLocation(m_programId, "a_texCoord");
        m_samplerHandle              = glGetUniformLocation(m_programId, "s_texture");
}
```

The last thing left to do with our shader is set it up ready for use, as shown in Listing 5-42.

*Listing 5-42.  TextureShader Setup*

```
void TextureShader::Setup(Renderable& renderable)
{
        assert(m_pTexture);
        Geometry* pGeometry = renderable.GetGeometry();
        if (pGeometry && m_pTexture)
        {
                Shader::Setup(renderable);


                glActiveTexture(GL_TEXTURE0);
                glBindTexture(GL_TEXTURE_2D, m_pTexture->GetId());
                glUniform1i(m_samplerHandle, 0);

                glTexParameteri(GL_TEXTURE_2D, GL_TEXTURE_WRAP_S, GL_CLAMP_TO_EDGE);
                glTexParameteri(GL_TEXTURE_2D, GL_TEXTURE_WRAP_T, GL_CLAMP_TO_EDGE);

                glTexParameteri(GL_TEXTURE_2D, GL_TEXTURE_MIN_FILTER, GL_LINEAR);
                glTexParameteri(GL_TEXTURE_2D, GL_TEXTURE_MAG_FILTER, GL_LINEAR);

                glVertexAttribPointer(
                        m_positionAttributeHandle,
                        pGeometry->GetNumVertexPositionElements(),
                        GL_FLOAT,
                        GL_FALSE,
                        pGeometry->GetVertexStride(),
                        pGeometry->GetVertexBuffer());
                        glEnableVertexAttribArray(m_positionAttributeHandle);

                glVertexAttribPointer(
                        m_texCoordAttributeHandle,
                        pGeometry->GetNumTexCoordElements(),
                        GL_FLOAT,
                        GL_FALSE,
```

```
                    pGeometry->GetVertexStride(),
                    &static_cast<GLfloat*>(pGeometry->GetVertexBuffer())
                                           [pGeometry->GetNumVertexPositionElements()]);
            glEnableVertexAttribArray(m_texCoordAttributeHandle);
        }
}
```

Listing 5-42 shows us what is required to set up the shader for use with a texture. After calling the parent object's Setup method, we then activate a texture sampler with OpenGL for our use using glActiveTexture. We then attach our texture to the GL_TEXTURE_2D unit and set our sampler location to be the texture unit zero. These steps are necessary to have OpenGL setup the correct texture for use in our shader at the correct location.

The next step is to set a wrapping format for our texture. Certain effects can be achieved using the wrapping value. Textures can be made to repeat or mirrored, for example, by specifying texture coordinate smaller or larger than zero and one. In our case, we will simply set the texture coordinates to be clamped to the range between zero and one.

We then specify a filtering type. Filtering is applied to a texture when it is not being drawn at one texel per screen pixel. When the texels are far away from the camera, multiple texels may be visible inside a single pixel. Linear filtering averages the four pixels in a block surrounding the point where the UV coordinates are pointing on the surface of the texture. The result is that the image is slightly blurred, and while this may not sound ideal, it helps to reduce a shimmering effect on textures as objects move toward and away from the camera.

We then specify the vertex data to OpenGL just like we did in the BasicShader. After specifying the vertex data, we specify the texture coordinate data. Everything looks the same for the most part, except that we pass the texture coordinate attribute location and the number of texture coordinate elements into glVertexAttribPointer. We then need to pass the address of the first texture coordinate into the last parameter. Remember that we discussed earlier that we would be using an array of structure formats for our data and that this means our vertex attributes are interleaved into a single array. You can see that we calculate the address of the first texture coordinate by casting the vertex buffer to a float pointer and then use an array index with the number of position elements to jump the pointer over the first position.

This is all we need for setting up our texture and shader for use. We can now look at how we go about making sure that OpenGL is in the correct state to handle our textures and shaders.

# Initializing Textures and Shaders

As we saw when we initialized OpenGL, the API has a context which is set up at a time when the Android OS informs us that it has created the window structures for our app. We also saw how setting up textures and shaders involves getting positions of variables from shader programs which have been linked or attached. These processes are carried out within the current context. The implication of this is that we need a valid context before we can carry out these operations on our shaders and textures. It also means that if the context is destroyed, which occurs if the user puts the phone to sleep, then each texture and shader must be reinitialized.

To ensure that this is possible, we will add a vector of textures and shaders which are in use to the Renderer, as shown in Listing 5-43.

*Listing 5-43. Renderer's Texture and Shader Vectors*

```
class Renderer
{
private:
        typedef std::vector<Shader*>               ShaderVector;
        typedef ShaderVector::iterator             ShaderVectorIterator;

        typedef std::vector<Texture*>              TextureVector;


        typedef TextureVector::iterator     TextureVectorIterator;

public:
        void AddShader(Shader* pShader);
        void RemoveShader(Shader* pShader);

        void AddTexture(Texture* pTexture);
        void RemoveTexture(Texture* pTexture);
};

void Renderer::AddShader(Shader* pShader)
{
        assert(pShader);
        if (m_initialized)
        {
                pShader->Link();
        }
        m_shaders.push_back(pShader);
}

void Renderer::RemoveShader(Shader* pShader)
{
        for (ShaderVectorIterator iter = m_shaders.begin(); iter != m_shaders.end(); ++iter)
        {
                Shader* pCurrent = *iter;
                if (pCurrent == pShader)
                {
                        m_shaders.erase(iter);
                        break;
                }
        }
}

void Renderer::AddTexture(Texture* pTexture)
{
        assert(pTexture);
        if (m_initialized)
        {
                pTexture->Init();
        }
        m_textures.push_back(pTexture);
}
```

```
void Renderer::RemoveTexture(Texture* pTexture)
{
        for (TextureVectorIterator iter = m_textures.begin(); iter != m_textures.end(); ++iter)
        {
                Texture* pCurrent = *iter;
                if (pCurrent == pTexture)
                {
                        m_textures.erase(iter);
                        break;
                }
        }
}
```

The preceding code is all we need to maintain a current list of textures and shaders in use. To reinitialize these when the phone becomes awake and the Renderer has been initialized or to initialize any which were added before the Renderer was ready, we add the code from Listing 5-44 to Renderer::Init after the OpenGL setup has completed.

*Listing 5-44. Reinitializing Textures and Shaders*

```
for (TextureVectorIterator iter = m_textures.begin(); iter != m_textures.end(); ++iter)
{
        Texture* pCurrent = *iter;
        pCurrent->Init();
}

for (ShaderVectorIterator iter = m_shaders.begin(); iter != m_shaders.end(); ++iter)
{
        Shader* pCurrent = *iter;
        pCurrent->Link();
}
```

# Loading Textures in a Task

Before we can load a texture, we need to specify the relevant variables required. We do this in Listing 5-45.

*Listing 5-45. Adding a Texture to Chapter5Task*

```
class Chapter5Task
        :       public Framework::Task
{
private:
        enum State
        {
                LOADING_FILE,
                CREATE_TEXTURE,
                RUNNING
        };

        State                           m_state;
```

```
Framework::File              m_file;
Framework::Renderer*         m_pRenderer;
Framework::Geometry          m_geometry;
Framework::TextureShader     m_textureShader;
Framework::Renderable        m_renderable;
Framework::Texture           m_texture;

void*                        m_pTGABuffer;
unsigned int                 m_readBytes;
unsigned int                 m_fileLength;
};
```

We'll look at what each is for as we move through the modified methods. Let's start with the constructor, as shown in Listing 5-46.

*Listing 5-46. Chapter5Task Constructor*

```
Chapter5Task::Chapter5Task(Framework::Renderer* pRenderer, const unsigned int priority)
        :        m_pRenderer(pRenderer)
        ,        Framework::Task(priority)
        ,        m_state(RUNNING)
        ,        m_file("test.tga")
        ,        m_pTGABuffer(NULL)
        ,        m_readBytes(0)
{
        m_renderable.SetGeometry(&m_geometry);
        m_renderable.SetShader(&m_textureShader);
}
```

Here you can see that we have set up the variables with default values, which includes specifying the filename test.tga.

Listing 5-47 shows the Start method.

*Listing 5-47. Chapter5Task Start*

```
float verts[] =
{
        -0.5f, 0.5f, 0.0f,
        0.0f, 1.0f,
        0.5f, 0.5f, 0.0f,
        1.0f, 1.0f,
        -0.5f, -0.5f, 0.0f,
        0.0f, 0.0f,
        0.5f, -0.5f, 0.0f,
        1.0f, 0.0f
};

bool Chapter5Task::Start()
{
        Framework::Geometry* pGeometry = m_renderable.GetGeometry();
        pGeometry->SetVertexBuffer(verts);
        pGeometry->SetNumVertices(4);
```

```
        pGeometry->SetIndexBuffer(indices);
        pGeometry->SetNumIndices(6);
        pGeometry->SetName("quad");

        pGeometry->SetNumVertexPositionElements(3);
        pGeometry->SetNumTexCoordElements(2);
        pGeometry->SetVertexStride(sizeof(float) * 5);

        bool success = false;
        if (m_file.Open())
        {
                m_fileLength = m_file.Length();

                m_pTGABuffer = new char[m_fileLength];

                m_state = LOADING_FILE;
                success = true;
        }

        return success;
}
```

Here we have modified the array of vertices to have the four corners of the texture coordinates specified at each position. The corresponding changes have been made to the Geometry class parameters, namely, the number of texture coordinates have been set to two and the vertex string to be the size of a float multiplied by five. This calculates our stride to be 20 bytes, which is easily verified. We have three floats for position and two for texture coordinates. A float is 4 bytes in size, so 5 times 4 is 20; perfect. An important point to notice with the texture coordinates is that they are "upside-down." While it would be normal for zero to be the top and one to be the bottom, TGA files actually save their image data vertically flipped. Rather than look at complex code for flipping the image data or preprocessing the files, we simply invert our texture coordinates here. All of the textures in this book are TGAs, so this is an acceptable approach, but this is an issue you will want to be aware of if you decide to use other image formats.

We then have a new block of code which opens our file, retrieves its length, and allocates an array of bytes large enough to store its entire contents. Our state variable is then set to LOADING_FILE; we'll take a look at the significance of that in the Update method, shown in Listing 5-48.

*Listing 5-48. Chapter5Task::Update()*

```
void Chapter5Task::Update()
{
        switch (m_state)
        {
        case LOADING_FILE:
        {
                void* pCurrentDataPos =
                        static_cast<char*>(m_pTGABuffer) + (sizeof(char) * m_readBytes);

                size_t bytesRead = 0;
                m_file.Read(pCurrentDataPos, 512 * 1024, bytesRead);
```

```
        m_readBytes += bytesRead;
        if (m_readBytes == m_fileLength)
        {
                m_state = CREATE_TEXTURE;
        }
    }


    break;

    case CREATE_TEXTURE:
    {
        Framework::TGAFile tgaFile(m_pTGABuffer);

        Framework::Texture::Header textureHeader;
        textureHeader.m_height = tgaFile.GetHeight();
        textureHeader.m_width = tgaFile.GetWidth();
        textureHeader.m_bytesPerPixel = 4;
        textureHeader.m_dataSize =
                textureHeader.m_height *
                textureHeader.m_width *
                textureHeader.m_bytesPerPixel;

        m_texture.SetData(textureHeader, tgaFile.GetImageData());

        m_pRenderer->AddShader(&m_textureShader);
        m_pRenderer->AddTexture(&m_texture);

        m_textureShader.SetTexture(&m_texture);

        m_pRenderer->AddRenderable(&m_renderable);

        m_state = RUNNING;
    }
    break;
    };
}
```

What we have in Update is a rudimentary state machine. A state machine is a code construct which specifies the current stage of an operation in an object. Our Task has three states: LOADING_FILE, CREATE_TEXTURE, and RUNNING. The following process shows how the states change.

1. The LOADING_FILE state reads the test.tga file into the allocated memory buffer in blocks of 512 kilobytes at a time. It calculates the current position to read into by offsetting into m_pTGABuffer by the number of bytes already read. File::Read passes out the number of bytes it read into the supplied buffer for each call, and we add that to the value in m_readBytes. Once the number of read bytes matches the size of the file, we can be satisfied that we are finished and move onto the next state, CREATE_TEXTURE.

2.  The CREATE_TEXTURE state takes the read file and creates an instance of TGAFile from it. We then create a Texture::Header object with the data from tgaFile and use this to initialize m_texture along with the image data from tgaFile.

3.  The texture and shader are then added to the Renderer, which will ensure that they are properly initialized. The texture is also added to the shader for rendering the quad and finally the renderable is added to the Renderer before we switch to the RUNNING state.

Before we move onto the next chapter, I'd like to show you what adding textures to geometry can achieve (see Figure 5-3).

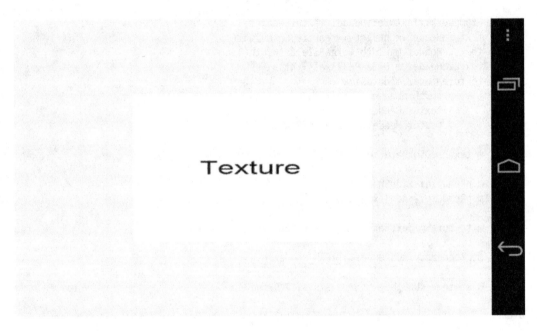

*Figure 5-3. A textured quad*

Rendering text is a complicated topic which we will not be covering in detail in this book, but by embedding text into a texture, we can add written words into our game engine. With the same simple rectangle we had earlier, texturing gives us a method to provide much more detail and data to our player.

# Summary

We didn't cover every single line of code necessary to get to this point; instead, I have focused on the main methods which are important to the tasks we have tried to achieve. I'd recommend that you take a look at the sample code which accompanies this chapter, build it, and use break points in the debugger to work out exactly how everything fits together.

I want to reiterate the benefits of writing a game engine. A lot of the code we have just covered is laborious to work through. The benefit of encapsulating this into reusable code is that you'll never have to write any of this again. It's quite clear to see from the Chapter5Task class that we can add geometry, textures, and shaders to future apps now with relative ease, which will increase our productivity moving forward, and that's exactly what we will do.

Part 1 of the book is now complete, and we have looked at video game development from its history to the present day and have begun to write code which we will hopefully use to affect its future. In the next section, we'll begin to look at code which will shape the gameplay of the game we are going to build, *Droid Runner*.

# Chapter 6

# Game Entities

All games are made up of different objects and the way that these objects behave. *Pac-Man* has objects such as Pac-Man himself, the ghosts, pac-dots, power pellets, and walls. Each of these objects has a different behavior. Pac-Man responds to the player's input and can change from being the prey to being the predator by eating a power pellet. This changes the behavior of the ghosts, who are placed into a state where they run away from the player.

Our game calls for a simpler set of behaviors, but we will construct the objects using state-of-the-art methods to get a feel for how modern games structure their game objects. Traditionally, game objects have been built with a normal class hierarchy, starting with a base class and adding specializations in each level up to the point where we have a class which is usable in-game. The problem with this approach is its inflexibility. Once a game reaches a reasonable level of complexity, it can be particularly difficult to add new types. There may also be problems related to diamond inheritance and particular objects not fitting into the hierarchy all that well, leading to the overly complex construction of objects which should in theory be quite simple.

Today, modern game architectures are more likely to be built using a component-based system. In this chapter, we will take a look at how we can construct objects using such a system.

We'll also look at an event system which will allow us to tell game objects about game events which they can then react to. This again is a modern system which is extremely useful and allows objects to opt in to events which they are interested in. Previously, the system which generates the event was responsible for notifying every object it thought was likely to need to react.

Finally, we'll move on to implementing the player and AI objects which will be used throughout our game.

## What Is a Game Entity?

The game entity is a very simple concept. Any object which exists in the game world is an entity. From cars to people, exploding barrels, power-ups, and projectiles, if the object is one which needs to be modeled in the game world to have an impact on gameplay, it is an entity.

There are also entities which may not be as clear to the beginner game programmer. These would be objects which must exist in the world but may not necessarily be visible. Lights, cameras, trigger boxes, and sound emitters could all be examples of game objects which could fall under this category. Figure 6-1 shows a traditional class hierarchy for vehicles.

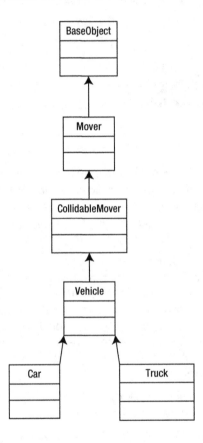

***Figure 6-1.*** *A vehicle object hierarchy*

Rather than use this hierarchy of classes to define the types of objects we will use in the game, we will have a single class called GameObject. Complex objects will be constructed by adding components to this object. We'll take a look at what types of components we will need later in this chapter; for now, Listing 6-1 shows the GameObject class.

*Listing 6-1. The Game Object Class*

```
class GameObject
{
        template <class T>
        friend T* component_cast(GameObject& object);

        template <class T>
        friend T* component_cast(GameObject* pObject);
```

```
private:
        typedef std::tr1::unordered_map<unsigned int, Component*>     ComponentUnorderedMap;
        typedef ComponentUnorderedMap::iterator             ComponentUnorderedMapIterator;
        ComponentUnorderedMap                       m_components;

        template <class T>
        T*     GetComponent() { return static_cast<T*>(GetComponent(T::GetId())); }

        Component*    GetComponent(unsigned int id);

public:
        GameObject();
        ~GameObject();

        template <class T>
        bool AddComponent();
};
```

Listing 6-1 contains some of the most complicated code which we've looked at so far, so we'll go through it line by line. The `friend` keyword in C++ is used to allow other classes or functions to call private methods which belong to instances of this class. In our case, we have defined a method named component_cast which will be used to convert an object into a pointer to a type of component. The component_cast method is overloaded to take a pointer or a reference to a GameObject for convenience so that we are not required to dereference pointers throughout our codebase. The methods are also templatized so that we can use the template syntax to specify which type of component we want to convert the object into.

We can then see a `typedef` for an `unordered_map` of Component pointers and another for an iterator of the map type.

The template method GetComponent is the method which will be called from the `friend` component_cast function which we'll look at shortly in Listing 6-2. This method calls the non-templatized version of GetComponent and passes the id obtained from the `static` GetId method from the template type. If the class passed as the type via the template does not contain a `static` GetId method, we will be given an error at compile time.

We then declare our constructor and destructor before also declaring another templatized method for adding components to the object.

Listing 6-2 shows the function definitions for the overloaded component_cast methods.

*Listing 6-2. component_cast*

```
template <class T>
T* component_cast(GameObject& object)
{
        return object.GetComponent<T>();
}
```

```
template <class T>
T* component_cast(GameObject* pObject)
{
        T* pComponent = NULL;
        if (pObject)
        {
            pComponent = pObject->GetComponent<T>();
        }

        return pComponent;
}
```

The major difference between the two methods is that the pointer-based version checks to see that the pointer is not null before calling GetComponent on the passed object. For programmers familiar with C++ cast types such as static_cast, this method of implementing the accessor for Component objects which our GameObject contains will be very familiar in use. The code in practice will look like that shown in Listing 6-3.

*Listing 6-3. component_cast example usage*

```
ComponentType* pComponent = component_cast<ComponentType>(pOurObject);
```

We will be looking at this more when we cover the Component implementations for *Droid Runner* later in this chapter.

Listing 6-4 shows GetComponent, which is a simple method.

*Listing 6-4. GetComponent*

```
Component* GameObject::GetComponent(unsigned int id)
{
        ComponentUnorderedMapIterator result = m_components.find(id);
        return result == m_components.end()
                ?       NULL
                :       result->second;
}
```

Our map is keyed using the id of each Component, so we can retrieve a Component from the map by simply calling find and passing the id as its argument.

The AddComponent method shown in Listing 6-5 does exactly what its name suggests: it adds a component to our object.

*Listing 6-5. AddComponent*

```
template <class T>
bool GameObject::AddComponent()
{
        bool added = false;

        ComponentUnorderedMapIterator result = m_components.find(T::GetId());
        if (result == m_components.end())
```

```
        {
                T* pNewComponent = new T(this);

                if (pNewComponent)
                {
                        std::pair<unsigned int, Component*> newComponent(
                                T::GetId(),
                                pNewComponent);
                        std::pair< ComponentUnorderedMapIterator, bool> addedIter =
                                                        m_components.insert(newComponent);
                        added = addedIter.second;
                }
        }

        return added;
}
```

First, it calls find on m_components to check if we have this type of Component already added to the object. If the Component does not already exist in the unordered_map, we create a new instance of the class type passed via the template parameter. The validity check on the pointer will help to prevent our code from crashing in the case where the object was not created. new generally fails in situations where we are out of memory, so we will likely see very bad things happening shortly after if it was not successful.

To add an element to unordered_map, we are required to create a std::pair. Our pair creates a mapping between the key, which in our case is the value returned by T::GetId(), and the pointer to the newly created component. m_components.insert is called with the pair passed as its argument. insert returns another pair which consists of an iterator into the map and a bool. If the new Component was successfully added to the map, the value of the bool will be true.

The last method of note in the GameObject is the destructor. We take a look at this in Listing 6-6.

*Listing 6-6. GameObject::~GameObject*

```
GameObject::~GameObject()
{
        for (ComponentUnorderedMapIterator iter = m_components.begin();
                iter != m_components.end();
                ++iter)
        {
                Component* pComponent = iter->second;
                if (pComponent)
                {
                        delete pComponent;
                        pComponent = NULL;
                }
        }
}
```

The destructor of GameObject has a simple job: it iterates over the m_components unordered_map and deletes each Component which was added.

The base class for a component is a simple piece of code and is shown in Listing 6-7.

*Listing 6-7. Component Declaration*

```
class Component
{
private:
        GameObject*     m_pOwner;

public:
        explicit Component(GameObject* pOwner)
                :       m_pOwner(pOwner)
        {
        }

        virtual ~Component()    {}

        virtual void Initialize()    = 0;

        GameObject* GetOwner() { return m_pOwner; }
};
```

As you can see, a Component will simply contain a pointer to its owner and a pure virtual initialization method. The GetOwner method will be useful later, as it allows Components to access the GameObject which they belong to and use component_cast to access other Components if necessary.

Now that we have a class which will encapsulate our objects and a base interface for components, we should take a look at the event system which will be used to communicate with the objects.

# Communicating with Game Objects via Events

The normal process for communicating with an object is to call the methods which make up the class. This requires that we have a suitable process for gaining access to the object and that we know which methods to call on that object. If we had a need to call the same method on multiple objects, we would increase the complexity of our code by requiring a method to collect all of the objects which we are going to call the method on. As game projects grow, these tasks become more and more difficult to manage properly and require proper planning and management to ensure that they do not consume too much time.

We can avoid all of these problems by switching to an event-based system. Rather than call methods on each class when we would like objects to carry out a task, we simply broadcast an event message. It is the responsibility of other objects to subscribe to the events which they wish to be informed of. It really is as simple as that.

## The Event Class

To get started, we'll take a look at the class which encapsulates an Event. The code can be seen in Listing 6-8.

*Listing 6-8. The Event Declaration*

```
typedef unsigned int EventID;

class Event
{
private:
        typedef std::vector<EventHandler*>      EventHandlerList;
        typedef EventHandlerList::iterator      EventHandlerListIterator;

        EventHandlerList            m_listeners;
        EventID                     m_id;

public:
        explicit Event(EventID eventId);
        ~Event();

        void Send();
        void SendToHandler(EventHandler& eventHandler);
        void AttachListener(EventHandler& eventHandler);
        void DetachListener(EventHandler& eventHandler);

        EventID     GetID()     const            { return m_id; }
};
```

The class for an Event is another simple class. You can see that we will be storing a list of EventHandler pointers in m_listeners. Our Event will also have an id field which we will ensure is unique to each Event.

The public methods Send, SendToHandler, AttachListener, and DetachListener are where the main work of the object is carried out.

Listing 6-9 shows the Send method.

*Listing 6-9. Event::Send()*

```
void Event::Send()
{
        for (EventHandlerListIterator iter = m_listeners.begin();
             iter != m_listeners.end();
             ++iter)
        {
                EventHandler* pEventHandler = *iter;
                assert(pEventHandler);
                if (pEventHandler)
                {
                        pEventHandler->HandleEvent(this);
                }
        }
}
```

This method simply loops over all of the members of the m_listeners list, retrieves the EventHandler pointer from the iterator, and calls EventHandler::HandleEvent on the object. Pretty simple. Listing 6-10 shows how we can send an Event to a single object.

*Listing 6-10. Event::SendToHandler()*

```
void Event::SendToHandler(EventHandler& eventHandler)
{
        for (EventHandlerListIterator iter = m_listeners.begin();
            iter != m_listeners.end();
            ++iter)
        {
            if (&eventHandler == *iter)
            {
                    eventHandler.HandleEvent(this);
            }
        }
}
```

Here you can see that we will send the event only to the specific object which is passed in the parameter, and only if that object exists in our list of listeners. We manage the list through the AttachListener and DetachListener methods. First, AttachListener as shown in Listing 6-11.

*Listing 6-11. Event::AttachListener()*

```
void Event::AttachListener(EventHandler& eventHandler)
{
        m_listeners.push_back(&eventHandler);
}
```

Attaching an object to the event is as simple as pushing its address onto m_listeners.

DetachListener is shown in Listing 6-12.

*Listing 6-12. Event::DetachListener()*

```
void Event::DetachListener(EventHandler& eventHandler)
{
        for (EventHandlerListIterator iter = m_listeners.begin();
            iter != m_listeners.end();
            ++iter)
        {
            if (&eventHandler == *iter)
            {
                    m_listeners.erase(iter);
                    break;
            }
        }
}
```

To remove a listener, we iterate over m_listeners and call erase on the iterator which matches the address of the EventHandler passed in the arguments.

What you may have noticed is that these methods do not protect against the same object being attached multiple times and will remove only a single instance of the listener from the list. I have left ensuring that objects are not added multiple times to calling code in the interests of simplicity.

# The EventHandler Classes

Now that we know what the Event class looks like, we will take a look at the EventHandler class in Listing 6-13.

*Listing 6-13. The EventHandler Class Declaration*

```
class EventHandler
{
public:
        virtual ~EventHandler()     {}

        virtual void HandleEvent(Event* pEvent) = 0;
};
```

This class couldn't really be any simpler. We provide a pure virtual method, HandleEvent, for our inherited classes to override.

# The EventManager

The EventManager is shown in Listing 6-14. The EventManager is the interface between the game code and the event system.

*Listing 6-14. The EventManager Class Declaration*

```
class EventManager
        :       public Singleton<EventManager>
{
        friend void SendEvent(EventID eventId);
        friend void SendEventToHandler(EventID eventId, EventHandler& eventHandler);
        friend bool RegisterEvent(EventID eventId);
        friend void AttachEvent(EventID eventId, EventHandler& eventHandler);
        friend void DetachEvent(EventID eventId, EventHandler& eventHandler);

private:
        typedef std::tr1::unordered_map<EventID, Event*>    EventMap;
        typedef EventMap::iterator                          EventMapIterator;

        EventMap                        m_eventMap;

        void SendEvent(EventID eventId);
        void SendEventToHandler(EventID eventId, EventHandler& eventHandler);
        bool RegisterEvent(EventID eventId);
        void AttachEvent(EventID eventId, EventHandler& eventHandler);
        void DetachEvent(EventID eventId, EventHandler& eventHandler);
```

```
public:
        EventManager();
        ~EventManager();
};
```

The first piece of important information to glean from Listing 6-14 is that we have made the class a Singleton object. The Singleton is a slightly contentious design pattern which allows us access to a single instance of a class from any point in the code base. Both of these properties are important for our EventManager implementation. For more details of how the Singleton is implemented, please take a look in the appendixes of this book.

## EventManager's Friend Functions

You can see from the class in Listing 6-14 that we have once again made use of the friend keyword to reduce the complexity of the code for the callers of this class. We'll take a look at the friend functions in Listing 6-15 to see why.

*Listing 6-15. EventManager's Friends*

```
inline void SendEvent(EventID eventId)
{
        EventManager* pEventManager = EventManager::GetSingletonPtr();
        assert(pEventManager);
        if (pEventManager)
        {
                pEventManager->SendEvent(eventId);
        }
}

inline void SendEventToHandler(EventID eventId, EventHandler& eventHandler)
{
        EventManager* pEventManager = EventManager::GetSingletonPtr();
        assert(pEventManager);
        if (pEventManager)
        {
                pEventManager->SendEventToHandler(eventId, eventHandler);
        }
}

inline bool RegisterEvent(EventID eventId)
{
        EventManager* pEventManager = EventManager::GetSingletonPtr();
        assert(pEventManager);
        if (pEventManager)
        {
                pEventManager->RegisterEvent(eventId);
        }
}
```

```
inline void AttachEvent(EventID eventId, EventHandler& eventHandler)
{
        EventManager* pEventManager = EventManager::GetSingletonPtr();
        assert(pEventManager);
        if (pEventManager)
        {
                pEventManager->AttachEvent(eventId, eventHandler);
        }
}

inline void DetachEvent(EventID eventId, EventHandler& eventHandler)
{
        EventManager* pEventManager = EventManager::GetSingletonPtr();
        assert(pEventManager);
        if (pEventManager)
        {
                pEventManager->DetachEvent(eventId, eventHandler);
        }
}
```

Each friend function wraps the code which retrieves the Singleton pointer for the object, validates that it has been created, and then calls through to the EventManager class methods of the same name. This reduces the six lines necessary for a safe call to a single line in the calling code, which should make for more readable and more productive code.

# Big O Notation

If you take another look at Listing 6-14, you can see that we have once again used an unordered_map to store our Events. We last used an unordered_map in the GameObject to store our Components, but we did not discuss at the time why we used this structure. Algorithms can be evaluated based on the amount of time they are expected to take to complete. The method for evaluating this time is called Big O Notation. Big O Notation doesn't measure time itself; rather, it gives us a method for evaluating how long an algorithm will take to complete for a given set of elements of size $n$.

When we access an unordered_map, we give the container the hash value and it converts that value into the address at which it has stored our element. This takes the same length of time regardless of how many elements are in our unordered_map and therefore is said to execute in constant time or O(1) in Big O Notation. If we had used a list container to store the elements, each new element in the list could increase the time taken to find any given element in a linear manner. In Big O Notation, this would be O($n$), and for a well-balanced tree container we would be looking at a Big O of O(log($n$)).

I chose to use unordered_map because the most common operation which we will carry out on components and events is retrieving them from their containers. As a game is trying to execute its code as quickly as possible and we may have situations where we have numerous events and components attached to any given object, it makes sense for us to make use of the O(1) property of unordered_map accesses for this purpose.

# EventManager's Interface Methods

Listing 6-16 shows the code used to call the Send and SendToHandler methods of the Event class.

*Listing 6-16. EventManager::SendEvent()*

```
void EventManager::SendEvent(EventID eventId)
{
        EventMapIterator result = m_eventMap.find(eventId);
        if (result != m_eventMap.end())
        {
                assert(result->second);
                if (result->second)
                {
                        result->second->Send();
                }
        }
}

void EventManager::SendEventToHandler(EventID eventId, EventHandler& eventHandler)
{
        EventMapIterator result = m_eventMap.find(eventId);
        if (result != m_eventMap.end())
        {
                assert(result->second);
                if (result->second)
                {
                        result->second->SendToHandler(eventHandler);
                }
        }
}
```

We retrieve the iterator from the m_eventMap container and then call the relevant method on the Event object which it contains.

The method in Listing 6-17 shows how we add a new event to the m_eventMap container.

*Listing 6-17. EventManager::RegisterEvent()*

```
bool EventManager::RegisterEvent(EventID eventId)
{
        bool added = false;

        EventMapIterator result = m_eventMap.find(eventId);
        if (result == m_eventMap.end())
        {
                Event* pNewEvent = new Event(eventId);

                if (pNewEvent)
```

```
        {
                std::pair<EventID, Event*> newEvent(eventId, pNewEvent);
                std::pair<EventMapIterator, bool> addedIter = m_eventMap.insert(newEvent);
                added = addedIter.second;
        }
    }

    assert(added);
    return added;
}
```

Just as we did with our unordered_map earlier, we create a new element, bundle it into a pair with its key, and insert the pair into the unordered_map.

Listing 6-18 shows the destructor of EventManager and the code required to clean the elements from m_eventMap.

*Listing 6-18. EventManager::~EventManager()*

```
EventManager::~EventManager()
{
    for (EventMapIterator iter = m_eventMap.begin(); iter != m_eventMap.end(); ++iter)
    {
        Event* pEvent = iter->second;
        if (pEvent)
        {
            delete pEvent;
            iter->second = NULL;
        }
    }

    m_eventMap.clear();
}
```

The last two methods of importance for the EventManager are the AttachEvent and DetachEvent methods. These are used to ensure that objects which wish to receive certain events are set up to do so and are shown in Listing 6-19.

*Listing 6-19. EventManager's AttachEvent and DetachEvent*

```
void EventManager::AttachEvent(EventID eventId, EventHandler& eventHandler)
{
    EventMapIterator result = m_eventMap.find(eventId);
    assert(result != m_eventMap.end());
    if (result != m_eventMap.end())
    {
        assert(result->second);
        result->second->AttachListener(eventHandler);
    }
}
```

```
void EventManager::DetachEvent(EventID eventId, EventHandler& eventHandler)
{
        EventMapIterator result = m_eventMap.find(eventId);
        assert(result != m_eventMap.end());
        if (result != m_eventMap.end())
        {
                assert(result->second);
                result->second->DetachListener(eventHandler);
        }
}
```

This is all we have for the EventManager class for now. In the next section, we'll create a Component which can be added to GameObjects and tell them to add themselves to the Renderer. We'll achieve this by using an Event which will be sent when the game should tell its objects to render.

# Rendering an Object

As we just touched upon, in this section we are going to look at putting the classes we have just gone over into practice by creating a RenderableComponent.

## The TransformComponent Class

Before we can render an object, we need to know where in the game world it should be placed. We'll store this information inside another Component, the TransformComponent, which is shown in Listing 6-20.

*Listing 6-20. The TransformComponent Class Declaration*

```
class TransformComponent
        :       public Component
{
private:
        static const unsigned int s_id = 0;

        Transform     m_transform;

public:
        static unsigned int GetId()    { return s_id; }

        explicit TransformComponent(GameObject* pOwner);
        virtual ~TransformComponent();

        virtual void Initialize();

        Transform& GetTransform()    { return m_transform; }
};
```

The TransformComponent's constructor, destructor, and Initialize methods are all empty, as they are not required to carry out any tasks. The TransformComponent's sole job is to provide our game objects with a Transform object.

# The Transform Class

The definition of the Transform class is shown in Listing 6-21.

*Listing 6-21. The Transform Class Declaration*

```
class Transform
{
private:
        Matrix3         m_rotation;
        Vector3         m_translation;
        float           m_scale;
        Matrix4         m_matrix;

public:
        Transform();
        virtual ~Transform();

        void                    Clone(const Transform& transform);

        void                    SetRotation(const Matrix3& rotation);
        const Matrix3&          GetRotation() const;

        void                    SetTranslation(const Vector3& translation);
        const Vector3&          GetTranslation() const;

        void                    SetScale(const float scale);
        const float             GetScale() const;

        void                    ApplyForward(const Vector3& in, Vector3& out) const;
        void                    ApplyInverse(const Vector3& in, Vector3& out) const;

        void                    UpdateMatrix();

        const Matrix4&          GetMatrix() const;
        void                    GetInverseMatrix(Matrix4& out) const;
        void                    GetInverseTransposeMatrix(Matrix4& out) const;
};
```

This Transform class is derived from the implementation provided by David Eberly on his website at http://www.geometrictools.com/. If you need to brush up on your math skills, I have provided a quick rundown of vectors and matrices in the appendixes of this book.

The accessor methods for the Transform class are fairly self-explanatory, so let's take a look at UpdateMatrix in Listing 6-22.

*Listing 6-22. Transform::UpdateMatrix()*

```
void Transform::UpdateMatrix()
{
        m_matrix.m_m[0] = m_rotation.m_m[0] * m_scale;
        m_matrix.m_m[1] = m_rotation.m_m[1];
```

```
        m_matrix.m_m[2]  = m_rotation.m_m[2];
        m_matrix.m_m[3]  = 0.0f;
        m_matrix.m_m[4]  = m_rotation.m_m[3];
        m_matrix.m_m[5]  = m_rotation.m_m[4] * m_scale;
        m_matrix.m_m[6]  = m_rotation.m_m[5];
        m_matrix.m_m[7]  = 0.0f;
        m_matrix.m_m[8]  = m_rotation.m_m[6];
        m_matrix.m_m[9]  = m_rotation.m_m[7];
        m_matrix.m_m[10] = m_rotation.m_m[8] * m_scale;
        m_matrix.m_m[11] = 0.0f;
        m_matrix.m_m[12] = m_translation.m_x;
        m_matrix.m_m[13] = m_translation.m_y;
        m_matrix.m_m[14] = m_translation.m_z;
        m_matrix.m_m[15] = 1.0f;
}
```

UpdateMatrix does exactly what its name suggests: it updates the internal matrix with the current state of the transform. Each member of the 3×3 rotation matrix is copied to the correct entry of the 4×4 transform matrix as well as being scaled where appropriate on the diagonal of the matrix. The translation values are copied into the translation entries of the matrix at positions 12, 13, and 14, just as OpenGL would expect.

GetMatrix simply returns a reference to our internal matrix which we saw set up in Listing 6-22, so we'll move on to look at the method GetInverseMatrix, shown in Listing 6-23.

*Listing 6-23. Transform::GetInverseMatrix()*

```
void Transform::GetInverseMatrix(Matrix4& out) const
{
        float invScale = 1.0f / m_scale;
        out.m_m[0]  = m_rotation.m_m[0] * invScale;
        out.m_m[1]  = m_rotation.m_m[3];
        out.m_m[2]  = m_rotation.m_m[6];
        out.m_m[3]  = 0.0f;
        out.m_m[4]  = m_rotation.m_m[1];
        out.m_m[5]  = m_rotation.m_m[4] * invScale;
        out.m_m[6]  = m_rotation.m_m[7];
        out.m_m[7]  = 0.0f;
        out.m_m[8]  = m_rotation.m_m[2];
        out.m_m[9]  = m_rotation.m_m[5];
        out.m_m[10] = m_rotation.m_m[8] * invScale;
        out.m_m[11] = 0.0f;
        out.m_m[12] = -m_translation.m_x;
        out.m_m[13] = -m_translation.m_y;
        out.m_m[14] = -m_translation.m_z;
        out.m_m[15] = 1.0f;
}
```

If you have studied the mathematics behind matrices previously, you may already be aware that the inverse is the matrix which is used to reverse the effects of the original matrix. In terms of simple algebra 1 × 10 = 10. The inverse of multiplying by 10 is multiplying by 1/10, so 10 × (1/10) = 1. The inverse matrix carries out the same job. Calculating the inverse of a matrix is a computationally expensive process, but with games development a transform matrix has an inverse that is much simpler to calculate.

In this case, we can use some special properties. Since scaling is simple multiplication, we can multiply by the inverse multiple, and as you can see in the first line of GetInverseMatrix, we calculate the inverse scale by dividing 1 by m_scale.

The next special property we can take advantage of is the case of the rotation matrix. A rotation matrix is a special type of matrix known as an orthogonal matrix. This means that each row in the matrix represents a unit vector. In our case, each row of our rotation matrix should be a unit vector representing the x, y, and z axes of our rotation to be applied. The inverse of an orthogonal matrix is simply its transpose, so we're in luck as we can transpose the matrix very easily. Looking at Listing 6-23, you can see this in practice in the way we index into the arrays representing the matrices: notice how they don't exactly match. Rather than copying in the order 0, 1, 2, for instance, in the first row, we have taken the first column of 0, 3, 6.

Last but not least is the translation component. Translations can be simply thought of as addition operations, so we can work out the inverse by adding the negative value of translation vector elements.

You might agree that this was much simpler than calculating the inverse using traditional methods.

# The RenderableComponent

Now that we have a method for placing objects in the world, let's take a look at how we will render them (see Listing 6-24).

*Listing 6-24. RenderableComponent*

```
class RenderableComponent
        :       public Component
        ,       public EventHandler
{
private:
        static const unsigned int s_id = 1;

        Renderable          m_renderable;

public:
        static unsigned int GetId()     { return s_id; }

        explicit RenderableComponent(GameObject* pOwner);
        virtual ~RenderableComponent();

        virtual void Initialize();

        Renderable& GetRenderable()     { return m_renderable; }

        virtual void HandleEvent(Event* pEvent);
};
```

Once again, we have a very simple component. The only field is the Renderable, which we will be able to pass to the Renderer. The major difference between this declaration and that for the TransformComponent is that the RenderableComponent inherits from EventHandler along with Component. This means that we are required to override HandleEvent; its code is listed in Listing 6-25.

*Listing 6-25. RenderableComponent::HandleEvent()*

```
void RenderableComponent::HandleEvent(Event* pEvent)
{
        assert(pEvent);
        if (pEvent->GetID() == RENDER_EVENT)
        {
                TransformComponent* pTransformComponent =
                        component_cast<TransformComponent>(GetOwner());
                if (pTransformComponent)
                {
                        m_renderable.GetTransform().Clone(pTransformComponent->GetTransform());
                }

                assert(Renderer::GetSingletonPtr());
                Renderer::GetSingleton().AddRenderable(&m_renderable);
        }
}
```

Things are starting to come together for the first time in this method. The first task is to check if the event which we have been passed is the RENDER_EVENT. We then use the component_cast method we wrote earlier to cast the owner pointer to a TransformComponent pointer. Once we have a valid TransformComponent pointer, we clone its Transform into another Transform object which we have added to the Renderable class.

Another change to the code from Chapter 5 which you can see in this method is that we have inherited the Renderer from Singleton. This allows us to add the Renderable object to the Renderer directly from this call.

# The TransformShader Class

The next step involved in being able to render an object with a Transform is to create a Shader which supports a matrix. Listing 6-26 shows the declaration for our TransformShader.

*Listing 6-26. The TransformShader Class Declaration*

```
class TransformShader
        :        public Shader
{
private:
        Matrix4          m_projection;

        GLint            m_transformUniformHandle;
        GLint            m_positionAttributeHandle;
        GLint            m_colorAttributeHandle;
```

```
public:
        TransformShader();
        virtual ~TransformShader();

        virtual void Link();
        virtual void Setup(Renderable& renderable);
};
```

This shader will have a uniform for the transform and attributes for the vertex position and color. We also have a 4×4 matrix in the class. This is a temporary measure which will allow us to set up a projection matrix. We will be covering projections in more detail in Chapter 8 when we look at implementing game cameras.

Listing 6-27 shows the GLSL code for our vertex and fragment shader.

*Listing 6-27. TransformShader's Constructor*

```
TransformShader::TransformShader()
{
        m_vertexShaderCode =
                    "uniform mat4 u_mModel;                    \n"
                    "attribute vec4 a_vPosition;               \n"
                    "void main(){                              \n"
                    "    gl_Position = u_mModel * a_vPosition; \n"
                    "}                                         \n";

        m_fragmentShaderCode =
                    "precision highp float;                    \n"
                    "uniform vec4 a_vColor;                    \n"
                    "void main(){                              \n"
                    "    gl_FragColor = a_vColor;              \n"
                    "}                                         \n";
}
```

In the vertex shader we have a uniform mat4 matrix which will store the transform matrix passed from the Renderer. This matrix is used to multiply the vertex position and stores the result in gl_Position.

For the fragment shader, we have a uniform for the fragment color. This will allow us to use the shader to render multiple objects and have each one be a different color.

Now we'll take a look at the code required to gain access to the uniform and attribute locations in Listing 6-28.

*Listing 6-28. TransformShader::Link()*

```
void TransformShader::Link()
{
        Shader::Link();

        m_transformUniformHandle   = glGetUniformLocation(m_programId, "u_mModel");
        m_positionAttributeHandle  = glGetAttribLocation(m_programId, "a_vPosition");
        m_colorAttributeHandle     = glGetUniformLocation(m_programId, "a_vColor");
```

```
float halfAngleRadians  = 0.5f * 45.0f * (3.1415926536f / 180.0f);
float m_top             = 1.0f * (float)tan(halfAngleRadians);
float m_bottom          = -m_top;
float m_right           = (1280.0f / 720.0f) * m_top;
float m_left            = -m_right;
float m_near            = 1.0f;
float m_far             = 100.0f;

m_projection.m_m[0]     = (2.0f * m_near) / (m_right - m_left);
m_projection.m_m[1]     = 0.0f;
m_projection.m_m[2]     = 0.0f;
m_projection.m_m[3]     = 0.0f;
m_projection.m_m[4]     = 0.0f;
m_projection.m_m[5]     = (2.0f * m_near) / (m_top - m_bottom);
m_projection.m_m[6]     = 0.0f;
m_projection.m_m[7]     = 0.0f;
m_projection.m_m[8]     = -((m_right + m_left) / (m_right - m_left));
m_projection.m_m[9]     = -((m_top + m_bottom) / (m_top - m_bottom));
m_projection.m_m[10]    = (m_far + m_near) / (m_far - m_near);
m_projection.m_m[11]    = 1.0f;
m_projection.m_m[12]    = 0.0f;
m_projection.m_m[13]    = 0.0f;
m_projection.m_m[14]    = -(2.0f * m_near * m_far) / (m_far - m_near);
m_projection.m_m[15]    = 0.0f;
}
```

In this listing, you can see that we use glGetUniformLocation to retrieve the location of the transform u_mModel and glGetAttribLocation to get the locations for a_vPosition and a_vColor.

We then have a section of code which works out the sides of a shape called a frustum and uses this frustum to construct a perspective projection matrix. This topic will be covered in detail in Chapter 8 and will be built into a formal Camera class.

The TransformShader::Setup method in Listing 6-29 shows how we supply our matrix to the shader.

*Listing 6-29. TransformShader::Setup()*

```
void TransformShader::Setup(Renderable& renderable)
{
    Geometry* pGeometry = renderable.GetGeometry();
    if (pGeometry)
    {
        Shader::Setup(renderable);

        Matrix4 mMVP;
        renderable.GetTransform().GetMatrix().Multiply(m_projection, mMVP);
        glUniformMatrix4fv(m_transformUniformHandle, 1, false, mMVP.m_m);

        glVertexAttribPointer(
                m_positionAttributeHandle,
                pGeometry->GetNumVertexPositionElements(),
                GL_FLOAT,
                GL_FALSE,
```

```
            pGeometry->GetVertexStride(),
            pGeometry->GetVertexBuffer());
        glEnableVertexAttribArray(m_positionAttributeHandle);

        Vector4& color = renderable.GetColor();
        glUniform4f(m_colorAttributeHandle, color.m_x, color.m_y, color.m_z, color.m_w);
    }
}
```

We set up a temporary matrix, mMVP. This matrix stores the result of the multiplication of the renderable's matrix by the projection matrix. We then pass the matrix to OpenGL using glUniformMatrix4fv. The first parameter is the location of the transform uniform, and the second is the number of matrices to upload, which in our case is one. The next parameter is passed false, which tells the driver that we do not wish for it to transpose our matrix before sending it to the shader. Finally, we pass the pointer to the matrix data.

The next few lines set up the vertex data stream just as we have with shaders previously.

The last task in the function is to set the color uniform using glUniform4f. We pass this method the location of the color uniform in the shader and the four float values for our color's rgba values.

Now we have finally written a couple of components, a shader which supports transforms, and taken a look at how EventHandlers can respond to events. We will put these components to use in the next section, where we'll make a basic player GameObject and have it rendered in an app.

# The Player Object

Before we can work with a player object, we will create a task for this example app, shown in Listing 6-30.

*Listing 6-30. The Chapter6Task Class Declaration*

```
class Chapter6Task
        :       public Framework::Task
{
private:
        Framework::Geometry          m_geometry;
        Framework::TransformShader    m_transformShader;

        Framework::GameObject         m_playerObject;

public:
        Chapter6Task(const unsigned int priority);
        virtual ~Chapter6Task();

        // From Task
        virtual bool    Start();
        virtual void    OnSuspend();
        virtual void    Update();
        virtual void    OnResume();
        virtual void    Stop();
};
```

We have an instance of the Geometry class, a TransformShader, and a GameObject which we have named m_playerObject. Now let's take a look at the Start method, as shown in Listing 6-31.

*Listing 6-31. Chapter6Task::Start()*

```
bool Chapter6Task::Start()
{
        using namespace Framework;

        Renderer* pRenderer = Renderer::GetSingletonPtr();
        if (pRenderer)
        {
                pRenderer->AddShader(&m_transformShader);
        }

        m_geometry.SetVertexBuffer(verts);
        m_geometry.SetNumVertices(sizeof(verts) / sizeof(verts[0]));
        m_geometry.SetIndexBuffer(indices);
        m_geometry.SetNumIndices(sizeof(indices) / sizeof(indices[0]));
        m_geometry.SetName("android");

        m_geometry.SetNumVertexPositionElements(3);
        m_geometry.SetVertexStride(0);

        RegisterEvent(UPDATE_EVENT);
        RegisterEvent(RENDER_EVENT);
        RegisterEvent(JUMP_EVENT);

        m_playerObject.AddComponent<MovementComponent>();
        MovementComponent* pMovementComponent =
                component_cast<MovementComponent>(m_playerObject);
        if (pMovementComponent)
        {
                Framework::AttachEvent(Framework::UPDATE_EVENT, *pMovementComponent);
                Framework::AttachEvent(Framework::JUMP_EVENT, *pMovementComponent);
        }

        m_playerObject.AddComponent<TransformComponent>();
        TransformComponent* pTransformComponent =
                component_cast<TransformComponent>(m_playerObject);
        if (pTransformComponent)
        {
                Vector3 translation(-10.0f, 0.0f, 50.0f);
                Transform& transform = pTransformComponent->GetTransform();
                transform.SetTranslation(translation);
        }

        m_playerObject.AddComponent<RenderableComponent>();
        RenderableComponent* pRenderableComponent =
                component_cast<RenderableComponent>(m_playerObject);
```

```
        if (pRenderableComponent)
        {
                Renderable& renderable = pRenderableComponent->GetRenderable();
                renderable.SetGeometry(&m_geometry);
                renderable.SetShader(&m_transformShader);
                Vector4& color = renderable.GetColor();
                color.m_x = 0.0f;
                color.m_y = 1.0f;
                color.m_z = 0.0f;
                color.m_w = 1.0f;
                Framework::AttachEvent(Framework::RENDER_EVENT, *pRenderableComponent);
        }

        return true;
}
```

At long last, Listing 6-31 shows the client code which the user can write to use the Framework systems we have created for the Event, Component, and GameObject systems.

We begin the Start method by registering our TransformShader with the Renderer and then configuring the Geometry object. The number of vertices and indices are now calculated at runtime by dividing the size of the array containing the data by the size of a single element in the array using the sizeof operator.

We them move on to registering some events. We register UPDATE_EVENT, RENDER_EVENT, and JUMP_EVENT. We've already seen that the RenderableComponent will use the RENDER_EVENT to add the Renderable to the render queue, but we haven't yet seen the events for update and jump; we'll look at those soon.

At this point, we begin to add components to our GameObject. After adding a MovementComponent, we also add a TransformComponent and a RenderableComponent. After adding the RenderableComponent, we use component_cast to retrieve it from m_playerObject and then set the Geometry, Shader, and color we would like to use with its Renderable. Finally, we attach the RENDER_EVENT.

Before moving on to take a look at the MovementComponent, we'll take a look at the Update method, as shown in Listing 6-32.

*Listing 6-32.  Chapter6Task::Update()*

```
void Chapter6Task::Update()
{
        Framework::SendEvent(Framework::UPDATE_EVENT);
        Framework::SendEvent(Framework::RENDER_EVENT);
}
```

The beauty of the Event system is now becoming apparent. The code can be very clean in most areas. To update and render all GameObjects, we simply send the update and render events, and all GameObject instances which have these events attached will update and render. It couldn't be any simpler.

We'll now use this system to have the player interact with the game. The code will detect when the player has touched the screen and the player's character will jump in the air.

# Making the Player Jump

We'll begin this section by jumping straight into the code for the MovementComponent, as shown in Listing 6-33.

*Listing 6-33. The MovementComponent Class Declaration*

```
class MovementComponent
        :       public Framework::Component
        ,       public Framework::EventHandler
{
private:
        static const unsigned int s_id = 9;

        Framework::Vector3      m_acceleration;
        Framework::Vector3      m_velocity;

public:
        static unsigned int GetId()     { return s_id; }

        explicit MovementComponent(Framework::GameObject* pObject);
        virtual ~MovementComponent();

        virtual void Initialize();

        virtual void HandleEvent(Framework::Event* pEvent);
};
```

You can see that we have defined two Vector3 objects, one for acceleration and one for velocity. You might be able to tell from those names that in the HandleEvent method, we're going to take a look at some basic physics. Take a look at Listing 6-34.

*Listing 6-34. MovementComponent::HandleEvent()*

```
void MovementComponent::HandleEvent(Event* pEvent)
{
        if (pEvent->GetID() == JUMP_EVENT)
        {
                TransformComponent* pTransformComponent =
                        component_cast<TransformComponent>(GetOwner());
                assert(pTransformComponent);
                if (pTransformComponent &&
                    pTransformComponent->GetTransform().GetTranslation().m_y < FLT_EPSILON)
                {
                        static const float JUMP_ACCELERATION = 80.0f;
                        m_acceleration.m_y = JUMP_ACCELERATION;
                }
        }
        else if (pEvent->GetID() == UPDATE_EVENT)
        {
                TransformComponent* pTransformComponent =
                        component_cast<TransformComponent>(GetOwner());
```

```
            assert(pTransformComponent);
            if (pTransformComponent)
            {
                    const Vector3& position =
                            pTransformComponent->GetTransform().GetTranslation();
                    bool onFloor = false;
                    if (position.m_y < FLT_EPSILON)
                    {
                            onFloor = true;
                    }

                    bool falling = m_acceleration.m_y < 0.0f;

                    Timer& timer = Timer::GetSingleton();
                    Vector3 translation = m_velocity;
                    translation.Multiply(timer.GetTimeSim());
                    translation.Add(position);
                    if (falling && translation.m_y < 0.0f)
                    {
                            translation.m_y = 0.0f;
                    }

                    pTransformComponent->GetTransform().SetTranslation(translation);

                    Vector3 accel = m_acceleration;
                    accel.Multiply(timer.GetTimeSim());
                    m_velocity.Add(accel);

                    static const float GRAVITY_MULTIPLIER    = 15.0f;
                    static const float GRAVITY_CONSTANT    = -9.8f;
                    m_acceleration.m_y +=
                            GRAVITY_MULTIPLIER *
                            GRAVITY_CONSTANT *
                            timer.GetTimeSim();
                    if (falling && onFloor)
                    {
                            m_acceleration.m_y  = 0.0f;
                            m_velocity.m_y        = 0.0f;
                    }
            }
        }
    }
}
```

The first task carried out in Listing 6-34 is handling JUMP_EVENT. When this event is sent to the MovementComponent, we first use component_cast to get the TransformComponent from the owner object. For now, we are using the position of y to see if the player is currently on the ground and allowed to jump again. We'll address this in the next chapter, when we cover level collision, but for now if the player is allowed to jump we set his vertical acceleration.

Game physics is based on the mathematical concepts of derivatives and integration. The derivative of the position, or displacement, of the object is its velocity. The derivative of velocity is acceleration. Given this fact, if we have an acceleration that we can integrate to achieve the desired velocity, we can also integrate the velocity to get the new position.

The basic equation to calculate acceleration is as follows: acceleration = force / mass. For simplicity's sake, we are using a mass of 1, so for now we can simplify the equation to acceleration = force. Therefore, we can get away with just setting the acceleration value directly as we have done when the JUMP_EVENT is handled. The code in Listing 6-35 shows the integration of the position from the current velocity.

*Listing 6-35. Integrating Position*

```
Vector3 translation = m_velocity;
translation.Multiply(Timer::GetSingleton().GetTimeSim());
translation.Add(position);
```

This simple multiplication of the velocity by the current time step and addition to the position is a simple implementation of the numerical method known as Euler Integration. There are good reasons as to why you would not use Euler Integration in a commercial game title, but for our simple purposes and in the interests of speed we have used it here.

Euler Integration can be unstable and give unreliable positions if the acceleration is not constant and the time step varies from frame to frame, which could definitely occur when our game scene becomes busy. Fortunately, our acceleration is constant and our simple game should run at consistently high frame rates. For anyone who would like to look into a numerical integration technique which is more stable and highly recommended for game development, you should look into the fourth-order Runge Kutta integrator.

Listing 6-36 shows our Euler Integration of the acceleration into the velocity.

*Listing 6-36. Integrating Acceleration with Euler*

```
Vector3 accel = m_acceleration;
accel.Multiply(timer.GetTimeSim());
m_velocity.Add(accel);
```

Once again, we multiply by the current simulation time step and add to the existing value.

To make our player fall back down to the ground, we need to apply the force of gravity to our model. Again, we can simplify the code slightly by using a useful feature of gravity. The force of gravity is applied to objects and pulls them toward the ground. You might expect that as the equation for the force multiplies the acceleration by mass, larger objects may fall faster. That's not the case, as objects also have a property known as inertia which is also tied to mass. Therefore, the mass in the equation for gravity cancels with the mass in the equation for inertia, and we find that all objects on earth accelerate under gravity at a rate of roughly 9.8 meters per second. Listing 6-37 shows how we use of this value to make our object fall back to the ground.

*Listing 6-37. Applying Gravity to the Acceleration*

```
static const float GRAVITY_MULTIPLIER   = 15.0f;
static const float GRAVITY_CONSTANT    = -9.8f;
m_acceleration.m_y += GRAVITY_MULTIPLIER * GRAVITY_CONSTANT * timer.GetTimeSim();
```

At this point, we have a jump acceleration of 80 and a gravity multiplier of 15. I arrived at these numbers purely through trial and error. You can try out the sample code which accompanies this chapter and increase or decrease these numbers to see what effect they have on our jump simulation.

This code runs each frame when the UPDATE_EVENT is received, so once the player has jumped they will rise and then fall back down to the ground. The three if statements in the code block for the UPDATE_EVENT also help to decide when the jump should end by working out if the player was on the floor, is now on the floor after the update and if they are falling (due to the velocity being negative in the y direction).

The last piece of code to look at in this section is how we send the jump event (see Listing 6-38).

*Listing 6-38. Android::Android()*

```
Android::Android(android_app* pState, unsigned int priority)
    :    Task(priority)
{
    m_pState                = pState;
    m_pState->onAppCmd       = android_handle_cmd;
    m_pState->onInputEvent   = android_handle_input;
}
```

We've updated the previous android_app state object to hold another function pointer, this time for when input events are ready for the game. Listing 6-39 shows the function declaration.

*Listing 6-39. android_handle_input*

```
static int android_handle_input(struct android_app* app, AInputEvent* event)
{
    int handled = 0;
    if (AInputEvent_getType(event) == AINPUT_EVENT_TYPE_MOTION)
    {
        int action = AMotionEvent_getAction(event);
        if (action == AMOTION_EVENT_ACTION_DOWN)
        {
            Framework::SendEvent(Framework::JUMP_EVENT);
            handled = 1;
        }
    }
    return handled;
}
```

Our simple game requires the player to jump only when the player touches the screen. When the AMOTION_EVENT_ACTION_DOWN is received, we send our JUMP_EVENT and any EventHandlers listening for this event will be processed.

Now that we have a player object, we'll add an AI object which follows a path.

# A Basic AI Entity

To begin, we'll add another GameObject to the Chapter6Task class, as shown in Listing 6-40.

*Listing 6-40. Adding an AI Object*

```
private:
        Framework::Geometry          m_geometry;
        Framework::TransformShader    m_transformShader;

        Framework::GameObject         m_playerObject;
        Framework::GameObject         m_aiObject;
```

We add the setup code for this object to Chapter6Task::Start, as shown in Listing 6-41.

*Listing 6-41. Updating Chapter6Task::Start()*

```
m_playerObject.AddComponent<RenderableComponent>();
RenderableComponent* pRenderableComponent =
        component_cast<RenderableComponent>(m_playerObject);
if (pRenderableComponent)
{
        Renderable& renderable = pRenderableComponent->GetRenderable();
        renderable.SetGeometry(&m_geometry);
        renderable.SetShader(&m_transformShader);
        Vector4& color = renderable.GetColor();
        color.m_x = 0.0f;
        color.m_y = 1.0f;
        color.m_z = 0.0f;
        color.m_w = 1.0f;
        Framework::AttachEvent(Framework::RENDER_EVENT, *pRenderableComponent);
}

m_aiObject.AddComponent<TransformComponent>();
pTransformComponent = component_cast<TransformComponent>(m_aiObject);

m_aiObject.AddComponent<PatrolComponent>();
PatrolComponent* pPatrolComponent = component_cast<PatrolComponent>(m_aiObject);
if (pPatrolComponent)
{
        Vector3 startPoint(10.0f, -10.0f, 75.0f);
        pPatrolComponent->SetStartPoint(startPoint);
        Vector3 endPoint(15.0f, 7.5f, 25.0f);
        pPatrolComponent->SetEndPoint(endPoint);
        pPatrolComponent->SetSpeed(25.0f);
        Framework::AttachEvent(UPDATE_EVENT, *pPatrolComponent);
}

m_aiObject.AddComponent<RenderableComponent>();
pRenderableComponent = component_cast<RenderableComponent>(m_aiObject);
```

```
        if (pRenderableComponent)
        {
                Renderable& renderable = pRenderableComponent->GetRenderable();
                renderable.SetGeometry(&m_geometry);
                renderable.SetShader(&m_transformShader);
                Vector4& color = renderable.GetColor();
                color.m_x = 1.0f;
                color.m_y = 0.0f;
                color.m_z = 0.0f;
                color.m_w = 1.0f;
                Framework::AttachEvent(Framework::RENDER_EVENT, *pRenderableComponent);
        }

        return true;
}
```

We add a TransformComponent and a RenderableComponent to our AI object just as we did for the player. This time, however, we make the enemy object red whereas the player object was green.

The new Component which we add for the enemy object is a PatrolComponent, shown in Listing 6-42. This component is written to move back and forward between two points in space. We set the start and end points as well as the speed we would like the object to move at here. We also attach the PatrolComponent to UPDATE_EVENT.

*Listing 6-42. The PatrolComponent Class Declaration*

```
class PatrolComponent
        :       public Framework::Component
        ,       public Framework::EventHandler
{
private:
        Framework::Vector3      m_direction;
        Framework::Vector3      m_startPoint;
        Framework::Vector3      m_endPoint;
        Framework::Vector3*     m_pOriginPoint;
        Framework::Vector3*     m_pTargetPoint;
        float                   m_speed;

        static const unsigned int s_id = 10;

public:
        static unsigned int GetId()     { return s_id; }

        explicit PatrolComponent(Framework::GameObject* pObject);
        virtual ~PatrolComponent();

        virtual void Initialize();

        virtual void HandleEvent(Framework::Event* pEvent);
```

```
        void SetStartPoint(Framework::Vector3& startPoint);
        void SetEndPoint(Framework::Vector3& endPoint);
        void SetSpeed(float speed)      { m_speed = speed; }
};
```

The PatrolComponent has three Vector3 fields, one for the current direction of movement, one for the start point, and one for the end point. We also have two Vector3 pointers and a float for the speed. We'll look at how these pointers are used in Listing 6-45. First, we need to look at the SetStartPoint method, as shown in Listing 6-43.

*Listing 6-43. PatrolComponent::SetStartPoint()*

```
void PatrolComponent::SetStartPoint(Vector3& startPoint)
{
        m_startPoint.Set(startPoint);
        TransformComponent* pTransformComponent = component_cast<TransformComponent>(GetOwner());
        assert(pTransformComponent);
        if (pTransformComponent)
        {
                pTransformComponent->GetTransform().SetTranslation(m_startPoint);
        }
}
```

SetStartPoint sets the m_startPoint field to match the Vector3 passed in via the parameter. We also use this vector to set the position of the object's TransformComponent.

Next is the SetEndPoint method, as shown in Listing 6-44.

*Listing 6-44. PatrolComponent::SetEndPoint()*

```
void PatrolComponent::SetEndPoint(Vector3& endPoint)
{
        assert(m_startPoint.LengthSquared() > FLT_EPSILON);

        m_endPoint.Set(endPoint);

        m_direction = m_endPoint;
        m_direction.Subtract(m_startPoint);
        m_direction.Normalise();

        m_pOriginPoint = &m_startPoint;
        m_pTargetPoint = &m_endPoint;
}
```

The assert at the beginning of SetEndPoint is used to warn us when the SetStartPoint method has not been called. We need the start point to have been set so that we can calculate the initial direction of travel. We do this by subtracting the start point from the end point with the results being stored in m_direction. The direction is normalized so that we can use the unit normal as a parametric line when the component updates. Finally, we store the address of the start point in the m_pOriginPoint pointer and the address of the end point in the m_pTargetPoint pointer. Now we are ready to update our PatrolComponent, as shown in Listing 6-45.

*Listing 6-45. PatrolComponent::HandleEvent()*

```
void PatrolComponent::HandleEvent(Event* pEvent)
{
    if (pEvent->GetID() == Framework::UPDATE_EVENT && m_pTargetPoint)
    {
        assert(m_direction.LengthSquared() > FLT_EPSILON);
        assert(m_speed > 0.0f);

        TransformComponent* pTransformComponent =
            component_cast<TransformComponent>(GetOwner());
        assert(pTransformComponent);
        if (pTransformComponent)
        {
            Vector3 translation = m_direction;
            translation.Multiply(m_speed * Timer::GetSingleton().GetTimeSim());
            translation.Add(pTransformComponent->GetTransform().GetTranslation());
            pTransformComponent->GetTransform().SetTranslation(translation);

            Vector3 distance = *m_pTargetPoint;
            distance.Subtract(translation);
            if (distance.LengthSquared() < 2.0f)
            {
                Vector3* temp      = m_pTargetPoint;
                m_pTargetPoint     = m_pOriginPoint;
                m_pOriginPoint     = temp;

                m_direction = *m_pTargetPoint;
                m_direction.Subtract(*m_pOriginPoint);
                m_direction.Normalise();
            }
        }
    }
}
```

We decide if the current component is ready to be processed if we receive an UPDATE_EVENT and we have a valid m_pTargetPoint. If we do, we then assert on the validity of m_direction and the m_speed fields just to ensure that we don't have any problems at runtime.

Once we are satisfied that we are ready to process, we retrieve the TransformComponent for our object's owner. The assert here will fire if we have added a PatrolComponent to an object with no TransformComponent. We update the translation element of the Transform by using the direction multiplied by the speed and the current simulation time delta. We then add the velocity for the current frame to the old position of the object.

Once the position has been updated, we test to see if the object has reached the target point. We do this by subtracting the new position of the object from the position which we are currently travelling toward and checking if the squared length of the remaining vector is less than 2.

If we have reached the target point, we switch the m_pOriginPoint and m_pTargetPoint addresses and recalculate the direction of travel. This sends our object back toward the point it just came from.

I'm sure you've played basic games with enemies which just seem to travel back and forward with very little actual intelligence, and now you have just seen one method for achieving the same behavior in your own game.

At this point in the process of developing a game engine, we have a player object being rendered on the screen. A screenshot from the game in its current state is shown in Figure 6-2.

*Figure 6-2.* *Droid Runner's Current State*

# Summary

This was another whirlwind tour of topics related to how games are currently being produced by large companies. Some of the topics we just covered ranged from engine system and graphics programming to gameplay and AI programming and even a brief introduction to game physics. Each of these topics has many, many books written about them, and there's no way to do them all justice in a single chapter, but we have covered enough of the basics to give us a start with our own projects.

The component system is a cutting edge approach to creating game entities. This method is the beginning block required to create flexible and extensible systems which move forward with ease. By using such a system we can avoid the complexities involved with planning and maintaining a complex hierarchical tree of inheritance and duplication of code required when entities on different branches require similar behaviors. It also allows us to update the behavior of objects at runtime by adding and removing components on the fly. This could be a powerful method in AI development where you could add and remove components based on the current state of a complex player or AI object.

Our event system similarly reduces the complexity of our code by making it very easy to respond to events throughout or game. The simple examples which we have looked at so far involved responding to input, updating game objects and rendering those objects. Moving forward we will be able to add more and more events. Game events such as playing sounds and informing objects of collisions can all be handled with our event system. This system also gives individual objects a degree of control over their operation. A valid alternative for handling the case where we receive multiple jump events in the `MovementComponent` could have been to detach the jump event after the first time it is handled until such a time that we are ready to receive another jump event. There are many possible uses for such as system and we'll look at more as we move forward.

Now that we have two objects on the screen, it's time to look at building a world around them and make our app feel more like a game. In the next chapter we'll take a walk through a collision system and then build a level to play in.

# Chapter 7

# Building Game Levels with Collision

A key part of almost every game is having the ability to detect and react to collisions between different objects. Even when going back to look at classic games such as *Pong* or *Space Invaders* we can see that collisions have been integral to the gameplay experience.

It should come as no surprise that collision detection is handled using math. Some of the math involved can be particularly complicated if you have to deal with collisions between the polygon meshes of objects. In this chapter we're going to look at collisions at a higher level. Bounding volumes are used as a test to detect if two objects are candidates for collisions at a more detailed level. The design of our game is simple enough that this level of collision detection will be good enough.

Detecting collisions can also be a computationally expensive business, and this causes us to look for ways to optimize the collision detection stage in our engine. We will achieve this by splitting our scene into discrete sections and checking for collisions between objects only within these sections. This is known as the broad phase of the collision detection algorithm and the testing of individual objects is called the narrow phase.

Once we have determined that objects have collided, we have to carry out a collision response. This will be handled in our code by sending a collision event. We looked at the event and component systems in the previous chapter and will be building upon these as we implement our collision detection systems.

Now that we know what we will be looking at in this chapter, let's make a start.

## Representing Game World Objects with Collision Data

The meshes which we use to render game objects are becoming more and more complex as the capabilities of GPUs increase. This means that the meshes used for rendering objects are no longer suitable for use in collision detection systems. Detecting collisions between very complex objects can be so time-consuming that achieving real-time frame rates would simply be impossible. We have no need to detect collisions between different objects at that level of detail for our simple game, so we can optimize the collision detection process early by simply comparing the bounding volumes of our objects.

Bounding volumes are shapes which represent the extents of the space taken up by your model. 3D shapes such as spheres, cubes, and capsules are commonly used to represent these volumes. For our example, we're going to use a type of bounding volume known as an axis-aligned bounding box (AABB). An AABB is a cuboid with sides which lie parallel to the x, y, and z axes. As all of the sides of all AABBs are parallel to these axes, we can use a very quick algorithm to detect if two of our objects are colliding. This algorithm is known as the separating axis theorem. This sounds much more complicated than it actually is, and in fact, you've already implemented a 2D version of the algorithm in the simple *Breakout* game we developed in Chapter 2.

The easiest way to see how this algorithm works is to take a look at the code we use to implement it. Listing 7-1 shows the CollisionComponent which we will use to add to our objects.

*Listing 7-1. The Collision Component Class Declaration*

```
class CollisionComponent
        :       public Component
{
private:
        static const unsigned int s_id = 2;

        Vector3        m_min;
        Vector3        m_max;

public:
        static unsigned int GetId()        { return s_id; }

        explicit CollisionComponent(GameObject* pOwner);
        virtual ~CollisionComponent();

        virtual void Initialize();

        void SetMin(const Vector3& point)        { m_min = point; }
        void SetMax(const Vector3& point)        { m_max = point; }

        bool Intersects(CollisionComponent& target);
};
```

Our CollisionComponent has two Vector3 objects which will be used to store the extents of the bounding volume. The m_min Vector3 object will store all of the minimum values for the x, y, and z axes and the m_max will store the maximum values for the x, y, and z axes.

The Intersect method is where the work of the component will be carried out and where the separating axis algorithm will be implemented. Before we look at the code which accomplishes this, we will look at how the algorithm works in theory. Figure 7-1 shows a graph which we will use to think about the separating axis algorithm.

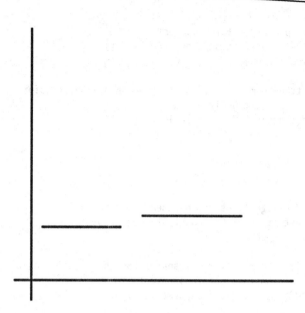

*Figure 7-1. The separating axis theorem*

As the name suggests, we detect overlapping objects by looking for gaps between them on each separate axis at a time. For an axis-aligned bounding box, each of the sides of the volume will be parallel to the corresponding axis in world space. If the preceding graph was looking along the z axis, the x axis would be going to the right and the y axis going up. This graph would allow us to visualize the gaps between the AABBs on the x axis.

If we were testing the second line against the first, then we would say that we know they are not overlapping as the left-hand edge of the line is further right than the right-hand edge of the first line. If we were testing the lines in the opposite situation and testing the first against the second, we would say that they are not overlapping because the right-hand edge of the first line is further left than the left-hand edge of the second line.

At runtime in our game, we cannot be sure which object is on which side, so we check against both situations. We also repeat this test against the edges on the y and z axes. It is also now clear why we need to store the min and max values of the lines in their respective Vector3 objects in the component: we need to know which side of the line is furthest left and which is furthest right for the algorithm to work easily.

Let's take a look at the implementation of CollisionComponent::Intersect now that we have covered the theory behind the algorithm (see Listing 7-2).

*Listing 7-2. CollisionComponent::Intersect()*

```
bool CollisionComponent::Intersects(CollisionComponent& target)
{
        bool intersecting = true;

        Vector3 thisMin = m_min;
        Vector3 thisMax = m_max;
```

```
TransformComponent* pThisTransformComponent =
        component_cast<TransformComponent>(GetOwner());
if (pThisTransformComponent)
{
        Transform& transform = pThisTransformComponent->GetTransform();
        thisMin.Add(transform.GetTranslation());
        thisMax.Add(transform.GetTranslation());
}

Vector3 targetMin = target.m_min;
Vector3 targetMax = target.m_max;

TransformComponent* pTargetTransformComponent =
        component_cast<TransformComponent>(target.GetOwner());
if (pTargetTransformComponent)
{
        Transform& transform = pTargetTransformComponent->GetTransform();
        targetMin.Add(transform.GetTranslation());
        targetMax.Add(transform.GetTranslation());
}

if (thisMin.m_x > targetMax.m_x ||
        thisMax.m_x < targetMin.m_x ||
        thisMin.m_y > targetMax.m_y ||
        thisMax.m_y < targetMin.m_y ||
        thisMin.m_z > targetMax.m_z ||
        thisMax.m_z < targetMin.m_z)
{
        intersecting = false;
}

    return intersecting;
}
```

The first task to be completed in the Intersect method is to translate the AABB of each object. We simply add the position from the TransformComponent for each object in the test to their bounding box rather than applying the entire transform. If the entire transform were applied, we would end up rotating the axis-aligned box, which would turn it into an oriented bounding box, and our AABB test would no longer be reliable. We are also ignoring the scale of the transform here as we know we are not using it, but if you were to decide to scale your objects, this would also need to be applied.

We then have an if test which determines if the objects are not overlapping. Thinking back to the graph in Figure 7-1, we can see that the min values represent the left-hand edges of the lines and the max values represent the right. We test each of the two cases where we know the objects are not overlapping for each axis. First, we check if the left-hand edge of the first object is further right than the right-hand edge of the second object. We then check if the right-hand edge of the first object is further left than the left-hand edge of the second object. If either of these conditions is true, then our objects are not overlapping. The same tests are then completed for the y and z axes. If any one of these tests is positive, we know that our objects do not overlap.

And that's all there is to detecting collisions between objects using axis-aligned bounding boxes. Collision detection is not always this trivial, but this is a good place to begin as it covers the basics of how we detect collisions between two objects in the world. At this point, we still don't really have much of a world, so we'll address this in the next section by creating a level.

# Building a Game Level

Now that we can make objects to collide, it's time to think about how we will position our objects in the game world. Side-scrolling games have been around for a long, long time, and many of the challenges which surround the placement of objects in side-scrolling game levels were solved over two decades ago. A prime example of this is the *Super Mario Bros.* series which built its levels out of uniform sized blocks. These blocks were known as tiles and they allowed the game developers to solve a number of problems which included limited memory for textures, limited color palettes and limited amounts of system RAM to store level data information. Therefore building levels from reusable blocks with repeating patterns was a very effective technique for building larger game levels than would otherwise be possible.

Our simple game will be built from this same basic technique. For the purposes of this book, our design is purposely written to be as simple as possible to demonstrate the techniques used to build games. The single block type we will use will simply be a platform for our player to stand on.

In the last chapter, we created game objects directly in the Chapter6Task class. This time, we'll be creating a class to contain our level, as this would allow us to create multiple levels in the future. Listing 7-3 shows the DroidRunnerLevel class declaration.

*Listing 7-3. The DroidRunnerLevel Class*

```
class DroidRunnerLevel
        :       public Framework::EventHandler
{
private:
        Framework::CollisionComponent*                  m_pPlayerCollisionComponent;

        Framework::Geometry                     m_sphereGeometry;
        Framework::Geometry                     m_cubeGeometry;
        Framework::TransformShader              m_transformShader;

        enum TileTypes
        {
                EMPTY = 0,
                BOX,
                AI,
                PLAYER
        };

        typedef std::vector<Framework::GameObject*>     GameObjectVector;
        typedef GameObjectVector::iterator              GameObjectVectorIterator;

        GameObjectVector                        m_levelObjects;
```

```
        void SetObjectPosition(
                Framework::GameObject* pObject,
                const unsigned int row,
                const unsigned int column);

        void AddMovementComponent(Framework::GameObject* pObject);

        void AddCollisionComponent(
                Framework::GameObject* pObject,
                const Framework::Vector3& min,
                const Framework::Vector3& max);

        void AddPatrolComponent(
                Framework::GameObject* pObject,
                const unsigned int startRow,
                const unsigned int startColumn,
                const unsigned int endRow,
                const unsigned int endColumn);

        void AddRenderableComponent(
                Framework::GameObject* pObject,
                Framework::Geometry& geometry,
                Framework::Shader& shader,
                Framework::Vector4& color);

        static const float          TILE_WIDTH      = 6.0f;
        static const float          TILE_HEIGHT     = 6.0f;

        Framework::Vector3          m_origin;

public:
        DroidRunnerLevel();
        ~DroidRunnerLevel();

        void Initialize(const Framework::Vector3& origin);

        virtual void HandleEvent(Framework::Event* pEvent);
};
```

The private section of the DroidRunnerLevel class is where we now find the Geometry and Shader objects for our scene. We still have a sphere, cube, and TransformShader for this chapter. In addition to these, we are also storing a pointer to the player object's CollisionComponent; we'll look at why we do this when we cover the code for DroidRunnerLevel::HandleEvent.

The enum TileTypes defines the different types of tiles which we will be supporting in our game level. We have a need for a player tile, an AI tile, and a box tile. These are the basic building blocks which we will be using to create our levels.

We define a vector and iterator for storing the GameObjects which belong to this level and then also some helper methods which will be used to construct the objects when the level is initialized.

Next, we have two static `floats`, which store the 2D dimensions of the tiles, and a `Vector3`, which stores the point in space which defines the origin of the level. All of our objects will be created offset from this origin.

The only public methods required by this class are the `constructor` and `destructor`, `Initialize` and `HandleEvent`. As usual, `HandleEvent` is an overridden virtual method which is defined in the `EventHandler` parent class.

The `Initialize` method listed in Listing 7-4 runs through the setup of our level.

*Listing 7-4. DroidRunnerLevel::Initialize*

```
void DroidRunnerLevel::Initialize(const Vector3& origin)
{
        m_sphereGeometry.SetVertexBuffer(sphereVerts);
        m_sphereGeometry.SetNumVertices(sizeof(sphereVerts) / sizeof(sphereVerts[0]));
        m_sphereGeometry.SetIndexBuffer(sphereIndices);
        m_sphereGeometry.SetNumIndices(sizeof(sphereIndices) / sizeof(sphereIndices[0]));
        m_sphereGeometry.SetName("android");

        m_sphereGeometry.SetNumVertexPositionElements(3);
        m_sphereGeometry.SetVertexStride(0);

        m_cubeGeometry.SetVertexBuffer(cubeVerts);
        m_cubeGeometry.SetNumVertices(sizeof(cubeVerts) / sizeof(cubeVerts[0]));
        m_cubeGeometry.SetIndexBuffer(cubeIndices);
        m_cubeGeometry.SetNumIndices(sizeof(cubeIndices) / sizeof(cubeIndices[0]));
        m_cubeGeometry.SetName("cube");

        m_cubeGeometry.SetNumVertexPositionElements(3);
        m_cubeGeometry.SetVertexStride(0);

        m_origin.Set(origin);

        CollisionManager::GetSingleton().AddCollisionBin();
        const Vector3 min(-3.0f, -3.0f, -3.0f);
        const Vector3 max(3.0f, 3.0f, 3.0f);

        const unsigned char tiles[] =
        {
            EMPTY,      EMPTY,      EMPTY,      EMPTY,      AI,      AI,      AI,      AI,
            EMPTY,      EMPTY,      EMPTY,      EMPTY,      BOX,     BOX,     BOX,     BOX,
            EMPTY,      PLAYER,     EMPTY,      EMPTY,      EMPTY,   EMPTY,   EMPTY,   EMPTY,
            BOX,        BOX,        BOX,        BOX,        BOX,     BOX,     BOX,     BOX
        };

        const unsigned int numTiles = sizeof(tiles) / sizeof(tiles[0]);

        const unsigned int numRows       = 4;
        const unsigned int rowWidth        = numTiles / numRows;
```

```cpp
for (unsigned int i=0; i<numTiles; ++i)
{
       if (tiles[i] == BOX)
       {
              const unsigned int row             = i / rowWidth;
              const unsigned int column       = i % rowWidth;

              GameObject* pNewObject = new GameObject();

              SetObjectPosition(pNewObject, row, column);
              AddCollisionComponent(pNewObject, min, max);

              Vector4 color(0.0f, 0.0f, 1.0f, 1.0f);
              AddRenderableComponent(
                     pNewObject,
                     m_cubeGeometry,
                     m_transformShader,
                     color);

              m_levelObjects.push_back(pNewObject);
       }
       else if (tiles[i] == PLAYER)
       {
              const unsigned int row               = i / rowWidth;
              const unsigned int column       = i % rowWidth;

              GameObject* pNewObject = new GameObject();

              SetObjectPosition(pNewObject, row, column);
              AddMovementComponent(pNewObject);

              AddCollisionComponent(pNewObject, min, max);

              MovementComponent* pMovementComponent =
                     component_cast<MovementComponent>(pNewObject);

              m_pPlayerCollisionComponent =
                     component_cast<CollisionComponent>(pNewObject);

              if (pMovementComponent && m_pPlayerCollisionComponent)
              {
                     m_pPlayerCollisionComponent->AddEventListener(pMovementComponent);
              }

              Vector4 color(0.0f, 1.0f, 0.0f, 1.0f);
              AddRenderableComponent(
                     pNewObject,
                     m_sphereGeometry,
                     m_transformShader,
                     color);
```

```
                        m_levelObjects.push_back(pNewObject);
            }
        else if (tiles[i] == AI)
        {
                const unsigned int row              = i / rowWidth;
                const unsigned int column            = i % rowWidth;

                unsigned int patrolEndRow            = 0;
                unsigned int patrolEndColumn      = 0;

                for (unsigned int j=i; j<numTiles; ++j)
                {
                    if (tiles[j] != AI)
                    {
                        i = j;

                        --j;
                        patrolEndRow              = j / rowWidth;
                        patrolEndColumn          = j % rowWidth;
                        break;
                    }
                }

                GameObject* pNewObject = new GameObject();

                SetObjectPosition(pNewObject, row, column);
                AddCollisionComponent(pNewObject, min, max);

                AddPatrolComponent(pNewObject, row, column, patrolEndRow, patrolEndColumn);

                Vector4 color(1.0f, 0.0f, 0.0f, 1.0f);
                AddRenderableComponent(
                        pNewObject,
                        m_sphereGeometry,
                        m_transformShader,
                        color);
            }
        }

    Renderer* pRenderer = Renderer::GetSingletonPtr();
    if (pRenderer)
    {
        pRenderer->AddShader(&m_transformShader);
    }
}
```

Initialize begins by initializing the Geometry and Shader classes just as we did in Chapter 6.

We then initialize the position of the origin vector, m_origin, with the value of origin which was passed as a parameter to the method.

A new collision bin is then added to the CollisionManager; we'll cover the CollisionManager in Listing 7-15.

An array of unsigned char values is then initialized to contain the layout of tiles which we would like to construct for the level. Here we have specified where the AI should patrol, where the world collision boxes should be placed, and where the starting position of the player should be. For now, we have split the level into four rows and eight columns. This level is large enough to fit onto a single screen; we will be expanding this level to cover multiple screens in Chapter 8.

The number of tiles is then calculated by dividing the size of the tile array by the size of a single element, and we use the fact that we will always have four rows to calculate the number of columns we have currently defined in the tile array.

A for loop is then used to pass over every element of the array. When we encounter an empty tile, no action is taken. If the tile is a box, then we will be creating a box object at this point in the world. First, we need to calculate which row and column we are occupying. We can work out the row by dividing the current index by the width of the row. For example, element 16 is the first tile of the third row: this would give us column 0 and row 2 (as we begin counting from row 0). We calculate the row using the divide operator, 16 / 8 = 2, and we can calculate the column using the mod (or remainder) operator, 16 % 8 = 0.

A new game object is created, and we set the position on the object which we derive in the SetObjectPosition method, which is shown in Listing 7-5.

*Listing 7-5. DroidRunnerLevel::SetObjectPosition*

```
void DroidRunnerLevel::SetObjectPosition(
        Framework::GameObject* pObject,
        const unsigned int row,
        const unsigned int column)
{
        assert(pObject);
        pObject->AddComponent<TransformComponent>();
        TransformComponent* pTransformComponent = component_cast<TransformComponent>(pObject);
        if (pTransformComponent)
        {
                Vector3 translation(m_origin);
                translation.m_x += TILE_WIDTH * column;
                translation.m_y -= TILE_HEIGHT * row;
                pTransformComponent->GetTransform().SetTranslation(translation);
        }
}
```

SetObjectPosition is a helper method which adds a TransformComponent to our object. The translation of the TransformComponent is then set to the position in world space which we would like our object to occupy. We calculate this by multiplying the width of the tile by the column index and then adding this to the x position of the origin of the level. Similarly, we calculate the y position by multiplying the height of a tile by the row index and subtracting this value from the origin y position.

After setting the position of the object in SetObjectPosition, DroidRunnerLevel calls AddCollisionComponent on the object; this method is shown in Listing 7-6.

*Listing 7-6. DroidRunnerLevel::AddCollisionComponent*

```
void DroidRunnerLevel::AddCollisionComponent(
        Framework::GameObject* pObject,
        const Framework::Vector3& min,
        const Framework::Vector3& max)
{
        assert(pObject);
        pObject->AddComponent<CollisionComponent>();
        CollisionComponent* pCollisionComponent = component_cast<CollisionComponent>(pObject);
        if (pCollisionComponent)
        {
                pCollisionComponent->SetMin(min);
                pCollisionComponent->SetMax(max);
                AttachEvent(COLLISION_EVENT, *pCollisionComponent);
                CollisionManager::GetSingleton().AddObjectToBin(0, pCollisionComponent);
        }
}
```

This is another straightforward helper method. We simply add a CollisionComponent to the object and initialize its min and max fields. We do have an update to make to the CollisionComponent at this point. We have registered a new event type name, COLLISION_EVENT, and have inherited the CollisionComponent from EventHandler. We look at CollisionComponent::HandleEvent in Listing 7-28. The CollisionComponent is also added to the CollisionManager's bin at index 0. We'll cover the CollisionManager in the following section of this chapter.

The last helper method applied to the box is AddRenderableComponent, shown in Listing 7-7.

*Listing 7-7. DroidRunnerLevel::AddRenderableComponent*

```
void DroidRunnerLevel::AddRenderableComponent(
        GameObject* pObject,
        Geometry& geometry,
        Shader& shader,
        Vector4& color)
{
        assert(pObject);
        pObject->AddComponent<RenderableComponent>();
        RenderableComponent* pRenderableComponent = component_cast<RenderableComponent>(pObject);
        if (pRenderableComponent)
        {
                Renderable& renderable = pRenderableComponent->GetRenderable();
                renderable.SetGeometry(&geometry);
                renderable.SetShader(&shader);
                Vector4& renderableColor = renderable.GetColor();
                renderableColor.Set(color);
                Framework::AttachEvent(Framework::RENDER_EVENT, *pRenderableComponent);
        }
}
```

This is another straightforward method which adds a RenderableComponent to our object and initializes its fields. In the case of the box, we specify the m_cubeGeometry, m_transformShader, and the color blue as the parameters to this method.

DroidRunnerLevel::Initialize can also create a player object when the tile is set to represent a player. The only differences between initializing a box and initializing a player are that the player is represented by the sphere geometry and the color green and has the method AddMovementComponent called with it as a parameter. This method is shown in Listing 7-8.

*Listing 7-8. DroidRunnerLevel::AddMovementComponent*

```
void DroidRunnerLevel::AddMovementComponent(GameObject* pObject)
{
        assert(pObject);
        pObject->AddComponent<MovementComponent>();
        MovementComponent* pMovementComponent = component_cast<MovementComponent>(pObject);
        if (pMovementComponent)
        {
                AttachEvent(JUMP_EVENT, *pMovementComponent);
                AttachEvent(UPDATE_EVENT, *pMovementComponent);
        }
}
```

Just as with the other helper methods, we add our target component to the object, in this case the MovementComponent, and initialize any data. The only initialization required for the MovementComponent is to attach the JUMP_EVENT and UPDATE_EVENT messages.

In the previous chapter's Listing 6-34, we saw that we stopped the MovementComponent from falling if it moved below 0 on the y axis. For this chapter, we would like to stop the player falling if they are resting on a box. We will look at how we achieve this in Listings 7-24 and 7-26, but for now we can see that the initialization code is adding the MovementComponent as a Listener object to the player's CollisionComponent.

The last type of tile which we will be handling is the AI type. Our AI tiles do not cover single tiles but cover a range of tiles which denote the path our AI object should patrol. Listing 7-9 recovers the code which works out the beginning and end of the patrol path.

*Listing 7-9. Calculating the AI Patrol Path*

```
const unsigned int row                  = i / rowWidth;
const unsigned int column             = i % rowWidth;

unsigned int patrolEndRow             = 0;
unsigned int patrolEndColumn      = 0;

for (unsigned int j=i; j<numTiles; ++j)
{
        if (tiles[j] != AI)
        {
                i = j;

                --j;
```

```
            patrolEndRow                    = j / rowWidth;
            patrolEndColumn                 = j % rowWidth;
            break;
        }
    }
}
```

As you can see, Listing 7-9 begins by working out the row and column for the current tile. We then use an inner loop to step along until we find a non-AI tile. At this point, we increase i to skip the AI tiles and then decrease j so that it is pointing at the last tile in the patrol path. The row and column of this end point are then calculated. This basic method for defining paths has a drawback in that we must always have a non-AI tile after the last tile in the path. This includes a path which ends at the end of a row; the first tile of the following row cannot be an AI path or this code will treat it as a continuation of the path from the previous row, and in addition the very last tile in the level cannot be an AI tile or the path will not terminate and will use tile 0, 0 as the end point.

Just as with the boxes and player objects, the AI object has a TransformComponent, CollisionComponent, and RenderableComponent added by our helper methods.

We also use AddPatrolComponent to add a PatrolComponent to our AI objects, as shown in Listing 7-10.

*Listing 7-10. DroidRunnerLevel::AddPatrolComponent*

```cpp
void DroidRunnerLevel::AddPatrolComponent(
      Framework::GameObject* pObject,
      const unsigned int startRow,
      const unsigned int startColumn,
      const unsigned int endRow,
      const unsigned int endColumn)
{
    assert(pObject);
    pObject->AddComponent<PatrolComponent>();
    PatrolComponent* pPatrolComponent = component_cast<PatrolComponent>(pObject);
    if (pPatrolComponent)
    {
        Vector3 startPoint(m_origin);
        startPoint.m_x += TILE_WIDTH * startColumn;
        startPoint.m_y -= TILE_HEIGHT * startRow;

        Vector3 endPoint(m_origin);
        endPoint.m_x += TILE_WIDTH * endColumn;
        endPoint.m_y -= TILE_HEIGHT * endRow;

        pPatrolComponent->SetStartPoint(startPoint);
        pPatrolComponent->SetEndPoint(endPoint);
        pPatrolComponent->SetSpeed(12.0f);

        AttachEvent(UPDATE_EVENT, *pPatrolComponent);
    }
}
```

AddPatrolComponent adds a PatrolComponent to the object and initializes the start and end fields. The positions in world space of the start and end points are calculated using the same method as we used to position the objects' TransformComponents.

Last but not least, DroidRunnerLevel::Initialize adds m_transformShader to the Renderer.

This method contains all of the code which we required to build our level. At this point, we are in a position where we have the objects in place but still do not have a method for detecting and responding to interactions between them. We'll look at how we determine if objects have collided in an efficient manner in the next section.

# Broad-Phase Filtering

Game levels can contain a substantial number of GameObjects. The simplest method for detecting collisions between objects is to brute force the operation. This involves testing every single object against every other object in the scene. Detecting collisions between objects can be a computationally expensive process. The large game engines used in modern FPS games, for example, may have a large number of destructible objects which must be tested against a large number of bullet objects in the world. Calculating the point and exact timing of impacts is essential in these destructible environments for gameplay, as players can very quickly tell if something has not deformed in the correct manner, or if their shots are not being counted against correct body parts.

When using the brute-force method, the number of collision tests to be carried out increases quadratically using the following equation, $x(x-1) / 2$. For ten objects, this gives a number of tests to be carried out as 45, which isn't too bad. For 1,000 objects, you're looking at having to test 499,500 times.

The process of reducing the number of objects to test between is known as broad-phase filtering. This pass on objects usually consists of a spatial algorithm. This means that we use the fact that objects are far apart to ignore any collision tests between these objects and only consider collisions between close objects.

## Quadtrees and Octrees

A Quadtree is a data structure which subdivides a 2D space into equally sized spaces; an Octree carries out the same job but includes the third dimension.

As Figure 7-2 shows, a Quadtree is used to subdivide a 2D space into equally sized sections at each level. First the outer section is split horizontally and vertically, creating four quarters. Each quarter is then split depending on the number of objects which exist in each section. The more objects which exist in a given area then the more subdivisions we will use to reduce the number of collisions between objects.

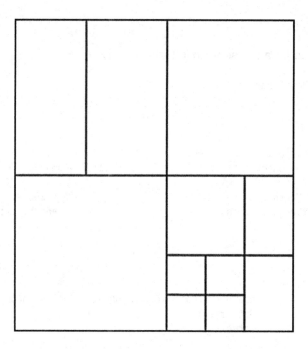

*Figure 7-2. A Quadtree*

An Octree behaves in exactly the same way but splits up a 3D space into equally sized cuboids with up to eight divisions per section instead of the four used by a Quadtree.

# Binary Space Partitions

A Binary Space Partition (or BSP) works in a similar fashion to the Quadtree and Octree in terms of subdividing space. *Doom* and *Quake* used this algorithm to render their scenes, as they were very efficient at culling geometry which should not be rendered in their 3D software rendering engines.

While the BSP is no longer used as a rendering algorithm due to its inefficient use of hardware 3D accelerators, it is still a valid choice to accelerate collision detection involving static geometry. The most common type of BSP involves splitting geometry using planes. A plane is an efficient piece of geometry for the task, as it has a simple test for determining which side of the plane an object sits.

The BSP structure is generated offline before the game is run and the algorithm operates by picking a root polygon, constructing a plane on which the polygon sits, and then continuing to pick polygons on each side of the plane to construct new planes. The process repeats until the subdivisions are at a fine-enough level of detail.

If you're building large outdoor levels with a large mesh, this is a valid technique to use.

# Broad-Phase Filtering in *Droid Runner*

Our needs for broad-phase filtering are much more modest. Our level is of a fixed height, and all objects exist on a 2D plane, so we can get away with splitting our level into equally sized bins. We've already seen that our level is defined with an array split into rows and columns, so we will use a bin for every eight columns.

# Collision Bins

We take a look at the code for a collision bin in Listing 7-11.

*Listing 7-11. The CollisionBin Class Declaration*

```
class CollisionBin
{
private:
        typedef std::vector<CollisionComponent*>            CollisionComponentVector;
        typedef CollisionComponentVector::iterator    CollisionComponentVectorIterator;

        CollisionComponentVector                            m_collisionObjects;
        CollisionComponentVectorIterator                    m_currentObject;

public:
        CollisionBin();
        ~CollisionBin();

        void                AddObject(CollisionComponent* pCollisionComponent);
        CollisionComponent*    GetFirst();
        CollisionComponent*    GetNext();
};
```

This is a simple class. As a bin, its task is simply to store a collection of objects and provide accessor methods to those objects. In this case, CollisionBin stores a vector of CollisionComponent pointers. The bin stores a current iterator which is used to supply the first and next objects to the calling class.

Listing 7-12 shows the code required to add a new object to the CollisionBin.

*Listing 7-12. CollisionBin::AddObject*

```
void CollisionBin::AddObject(CollisionComponent* pCollisionComponent)
{
        m_collisionObjects.push_back(pCollisionComponent);
}
```

The method AddObject has a simple job: it adds the passed CollisionComponent pointer to its array.

Listing 7-13 shows how GetFirst sets the internal iterator to be the beginning of the vector. The return statement uses the ternary operator to determine if the iterator points to a valid object. If so, we return the dereferenced iterator; if not, we return NULL.

*Listing 7-13. CollisionBin::GetFirst*

```
CollisionComponent* CollisionBin::GetFirst()
{
        m_currentObject = m_collisionObjects.begin();
        return m_currentObject != m_collisionObjects.end()
                ?            *m_currentObject
                :            NULL;
}
```

In Listing 7-14, we test the current iterator for a valid object twice in the method GetNext. We need to ensure that the iterator is not at the end of the vector before attempting to increment so that we ensure that we do not walk off the end. Once we have incremented the iterator, we again check if the iterator is valid before returning the dereferenced object or NULL.

*Listing 7-14. CollisionBin::GetNext*

```
CollisionComponent* CollisionBin::GetNext()
{
        CollisionComponent* pRet = NULL;

        if (m_currentObject != m_collisionObjects.end())
        {
                ++m_currentObject;
                pRet = m_currentObject != m_collisionObjects.end()
                        ?       *m_currentObject
                        :       NULL;
        }

        return pRet;
}
```

The bins themselves do not carry out any collision testing; they are just storage algorithms. The actual testing will be carried out by the CollisionManager.

# The Collision Manager

CollisionManager, the declaration of which is described in Listing 7-15, is responsible for storing the collision bins and providing an interface for collision testing to the rest of the code.

*Listing 7-15. The CollisionManager Class Declaration*

```
class CollisionManager
        :       public Singleton<CollisionManager>
{
private:
        typedef std::vector<CollisionBin>       CollisionBinVector;

        CollisionBinVector              m_collisionBins;

public:
        CollisionManager();
        ~CollisionManager();

        void AddCollisionBin();
        void AddObjectToBin(const unsigned int binIndex, CollisionComponent* pObject);
        void TestAgainstBin(const unsigned int binIndex, CollisionComponent* pObject);
};
```

We make use of the vector once again in this class, this time storing a vector of CollisionBin instances. We provide public methods for creating new bins, for adding CollisionComponents to bins, and for testing a single object against all others in the bin.

In AddCollisionBin, we push a new bin onto the back of the vector. This is shown in Listing 7-16.

*Listing 7-16. CollisionManager::AddCollisionBin*

```
void CollisionManager::AddCollisionBin()
{
        m_collisionBins.push_back();
}
```

AddObjectToBin, described in Listing 7-17, asserts that the index supplied is lower than the size of the bin vector. It then calls AddObject on the bin found at binIndex.

*Listing 7-17. CollisionManager::AddObjectToBin*

```
void CollisionManager::AddObjectToBin(const unsigned int binIndex, CollisionComponent* pObject)
{
        assert(binIndex < m_collisionBins.size());
        m_collisionBins[binIndex].AddObject(pObject);
}
```

# Narrow-Phase Collision Detection

Narrow-phase collision detection is concerned with accelerating the process of determining if two specific objects have collided. The entire process of filtering collisions is based on the assumption that the most expensive part of the collision detection algorithm is the intersection tests between geometric primitives. This may be triangles, rays, or whatever other type of geometry is used to represent the surface of the object. For modern video games, the detail required in models results in meshes which consist of thousands of geometric primitives, and testing each of these would be expensive.

We've already discussed our approach to this earlier in the chapter: we will be approximating our objects using axis-aligned bounding boxes. If we were building humanoid characters, we would have an overall bounding volume and then a volume roughly representing each body part. This may mean having a sphere for a head, capsules for the upper and lower sections of limbs, and an AABB for the torso.

Due to our test being very simple, the entire algorithm fits into a single method. CollisiongManager::TestAgainstBin is listed in Listing 7-18.

*Listing 7-18. CollisionManager::TestAgainstBin*

```
void CollisionManager::TestAgainstBin(const unsigned int binIndex, CollisionComponent* pObject)
{
        assert(binIndex < m_collisionBins.size());
        CollisionBin& bin = m_collisionBins[binIndex];
        CollisionComponent* pBinObject = bin.GetFirst();
        while (pBinObject)
        {
                if (pBinObject != pObject &&
                        pBinObject->Intersects(*pObject))
                {
```

```
                    CollisionEventData collisionData;
                    collisionData.m_pCollider = pBinObject->GetOwner();
                    SendEventToHandler(
                            COLLISION_EVENT,
                            *static_cast<EventHandler*>(pObject),
                            &collisionData);
                }
                pBinObject = bin.GetNext();
            }
        }
}
```

We pass the object which we'd like to test against the bin as a parameter. The brute-force method we discussed earlier would involve testing every object in a bin against every other; however, we know that we're only ever interested in testing against the player object which gives us a good optimization.

The method simply loops over each object in the bin and calls the Intersect method if the objects are not the same. When the Intersect method returns true, we send COLLISION_EVENT to the CollisionComponent passed as a parameter.

The CollisionEventData structure simply holds a pointer to the GameObject we have collided with. We look at this structure in Listing 7-19.

*Listing 7-19. The CollisionEventData Structure*

```
struct CollisionEventData
{
    GameObject*     m_pCollider;
};
```

The TestAgainstBin method highlights an update which we will make to the event system. Often when sending an event it is convenient to pass data along with the event. In this case, we would like to know which object we have collided with.

To facilitate sending data with an event, we have added a void pointer to the event class. We have also added void pointers to the Send and SendToHandler methods. We do this in Listings 7-20 and 7-21.

*Listing 7-20. Updating the Event Class*

```
        EventHandlerList               m_listeners;
        EventID                        m_id;
        void*                          m_pData;

public:
        explicit Event(EventID eventId);
        ~Event();

        void Send(void* pData);
        void SendToHandler(EventHandler& eventHandler, void* pData);
        void AttachListener(EventHandler& eventHandler);
        void DetachListener(EventHandler& eventHandler);
```

*Listing 7-21. Updating Event::Send and Event::SendToHandler*

```
void Event::Send(void* pData)
{
        m_pData = pData;
        for (EventHandlerListIterator iter = m_listeners.begin();
                iter != m_listeners.end();
                ++iter)
        {

void Event::SendToHandler(EventHandler& eventHandler, void* pData)
{
        m_pData = pData;
        for (EventHandlerListIterator iter = m_listeners.begin();
                iter != m_listeners.end();
                ++iter)
        {
```

Along with this change, each of the Send and SendToHandler methods which pass the event along to and from the EventManager will also be required to be updated to include the void pointer parameter.

Now that we have a method to detect collisions and an event which tells an object when it has been involved in a collision, we can write code to respond to these collisions.

# Responding to Collisions

Our game design calls for two distinct responses to the collisions which occur. We can be supported on top of boxes, or we can be killed by hitting the side of boxes or by hitting enemies.

Our player object's update code is mostly contained within the MovementComponent. The trouble we have now is getting the COLLISION_EVENT from the CollisionComponent to the objects which are interested in the specific collision data.

We will achieve this by turning to the Observer pattern. What we want to do in this instance is have objects which can be notified using a specific method when the CollisionEvent occurs. The CollisionListener interface will be used to achieve this and is shown in Listing 7-22.

*Listing 7-22. The CollisionListener Interface*

```
class CollisionListener
{
public:
        virtual void HandleCollision(CollisionEventData* pData) = 0;
};
```

In Listing 7-23, the MovementComponent inherits from this class.

*Listing 7-23. Updating the MovementComponent*

```
class MovementComponent
        :       public Framework::Component
        ,       public Framework::EventHandler
```

```
        ,        public Framework::CollisionListener
{
private:
        static const unsigned int s_id = 9;
public:


        virtual void HandleCollision(Framework::CollisionEventData* pData);
};
```

The method body in Listing 7-24 handles the collision.

*Listing 7-24. MovementComponent::HandleCollision*

```
void MovementComponent::HandleCollision(Framework::CollisionEventData* pData)
{
        PatrolComponent* pPatrolComponent = component_cast<PatrolComponent>(pData->m_pCollider);
        if (pPatrolComponent)
        {
                // We're colliding with an AI; we're dead!
        }
        else
        {
                // We're colliding with a block
                TransformComponent* pColliderTransformComponent =
                        component_cast<TransformComponent>(pData->m_pCollider);

                CollisionComponent* pColliderCollisionComponent =
                        component_cast<CollisionComponent>(pData->m_pCollider);

                assert(pColliderTransformComponent && pColliderCollisionComponent);

                const Vector3& translation =
                        pColliderTransformComponent->GetTransform().GetTranslation();

                Vector3 minPosition(pColliderCollisionComponent->GetMin());
                minPosition.Add(translation);

                TransformComponent* pObjectTransformComponent =
                        component_cast<TransformComponent>(GetOwner());

                if (pObjectTransformComponent->GetTransform().GetTranslation().m_x <
                        minPosition.m_x)
                {
                        // We're dead because we've hit the side of the block
                }
                else
                {
                        SetIsSupported(
                                true,
                                pColliderCollisionComponent->GetMax().m_y + translation.m_y);
                }
        }
}
```

As you can see here, we determine if the object we have hit is a box or AI by checking if it has a PatrolComponent; boxes do not have these.

If it's a box, we then need to determine if we have hit the top or the side. To do this, we get the TransformComponent and CollisionComponent for the collider object.

As we'll be moving from left to right, we will only ever die from hitting the left-hand side of the box, so we need to check the min position of the bounding box. The min position is translated into world space and stored in the minPosition vector. We then get the TransformComponent for our MovementComponent's owner. If the x position of the object's translation is to the left of the box's minimum left position, we decide that we have hit the side of the box. If we are to the right of the left position, we have hit the top.

If we are on top of the box, we call SetIsSupported and pass the translated top of the bounding box. It is shown in Listing 7-25.

*Listing 7-25. MovementComponent::SetIsSupported*

```
void MovementComponent::SetIsSupported(bool isSupported, float floor = 0.0f)
{
        m_isSupported = isSupported;
        m_floor = floor;
}
```

To allow the player to sit on top of the box, we also have to update the HandleEvent method; we do this in Listing 7-26.

The SetIsSupported method simply sets the m_isSupported field and the m_floor field.

*Listing 7-26. Updating MovementComponent::HandleEvent*

```
else if (pEvent->GetID() == UPDATE_EVENT)
{
        TransformComponent* pTransformComponent = component_cast<TransformComponent>(GetOwner());
        assert(pTransformComponent);
        CollisionComponent* pCollisionComponent = component_cast<CollisionComponent>(GetOwner());
        assert(pCollisionComponent);
        if (pTransformComponent && pCollisionComponent)
        {
                const Vector3& position = pTransformComponent->GetTransform().GetTranslation();

                bool falling = m_acceleration.m_y < 0.0f;

                Vector3 bvMin = pCollisionComponent->GetMin();

                Vector3 translation = m_velocity;
                translation.Multiply(Timer::GetSingleton().GetTimeSim());
                translation.Add(position);

                const float offsetFloor = m_floor - bvMin.m_y;
                if (m_isSupported && falling && (translation.m_y < offsetFloor))
```

```
        {
                translation.m_y = offsetFloor;
        }

        pTransformComponent->GetTransform().SetTranslation(translation);

        Timer& timer = Timer::GetSingleton();
        Vector3 accel = m_acceleration;
        accel.Multiply(timer.GetTimeSim());
        m_velocity.Add(accel);

        static const float GRAVITY_MULTIPLIER    = 15.0f;
        static const float GRAVITY_CONSTANT   = -9.8f;
        m_acceleration.m_y += GRAVITY_MULTIPLIER * GRAVITY_CONSTANT * timer.GetTimeSim();
        if (falling && m_isSupported)
        {
                m_acceleration.m_y   = 0.0f;
                m_velocity.m_y       = 0.0f;
        }
    }

    // Always undo support after an update: we'll be resupported if we are colliding with a block.
    SetIsSupported(false);
}
```

Now that we are testing for collisions, the decision on whether we are supported or not is made for us. In this case, we need to get the CollisionComponent so that we can determine how far our translation sits from the bottom of the object. We do this by subtracting the bounding volume's minimum y position from the floor value.

We then test to see if our position should be fixed to the floor. It should be if we are supported, are falling, and our translation's y field is below our offsetFloor value.

Our acceleration and velocity are cleared if we are falling and we are supported on a surface.

Finally, we always want to clear the supported flag. Our collision system will retest to determine if we are still colliding with the box we are resting upon and we will be set to supported once more next frame if we are.

Now we know how the MovementComponent handles the collision. We haven't yet handled the death case, as we aren't yet moving. We will cover dying in Chapter 8 once we make the player move along with a camera. We also don't yet know how the CollisionListener interface is used. We need to take another look at an updated CollisionComponent and do this in Listing 7-27.

*Listing 7-27. Adding Listeners to the CollisionComponent Class*

```
class CollisionComponent
        :      public Component
        ,      public EventHandler
{
private:
        static const unsigned int s_id = 2;
```

```
        Vector3        m_min;
        Vector3        m_max;

        typedef std::vector<CollisionListener*>          CollisionListenerVector;
        typedef CollisionListenerVector::iterator        CollisionListenerVectorIterator;

        CollisionListenerVector                          m_eventListeners;
public:
        static unsigned int GetId()        { return s_id; }

        explicit CollisionComponent(GameObject* pOwner);
        virtual ~CollisionComponent();

        .
        .
        .

        void AddEventListener(CollisionListener* pListener)
        {
                m_eventListeners.push_back(pListener);
        }
};
```

We saw the call to AddEventListener in Listing 7-4, so we've come full circle from when we initially created our objects. Managing the listeners is as simple as maintaining a vector of pointers to the CollisionListener objects.

The CollisionComponent is not concerned with responding to collisions itself; it simply needs to distribute the COLLISION_EVENT data to the objects which are interested in collisions involving this object. In Listing 7-28, we traverse the vector of CollisionListener objects and call their HandleCollision method.

*Listing 7-28. CollisionComponent::HandleEvent*

```
void CollisionComponent::HandleEvent(Event* pEvent)
{
        if (pEvent->GetID() == COLLISION_EVENT)
        {
                CollisionEventData* pCollisionData =
                        static_cast<CollisionEventData*>(pEvent->GetData());
                if (pCollisionData && pCollisionData->m_pCollider)
                {
                        for (CollisionListenerVectorIterator iter = m_eventListeners.begin();
                                iter != m_eventListeners.end();
                                ++iter)
                        {
                                (*iter)->HandleCollision(pCollisionData);
                        }
                }
        }
}
```

Now that the collision handling is all hooked up, we need to trigger the system each frame to detect collisions.

# Running the Collision Test

Collisions are best detected after the objects in the scene have been updated. To achieve this, we will register a new event, POSTUPDATE_EVENT.

We saw in Listing 7-3 that the DroidRunnerLevel class was storing a pointer to the player object's CollisionComponent. We also saw in the section on narrow-phase collision detection that we can optimize our detection algorithm by testing only the player's object for collisions. These two facts go hand in hand. We use our stored pointer to test for collisions in Listing 7-29.

*Listing 7-29. DroidRunnerLevel::HandleEvents*

```
void DroidRunnerLevel::HandleEvent(Event* pEvent)
{
        if (pEvent->GetID() == POSTUPDATE_EVENT && m_pPlayerCollisionComponent)
        {
                CollisionManager::GetSingleton().TestAgainstBin(0, m_pPlayerCollisionComponent);
        }
}
```

That's all the code we need for running our collision detection algorithm.

Listing 7-30 shows the update to the chapter's Update method, which is required to trigger POSTUPDATE_EVENT. Here we ensure that any tasks which should be completed after the update are completed in the correct order.

*Listing 7-30. Triggering POSTUPDATE_EVENT*

```
void Chapter7Task::Update()
{
        if (Renderer::GetSingleton().IsInitialized())
        {
                Framework::SendEvent(Framework::UPDATE_EVENT);
                Framework::SendEvent(Framework::POSTUPDATE_EVENT);
                Framework::SendEvent(Framework::RENDER_EVENT);
        }
}
```

That's all we need for collision detection for our game. There is one more change that we need to make to the Renderer which you should be aware of.

# Using the Z Buffer

When objects are rendered to the frame buffer, the default behavior is to render every single pixel to the screen. Problems arise when an object is rendered but should be behind an object which has been rendered previously. As the pixels are always written to the frame buffer, our second object will overwrite the first even though we'd prefer it not to.

We can solve this issue by using the z buffer. A z buffer, or depth buffer, stores the depth of each rendered pixel when it is written to the frame buffer. Each pixel in the depth buffer is initially set to 1. After the vertices for an object are transformed and ready for fragment shading, the z value of each fragment will be calculated and will contain a depth between 0 and 1. If the new fragment's depth is less than the existing depth at that position, it is processed in the fragment shader and the color is written to the frame buffer. If the depth is greater than the existing pixel, that fragment is discarded and the existing value in the frame and depth buffers will be retained.

We enable depth testing in OpenGL by doing the following.

1. Select an EGL configuration which supports a depth buffer, shown in Listing 7-32.

   *Listing 7-31. EGL Depth Configuration Attributes*

   ```
   const EGLint attribs[] =
   {
           EGL_RENDERABLE_TYPE, EGL_OPENGL_ES2_BIT,
           EGL_SURFACE_TYPE, EGL_WINDOW_BIT,
           EGL_BLUE_SIZE, 8,
           EGL_GREEN_SIZE, 8,
           EGL_RED_SIZE, 8,
           EGL_DEPTH_SIZE, 24,
           EGL_NONE
   };
   ```

2. Enable the depth test (Listing 7-32).

3. Clear the depth buffer (Listing 7-32).

   *Listing 7-32. Enabling GL_DEPTH_TEST and Clearing the Depth Buffer*

   ```
   void Renderer::Update()
   {
           if (m_initialized)
           {
                   glEnable(GL_DEPTH_TEST);
                   glClearColor(0.95f, 0.95f, 0.95f, 1);

                   glClear(GL_COLOR_BUFFER_BIT | GL_DEPTH_BUFFER_BIT);
   ```

The three altered lines in Listings 7-31 and 7-32 are all that were required to enable depth testing in our game code. From now on, we can be sure that all of the pixels in our scene are those which were rasterized as part of objects which were closest to the camera.

# Summary

This chapter has been a whirlwind introduction to building game levels and collision detection systems. What we've seen is that the challenges which surround game levels are largely those which involve creating the objects to populate the level. In our game, we have used the tried and tested tiling method from older-style 2D games to build a 3D level out of equally sized blocks.

The major benefit of using such a system when learning game programming is that it's very easy to create computationally. Modern games are more likely to use offline tools to build levels which can be preprocessed before being loaded at runtime. Many of the problems which are faced by these systems, however, are the same as we have seen in this chapter and which we began to address in the previous chapter, namely, how to communicate between objects and how to manage large numbers of objects. Our component and event systems made some of these tasks trivial when it came to building the initial level.

Once we had our level data in place, we took a look at calculating collisions between the objects. We learned why broad-phase filtering of objects is important to reduce the number of pairs which we need to test and also why a narrow phase helps reduce the computational complexity of the collision tests themselves. We have applied these lessons to our game by creating a binning system which allows us to store objects together in any way the game code chooses, and we have implemented the most optimal test algorithm for our game where we are concerned only with the effects of collisions on a single object.

To end the chapter, we took a little detour into graphics programming and looked at how to enable depth testing to ensure that the pixels being rendered to the frame buffer are actually the pixels we would like to see.

In the next chapter, we will be expanding our level significantly and be making better use of the discrete bins in our collision manager. We will also look at creating a game camera, moving the player through the level, and writing the code which will determine what to do when the player dies. We'll also be looking at how we can use the camera object to reduce the amount of geometry which we will be sending to the GPU.

# Chapter 8

# Virtual Cameras

Cameras are an obvious tool for photographers and filmmakers. They enable the artist to capture the living world around them by using position and settings which control the capture of light to create a representation of their chosen scene. Video games are no different.

Until now, our scene has remained essentially static, but this wouldn't make for a particularly fun game. Most of you will have played 3D games before, and I'm sure you would agree that the ability to move through the world is a key aspect of what makes a game compelling. This would not be possible without defining a camera.

In the fields of photography and filmmaking, cameras are a relatively easy-to-understand concept. To capture a different point of view, you simply move the camera to a position where it captures the scene as you would like to portray it. Cameras in 3D graphics are not quite that simple. In this chapter, we're going to look at how we define a camera game object and how we use the object to move through our *Droid Runner* level.

Let's begin and take a look at the theory behind game cameras.

## The Model and View Matrices

As we have already seen, we can move objects around in a 3D world by altering a transform matrix, supplying that matrix to the vertex shader, and multiplying the vertices by this matrix. The transform matrix contains scaling, rotation, and translation elements which affect the size, orientation, and position of a game object.

Figure 8-1 shows the effects of the scale matrix on a game object.

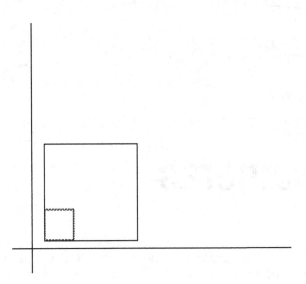

*Figure 8-1.* *Scaling a cube*

The rotation elements of a transform rotate vertices around the object's origin. This is shown in Figure 8-2.

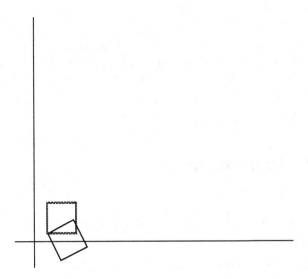

*Figure 8-2.* *The effects of rotation on a game object*

The translation components of a transform matrix are responsible for moving the object in 3D space. Figure 8-3 shows the offset applied to a game object's position.

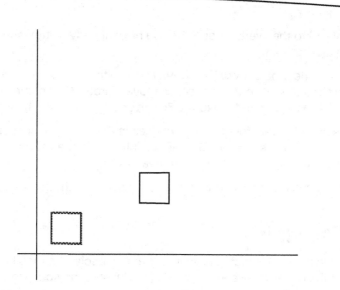

*Figure 8-3. Translating a game object*

The TransformComponent which we created Listing 6-20 was responsible for storing this transform information on a per-object basis. The vertex shader code in Listing 6-28 was used to apply the transform matrix to the vertices as they are processed in the rendering pipeline.

Our camera object will be a game object just like any other. It will be moved around the scene by updating its Transform contained in its TransformComponent, but the camera itself will not be rendered; instead the position and orientation of the camera will be used to manipulate the other objects in the scene.

In Chapter 5, we introduced the concept of the canonical view volume. We discussed that the vertex shader was responsible for transforming vertices to a position relative to this volume. Up until now, our lack of a camera model has meant that we have had to move objects around in world space to have them appear properly within this volume. It will now be the responsibility of the camera to modify vertices to fit into this volume.

When we are taking pictures with a camera, we know that we can move the camera around to get a different view of the scene. We can achieve the same effect in our game world by manipulating the camera by using its TransformComponent; however, this will not help us manipulate the vertices of other objects in the vertex shader. We must visualize the camera in the rendering pipeline as an object which never moves. All other objects must be moved around relative to the camera object. To help with this, imagine that you were taking a family portrait with a camera. If you decided that you would actually like the shot taken from a position slightly to your right, you could take a step to your right. In 3D games, this isn't possible, as the camera in the rendering pipeline is essentially fixed, so we must imagine that we have to move the objects in the world instead. In our visualization, you could imagine that to get the same view of the scene, rather than taking a step to the right you could ask the people in the picture to take a step to the left. You would have stayed still with the camera but you would get the same angle to take the picture of your subjects as if you had stepped to the left.

We achieve this in 3D mathematics by applying the inverse of a transform. The easiest part of the transform to visualize this for is the translation component. If our camera object's translation contains a positive offset of ten units along the z axis, we would manipulate every other object in the scene by applying an offset of −10 to their vertex positions. We have already written a method for obtaining an inverse transform in Listing 6-23.

To quickly recap, our camera object will be a `GameObject` with a `TransformComponent` like any other. We will apply forward transforms to the camera to move it around the game world. We will supply the inverse matrix of the camera's `Transform` to the `Renderer` to be used as the view matrix.

This covers two bases of the transformation of vertices in the fragment shader. The model matrix manipulates the object's vertices from its local space into world space. The view matrix then manipulates the vertex from world space into camera or view space.

The last piece if the process for transforming vertices in a vertex shader is the projection matrix.

# The Projection Matrix

To understand why the projection matrix is so important, especially in mobile development, we must once again consider the canonical view volume. This volume is the space in which vertices sit after they have been processed through a vertex shader. The canonical view volume is a cube with sides of equal dimensions in OpenGL ES 2.0 (it may have different properties in other APIs; DirectX, for example, uses a cube which only ranges from 0 to 1 on the z axis). If you see a range of Android devices sitting side by side, it is immediately apparent that the screens may all be different sizes.

The sizes of the devices themselves are not a problem, as our game will just stretch to fit the larger screens. The problem comes from screens with different aspect ratios. We calculate the aspect ratio by dividing the width by the height. My current device is a Galaxy Nexus with a screen resolution of 1280 * 720 and an aspect ratio of 1.778. The screen resolution of the original Asus Transformer was 1280 * 800, giving an aspect ratio of 1.6. These may not seem like significant differences; however, they directly impact our output. If we didn't correct for the device aspect ratio, we would allow the cube view volume to be stretched horizontally to fit the device's screen. Squares would become rectangles and spheres would not appear as perfect circles.

This is one of the problems solved by the projection matrix.

There are two distinct types of projection matrix commonly used in 3D graphics. One is the orthographic projection and the other perspective projection. The key property of orthographic projection is that parallel lines remain parallel after projection. Perspective projection does not maintain parallel lines, and this allows us to create a sense of perspective, as the name suggests. Most of us will be aware of the concept of a vanishing point. This effect in drawing is achieved by having parallel lines converge on a single point in the distance, and this is the same effect we get from using perspective projection.

Figure 8-4 shows the cuboid orthographic projection volume and the frustum for a perspective view volume overlaid onto the canonical view volume from a top-down view.

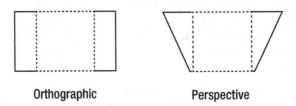

Orthographic          Perspective

*Figure 8-4. The projection view volumes*

As Figure 8-4 shows, the perspective view volume is represented by a frustum. The near plane of the frustum is mapped onto the cube in the same manner as the far plane. As the far plane is much wider, objects which are at the back of the frustum are squashed in size to fit into the canonical view volume. This squashing of objects the further they are from the camera is how we achieve the sense of perspective. This squashing does not occur with orthographic projection and objects appear to be the same size regardless of how close they are to the camera.

We will be using the perspective method of projection in our camera, and we will look at how we achieve this in the next section.

# Defining a Camera Object

As with all of our other objects so far, our camera will be a GameObject with a new component type, CameraComponent.

The class declaration in Listing 8-1 shows the interface for the CameraComponent. We have the usual static int and GetId method to add support for the component system.

*Listing 8-1. The CameraComponent Class Declaration. CameraComponent.h*

```
class CameraComponent
        :       public Component
        ,       public EventHandler
{
private:
        static const unsigned int s_id = 3;
        float               m_frustumParameters[Renderer::NUM_PARAMS];
public:
        static unsigned int GetId()       { return s_id; }
        explicit CameraComponent(GameObject* pOwner);
        virtual ~CameraComponent();

        virtual void Initialize() {}
        void SetFrustum(
                const float verticalFieldOfView,
                const float aspectRatio,
                const float near,
                const float far);

        virtual void HandleEvent(Event* pEvent);
};
```

We then see storage for the frustum parameters. These parameters define the bounds of the edges of the view frustum. There is a parameter for each of the top, bottom, left, right, near, and far planes of the frustum.

We also have two public methods, `SetFrustum` and `HandleEvent`.

We'll take a look at `SetFrustum` in listing 8-2.

*Listing 8-2. CameraComponent::SetFrustum. CameraComponent.cpp*

```
void CameraComponent::SetFrustum(
        const float verticalFieldOfView,
        const float aspectRatio,
        const float near,
        const float far)
{
        float halfAngleRadians  = 0.5f * verticalFieldOfView * (3.1415926536f / 180.0f);

        m_frustumParameters[Renderer::TOP]      = near * (float)tan(halfAngleRadians);
        m_frustumParameters[Renderer::BOTTOM]   = -m_frustumParameters[Renderer::TOP];
        m_frustumParameters[Renderer::RIGHT]    =
                aspectRatio * m_frustumParameters[Renderer::TOP];
        m_frustumParameters[Renderer::LEFT]     = -m_frustumParameters[Renderer::RIGHT];
        m_frustumParameters[Renderer::NEAR]     = near;
        m_frustumParameters[Renderer::FAR]      = far;
}
```

`SetFrustum` calculates the frustum parameters from the passed-in parameters. We will calculate our frustum based on the aspect ratio of the screen and a vertical field of view in degrees. The field of view is an angle which denotes how wide the frustum will be: the larger the field of view, the larger the difference between the width of the near and far planes.

A larger field of view will give us an effect of zooming out on a traditional camera; a narrower field of view gives us a sense of zooming in on an object. The most common example of this effect would be a sniper scope in first-person shooter games. The scope view will have a much narrower field of view and the scale of distant objects is greatly increased in the frame buffer.

Our frustum is calculated in halves, and the opposite half is simply its counterpart negated. Since we are calculating in halves, we multiply the vertical field of view by 0.5f. We then multiply `verticalFieldOfView` by 3.1415926536f / 180.0f; this converts the past angle from degrees to radians. Combined, this gives us the field `halfAngleRadians`.

The top of the frustum is calculated by getting the tan of the half angle in radians multiplied by the near value. This is simple trigonometry, where tan(x) = opposite / adjacent, and in our case the distance of the near plane is the adjacent, so opposite = adjacent * tan(x). The tan method in C++ takes angles in radians, and this was the reason for the conversion into radians in the first line in this method. It's normal that people are more accustomed to dealing with degrees, so we pass our angle in degrees and convert internally.

The bottom of the frustum is simply the negative of the top.

Our right parameter is the top parameter multiplied by the supplied aspect ratio; left is simply the negative of right. These lines show why we have used the vertical field of view method for calculating the dimensions of the frustum. By supplying a vertical field of view, we have locked the height of the frustum on all devices. This will be consistent regardless of whether our aspect ratio is 16:9, 16:10, or something else entirely. In the cases where our aspect ratio is wider, we will be able to see more of the scene at each side, and the opposite is true when the screen is narrower. Vertical field of view works in our case because we are developing a game for the landscape orientation; if you were developing for a portrait orientation, you might want to consider using a locked horizontal field of view.

The distances of the near and far planes are stored as supplied in the function parameters.

Updating the CameraComponent involves supplying the current state of the camera to the Renderer so that we can properly render the objects in our scene (see Listing 8-3).

*Listing 8-3. CameraComponent::HandleEvent. CameraComponent.cpp*

```cpp
void CameraComponent::HandleEvent(Event* pEvent)
{
        if (pEvent->GetID() == POSTUPDATE_EVENT)
        {
                TransformComponent* pTransformComponent =
                        component_cast<TransformComponent>(GetOwner());
                assert(pTransformComponent);
                Renderer& renderer = Renderer::GetSingleton();

                Matrix4 inverseCamera;
                pTransformComponent->GetTransform().GetInverseMatrix(inverseCamera);
                renderer.SetViewMatrix(inverseCamera);
                renderer.SetFrustum(m_frustumParameters);
        }
}
```

The CameraComponent reacts to the POSTUPDATE_EVENT to ensure that the TransformComponent has been updated in the UPDATE_EVENT if necessary.

We obtain a pointer to our owner's TransformComponent and ask it for the inverse of its Transform object. We discussed why we should use the inverse of the camera's Transform earlier in this chapter.

The inverse view matrix and current frustum parameters are supplied to the Renderer via the SetViewMatrix and SetFrustum methods.

Now that we have a CameraComponent to add to a game object and simulate a virtual camera, we need to look at how we update the Renderer to accommodate the view and projection matrices.

# Updating the Renderer

Now that we have a method for representing a Camera as a GameObject, we need to add support for view and projection matrices to our Renderer.

We do this in Listing 8-4 by adding the following updates to the Renderer class.

*Listing 8-4. Adding View and Projection Matrix Support to Renderer. Renderer.h*

```cpp
class Renderer
        :       public Task
        ,       public Singleton<Renderer>
```

```
{
public:
        enum FrustumParameters
        {
                TOP,
                BOTTOM,
                RIGHT,
                LEFT,
                NEAR,
                FAR,
                NUM_PARAMS
        };

private:
        android_app*    m_pState;
        EGLDisplay      m_display;
        EGLContext      m_context;
        EGLSurface      m_surface;
        Int             m_width;
        Int             m_height;
        Bool            m_initialized;

        typedef std::vector<Shader*>        ShaderVector;
        typedef ShaderVector::iterator      ShaderVectorIterator;

        typedef std::vector<Texture*>       TextureVector;
        typedef TextureVector::iterator     TextureVectorIterator;

        typedef std::vector<Renderable*>    RenderableVector;
        typedef RenderableVector::iterator  RenderableVectorIterator;

        RenderableVector m_renderables;
        TextureVector    m_textures;
        ShaderVector     m_shaders;

        float            m_frustumParameters[NUM_PARAMS];

        Matrix4          m_viewMatrix;
        Matrix4          m_projectionMatrix;

        void Draw(Renderable* pRenderable);
public:
        explicit Renderer(android_app* pState, const unsigned int priority);
        virtual ~Renderer();
        void Init();
        void Destroy();

        void AddRenderable(Renderable* pRenderable);
        void AddShader(Shader* pShader);
        void RemoveShader(Shader* pShader);

        void AddTexture(Texture* pTexture);
        void RemoveTexture(Texture* pTexture);
```

```
// From Task
virtual bool      Start();
virtual void      OnSuspend();
virtual void      Update();
virtual void      OnResume();
virtual void      Stop();

bool IsInitialized() { return m_initialized; }
void              SetViewMatrix(const Matrix4& viewMatrix)
{
        m_viewMatrix = viewMatrix;
}

const Matrix4&    GetViewMatrix() const              { return m_viewMatrix; }

void              SetFrustum(const float frustumParameters[]);
const Matrix4&    GetProjectionMatrix() const    { return m_projectionMatrix; }

int               GetWidth() cons                { return m_width; }
int               GetHeight() const              { return m_height; }
};
```

The first addition is the enum which adds the definitions of the six frustum parameters. There is also a float array to store the parameters and two matrices to store the view and projection matrices.

There are then accessor methods for getting and setting the new fields.

The only method which is not straightforward is the SetFrustum method. The CameraComponent::SetFrustum method took in the vertical field of view and aspect ratio to build the frustum parameters necessary for creating the bounds of the virtual camera frustum. Renderer's SetFrustum method takes these parameters as input and builds a projection matrix from them. We take a look at this method in Listing 8-5.

*Listing 8-5. Renderer::SetFrustum. Renderer.cpp*

```
void Renderer::SetFrustum(const float frustumParameters[])
{
        for (unsigned int i=0;  i<NUM_PARAMS; ++i)
        {
                m_frustumParameters[i] = frustumParameters[i];
        }

        m_projectionMatrix.m_m[0] =
                (2.0f * m_frustumParameters[NEAR]) /
                (m_frustumParameters[RIGHT] - m_frustumParameters[LEFT]);
        m_projectionMatrix.m_m[1]        = 0.0f;
        m_projectionMatrix.m_m[2]        = 0.0f;
        m_projectionMatrix.m_m[3]        = 0.0f;

        m_projectionMatrix.m_m[4]        = 0.0f;
        m_projectionMatrix.m_m[5]        =
                (2.0f * m_frustumParameters[NEAR]) /
                (m_frustumParameters[TOP] - m_frustumParameters[BOTTOM]);
```

```
        m_projectionMatrix.m_m[6]        = 0.0f;
        m_projectionMatrix.m_m[7]        = 0.0f;
        m_projectionMatrix.m_m[8]        =
                -((m_frustumParameters[RIGHT] + m_frustumParameters[LEFT]) /
                (m_frustumParameters[RIGHT] - m_frustumParameters[LEFT]));
        m_projectionMatrix.m_m[9]        =
                -((m_frustumParameters[TOP] + m_frustumParameters[BOTTOM]) /
                (m_frustumParameters[TOP] - m_frustumParameters[BOTTOM]));
        m_projectionMatrix.m_m[10]       =
                (m_frustumParameters[FAR] + m_frustumParameters[NEAR]) /
                (m_frustumParameters[FAR] - m_frustumParameters[NEAR]);
        m_projectionMatrix.m_m[11]       = 1.0f;
        m_projectionMatrix.m_m[12]       = 0.0f;
        m_projectionMatrix.m_m[13]       = 0.0f;
        m_projectionMatrix.m_m[14]       =
                -(2.0f * m_frustumParameters[NEAR] * m_frustumParameters[FAR]) /

                (m_frustumParameters[FAR] - m_frustumParameters[NEAR]);
        m_projectionMatrix.m_m[15]       = 0.0f;
}
```

The perspective projection matrix is created by combining a scaling matrix with a matrix which modifies the vertices to be squashed into and a matrix which is used to prepare the vertices for a step in the rendering pipeline known as the perspective divide.

The math involved in perspective projection can become quite complicated, so we won't go into details here, as all we need to know is that the preceding code will create a perspective projection matrix which is suitable for transforming vertices into the canonical view volume used by OpenGL ES 2.0 on Android.

# Concatenating the Model, View, and Projection Matrices

A property of matrix transforms which we are going to rely on is that of concatenation. Matrices can be multiplied together, and their respective transforms will be combined into a single matrix. The order in which these matrices are multiplied is very important. In our case, we want to ensure that we apply the model transform, then the view transform, and finally the projection transform. We achieve this by starting with the model matrix and multiplying it by the view matrix. We then take the resulting matrix and multiply it by the projection matrix.

This code is found in TransformShader::Setup, which we can see in Listing 8-6.

*Listing 8-6. Updating TransformShader::Setup. TransformShader.cpp*

```
void TransformShader::Setup(Renderable& renderable)
{
        Geometry* pGeometry = renderable.GetGeometry();
        if (pGeometry)
        {
                Shader::Setup(renderable);
                Renderer& renderer = Renderer::GetSingleton();
                const Matrix4& viewMatrix = renderer.GetViewMatrix();
```

```
const Matrix4& projectionMatrix = renderer.GetProjectionMatrix();
Matrix4 modelViewMatrix;
renderable.GetTransform().GetMatrix().Multiply(viewMatrix, modelViewMatrix);
Matrix4 modelViewProjectionMatrix;
modelViewMatrix.Multiply(projectionMatrix, modelViewProjectionMatrix);
glUniformMatrix4fv(
        m_transformUniformHandle,
        1,
        false,
        modelViewProjectionMatrix.m_m);

    glVertexAttribPointer(
            m_positionAttributeHandle,
            pGeometry->GetNumVertexPositionElements(),
            GL_FLOAT,
            GL_FALSE,
            pGeometry->GetVertexStride(),
            pGeometry->GetVertexBuffer());
    glEnableVertexAttribArray(m_positionAttributeHandle);
    Vector4& color = renderable.GetColor();
    glUniform4f(
            m_colorAttributeHandle,
            color.m_x,
            color.m_y,
            color.m_z,
            color.m_w);
  }
}
```

The updated code in Listing 8-6 shows how we concatenate the matrices together.

The Renderable's Transform provides the model matrix for this object. We multiply this model matrix by viewMatrix, which we have obtained from the Renderer. The resulting matrix, modelViewMatrix, is then multiplied by projectionMatrix, also obtained from the Renderer.

The final matrix is then supplied to OpenGL via the glUniformMatrix4fv call (at the end of the bold code block in Listing 8-6).

Now that our framework has been updated to support camera objects, we should add code to update the position of our camera each frame.

# Updating the Camera's Transform

The design of *Droid Runner* which we laid out in Chapter 3 calls for our game to update the player's position automatically from left to right. If we didn't update the camera at the same time as the player, our player's GameObject would move off the screen and the player would not be able to see the action.

There are a few options for how we could address such a situation. We could choose to update the camera's position in exactly the same manner as the player object each frame and rely on the two objects moving at the same rate to keep the player's GameObject on the screen.

Another option would be to "attach" the camera to the player's object and to have the camera update its position each frame using an offset from the player's position. This is the method I have decided to use.

To achieve this, we will create a new component, BoundObjectComponent, and the declaration for this component is shown in Listing 8-7.

*Listing 8-7. The BoundObjectComponent Class Declaration. BoundObjectComponent.h*

```cpp
class BoundObjectComponent
        :       public Component
        ,       public EventHandler
{
private:
        static const unsigned int s_id = 4;
        Transform                               m_offsetTransform;

        const TransformComponent*               m_pBoundObject;

public:
        static unsigned int GetId()      { return s_id; }
        explicit BoundObjectComponent(GameObject* pOwner);
        virtual ~BoundObjectComponent();

        virtual void Initialize() {}
        Transform&      GetTransform()                  { return m_offsetTransform; }
        const Transform&    GetTransform() const        { return m_offsetTransform; }

        void            SetBoundObject(const TransformComponent* pComponent)
        {
                m_pBoundObject = pComponent;
        }

        const TransformComponent*       GetBoundObject() const  { return m_pBoundObject; }
        virtual void HandleEvent(Event* pEvent);
};
```

The BoundObjectComponent is set up in the same way as our other Component classes and EventHandlers. The important fields are m_offsetTransform and m_pBoundObject.

m_offsetTransform will store the Transform information for the offset from the parent object. m_pBoundObject will store a pointer to the TransformComponent for the object which we wish to track through the level.

All of the hard work carried out by this Component is contained in the HandleEvent method. We take a look at this method in Listing 8-8.

*Listing 8-8. BoundObjectComponent::HandleEvent. BoundObjectComponent.cpp*

```cpp
void BoundObjectComponent::HandleEvent(Event* pEvent)
{
    if (pEvent->GetID() == UPDATE_EVENT && m_pBoundObject)
    {
        TransformComponent* pTransformComponent =
            component_cast<TransformComponent>(GetOwner());
        assert(pTransformComponent);
        Transform& ourTransform = pTransformComponent->GetTransform();
        const Transform& boundTransform = m_pBoundObject->GetTransform();
        Vector3 translation = m_offsetTransform.GetTranslation();
        translation.Add(boundTransform.GetTranslation());
        ourTransform.SetTranslation(translation);
        ourTransform.UpdateMatrix();
    }
}
```

As you can see, HandleEvent is attached to UPDATE_EVENT. When this object is being updated, we get the Transform of our owner object and the Transform of the object we are bound to.

The most interesting piece of code are the three lines where we create a new Vector3, translation. The initial value is initialized to match the translation of m_offsetTransform. We then add the translation of our bound object and set our Transform to contain the newly calculated translation. Finally, we update the matrix stored by our Transform object.

This code will allow our camera to follow the player object through our level. As the player jumps, the camera will rise and fall with the player, and once we write the code to have the player move to the right through the level, the camera will follow along.

Now it's time to tie everything together and add a GameObject with a CameraComponent to our level.

# Adding a Camera to DroidRunnerLevel

Our camera object will be added to our list of level objects. Let's take a look at the code in Listing 8-9.

*Listing 8-9. An Update to DroidRunnerLevel::Initialize. DroidRunnerLevel.cpp*

```cpp
void DroidRunnerLevel::Initialize(const Vector3& origin)
{
    m_sphereGeometry.SetVertexBuffer(sphereVerts);
    m_sphereGeometry.SetNumVertices(sizeof(sphereVerts) / sizeof(sphereVerts[0]));
    m_sphereGeometry.SetIndexBuffer(sphereIndices);
    m_sphereGeometry.SetNumIndices(sizeof(sphereIndices) / sizeof(sphereIndices[0]));
    m_sphereGeometry.SetName("android");
    m_sphereGeometry.SetNumVertexPositionElements(3);
    m_sphereGeometry.SetVertexStride(0);
```

```
m_cubeGeometry.SetVertexBuffer(cubeVerts);
m_cubeGeometry.SetNumVertices(sizeof(cubeVerts) / sizeof(cubeVerts[0]));
m_cubeGeometry.SetIndexBuffer(cubeIndices);
m_cubeGeometry.SetNumIndices(sizeof(cubeIndices) / sizeof(cubeIndices[0]));
m_cubeGeometry.SetName("cube");
m_cubeGeometry.SetNumVertexPositionElements(3);
m_cubeGeometry.SetVertexStride(0);

m_origin.Set(origin);
CollisionManager::GetSingleton().AddCollisionBin();
const Vector3 min(-3.0f, -3.0f, -3.0f);
const Vector3 max(3.0f, 3.0f, 3.0f);

TransformComponent* pPlayerTransformComponent = NULL;
const unsigned char tiles[] =
{
        EMPTY,   EMPTY,  EMPTY,  EMPTY,  AI,     AI,     AI,     AI,
        EMPTY,   EMPTY,  EMPTY,  EMPTY,  BOX,    BOX,    BOX,    BOX,
        EMPTY,   PLAYER, EMPTY,  EMPTY,  EMPTY,  EMPTY,  EMPTY,  EMPTY,
        BOX,     BOX,    BOX,    BOX,    BOX,    BOX,    BOX,    BOX
};

const unsigned int numTiles = sizeof(tiles) / sizeof(tiles[0]);
const unsigned int numRows  = 4;
const unsigned int rowWidth = numTiles / numRows;

for (unsigned int i=0; i<numTiles; ++i)
{
        if (tiles[i] == BOX)
        {
                const unsigned int row     = i / rowWidth;
                const unsigned int column  = i % rowWidth;

                GameObject* pNewObject = new GameObject();
                SetObjectPosition(pNewObject, row, column);
                AddCollisionComponent(pNewObject, min, max);
                Vector4 color(0.0f, 0.0f, 1.0f, 1.0f);
                AddRenderableComponent(
                        pNewObject,
                        m_cubeGeometry,
                        m_transformShader,
                        color);

                m_levelObjects.push_back(pNewObject);
        }
        else if (tiles[i] == PLAYER)
        {
                const unsigned int row     = i / rowWidth;
                const unsigned int column  = i % rowWidth;

                GameObject* pNewObject = new GameObject();
                SetObjectPosition(pNewObject, row, column);
```

```
                AddMovementComponent(pNewObject);
                AddCollisionComponent(pNewObject, min, max);
                MovementComponent* pMovementComponent =
                        component_cast<MovementComponent>(pNewObject);
                m_pPlayerCollisionComponent =
                        component_cast<CollisionComponent>(pNewObject);
                if (pMovementComponent && m_pPlayerCollisionComponent)
                {
                        m_pPlayerCollisionComponent->AddEventListener(pMovementComponent);
                }

                pPlayerTransformComponent = component_cast<TransformComponent>(pNewObject);
                Vector4 color(0.0f, 1.0f, 0.0f, 1.0f);
                AddRenderableComponent(
                        pNewObject,
                        m_sphereGeometry,
                        m_transformShader,
                        color);

                m_levelObjects.push_back(pNewObject);
        }
        else if (tiles[i] == AI)
        {
                const unsigned int row              = i / rowWidth;
                const unsigned int column           = i % rowWidth;

                unsigned int patrolEndRow           = 0;
                unsigned int patrolEndColumn        = 0;

                for (unsigned int j=i; j<numTiles; ++j)
                {
                        if (tiles[j] != AI)
                        {
                                i = j;
                                --j;
                                patrolEndRow        = j / rowWidth;
                                patrolEndColumn     = j % rowWidth;
                                break;
                        }
                }

                GameObject* pNewObject = new GameObject();
                SetObjectPosition(pNewObject, row, column);
                AddCollisionComponent(pNewObject, min, max);
                AddPatrolComponent(pNewObject, row, column, patrolEndRow, patrolEndColumn);
                Vector4 color(1.0f, 0.0f, 0.0f, 1.0f);
                AddRenderableComponent(
                        pNewObject,
                        m_sphereGeometry,
                        m_transformShader,
                        color);
```

```
                        m_levelObjects.push_back(pNewObject);
            }
    }

    // Create a camera object
    GameObject* pCameraObject = new GameObject();

    pCameraObject->AddComponent<TransformComponent>();
    pCameraObject->AddComponent<BoundObjectComponent>();
    BoundObjectComponent* pBoundObjectComponent =
            component_cast<BoundObjectComponent>(pCameraObject);
    assert(pBoundObjectComponent);
    pBoundObjectComponent->SetBoundObject(pPlayerTransformComponent);
    pBoundObjectComponent->GetTransform().SetTranslation(Vector3(6.0f, 4.25f, -45.0f));
    AttachEvent(UPDATE_EVENT, *pBoundObjectComponent);
    pCameraObject->AddComponent<CameraComponent>();
    CameraComponent* pCameraComponent = component_cast<CameraComponent>(pCameraObject);
    assert(pCameraComponent);
    const Renderer& renderer = Renderer::GetSingleton();
    float width = static_cast<float>(renderer.GetWidth());
    float height = static_cast<float>(renderer.GetHeight());
    pCameraComponent->SetFrustum(35.0f, width / height, 1.0f, 100.0f);
    AttachEvent(POSTUPDATE_EVENT, *pCameraComponent);
    m_levelObjects.push_back(pCameraObject);
    Renderer* pRenderer = Renderer::GetSingletonPtr();
    if (pRenderer)
    {
            pRenderer->AddShader(&m_transformShader);
    }

    m_initialized = true;
}
```

Our updated DroidRunnerLevel::Initialize method now has the code necessary to create a camera object from the new Components which we have created in this chapter.

The first change involves caching a pointer to the player object's TransformComponent. This is necessary for binding the camera to the player object once it is created.

The camera itself requires a TransformComponent, a BoundObjectComponent, and a CameraComponent. It is the first game object we have created which does not have a RenderableComponent. The BoundObjectComponent is bound to the player and the offset is set to Vector3(6.0f, 4.25f, -45.0f). This offset means that the player object is slightly below and slightly to the left of the camera in the scene. This will allow the player to see ledges at a height above the player and more of the scene which is coming into the right of the view.

The SetFrustum method is called with a vertical field of view of 35 degrees. The aspect ratio is calculated by dividing the width of the frame buffer by the height of the frame buffer. The width and height of the frame are held by the Renderer, and these are retrieved from EGL when the Renderer is initialized.

This leads to another change which is required. Previously, we were initializing the level in `Chapter7Task::Start`. For Chapter 8, the `CameraComponent` requires the display to be initialized so that we can access the width and height of the frame buffer. We look at how we achieve this in Listing 8-10.

*Listing 8-10. Chapter8Task::Update. Chapter8Task.cpp*

```
void Chapter8Task::Update()
{
        if (Renderer::GetSingleton().IsInitialized())
        {
                if (!m_level.IsInitialized ())
                {
                        Framework::Vector3 levelOrigin(-21.0f, 7.75f, 35.0f);
                        m_level.Initialize(levelOrigin);
                        Framework::AttachEvent(POSTUPDATE_EVENT, m_level);
                }

                Framework::SendEvent(Framework::UPDATE_EVENT);
                Framework::SendEvent(Framework::POSTUPDATE_EVENT);
                Framework::SendEvent(Framework::RENDER_EVENT);
        }
}
```

As you can see, we now don't do any work in `Update` until after the `Renderer` has been initialized. We set a bool in Listing 8-9 at the very end of `DroidRunnerLevel::Initialize`, and we call `Initialize` on `m_level` if it only has not already been done.

Delaying our update until after the Renderer and Level have both been initialized is part of our app trying to be a good citizen within the Android ecosystem. We'll look at how we can update our Renderer and Android classes to be better behaved when we pause and resume.

# Proper App Behavior When Pausing and Resuming

Until now, our app has not been behaving properly when the Android ecosystem sends us pause and resume events. Listing 4-14 contained code which our app used to detect if it should be paused or resumed, but we have not as of yet made any practical use of this information. When we receive a pause event while executing an OpenGL app, the phone will have destroyed our OpenGL context and rendering surfaces. This doesn't have a fatal effect on our app, but if you look at the output coming from LogCat, you will be able to see a stream of red output errors in the log. We can prevent these errors from occurring by stopping our game from rendering at this point.

## Adding Events for Pausing and Resuming

We'll handle the pause and resume events by adding new events to broadcast when these occur. Listing 8-11 shows the new events.

*Listing 8-11. The PAUSEAPP_EVENT and RESUMEAPP_EVENT Definitions. EventId.h*

```
static const EventID UPDATE_EVENT           = 0;
static const EventID POSTUPDATE_EVENT       = 1;
static const EventID RENDER_EVENT           = 2;
```

```
static const EventID JUMP_EVENT           = 3;
static const EventID COLLISION_EVENT      = 4;
static const EventID PAUSEAPP_EVENT       = 5;
static const EventID RESUMEAPP_EVENT      = 6;
```

We register these events using RegisterEvent in Application::CreateSingletons, shown in Listing 8-12.

*Listing 8-12. Registering PAUSEAPP_EVENT and RESUMEAPP_EVENT. Application.cpp*

```
void Application::CreateSingletons()
{
        new Timer(Task::TIMER_PRIORITY);
        new Renderer(m_pAppState, Task::RENDER_PRIORITY);
        new EventManager();
        new CollisionManager();

        RegisterEvent(PAUSEAPP_EVENT);
        RegisterEvent(RESUMEAPP_EVENT);
}
```

Now that the events are registered, Listing 8-13 shows how we send them from within android_handle_cmd.

*Listing 8-13. Sending PAUSEAPP_EVENT and RESUMEAPP_EVENT. Android.cpp*

```
static void android_handle_cmd(struct android_app* app, int32_t cmd)
{
        switch (cmd)
        {
        case APP_CMD_INIT_WINDOW:
                {
                        assert(Renderer::GetSingletonPtr());
                        Renderer::GetSingleton().Init();
                }
                break;
        case APP_CMD_DESTROY:
                {
                        assert(Renderer::GetSingletonPtr());
                        Renderer::GetSingleton().Destroy();
                }
                break;
        case APP_CMD_TERM_WINDOW:
                {
                        assert(Renderer::GetSingletonPtr());
                        Renderer::GetSingleton().Destroy();
                }
                break;
        case APP_CMD_RESUME:
                {
                        SendEvent(RESUMEAPP_EVENT);
                }
```

```
                break;
        case APP_CMD_PAUSE:
                {
                        SendEvent(PAUSEAPP_EVENT);
                }
                break;
        }
}
```

You can remove the static methods and `m_bPaused` field from this class as we will no longer be using these.

## Handling the Pause and Resume Events in the Renderer

Objects which are interested in learning when the app has been paused and resumed by the system can now attach to these events. Listing 8-14 shows our Renderer being updated to inherit from EventHandler.

*Listing 8-14. Adding Pause and Resume Support to Renderer. Renderer.h*

```
class Renderer
        :       public Task
        ,       public EventHandler
        ,       public Singleton<Renderer>
{
public:
        enum FrustumParameters
        {
                TOP,
                BOTTOM,
                RIGHT,
                LEFT,
                NEAR,
                FAR,
                NUM_PARAMS
        };

private:
        android_app*        m_pState;
        EGLDisplay          m_display;
        EGLContext          m_context;
        EGLSurface          m_surface;
        int                 m_width;
        int                 m_height;
        bool                m_initialized;
        bool m_paused;

        typedef std::vector<Shader*>            ShaderVector;
        typedef ShaderVector::iterator          ShaderVectorIterator;
```

```
        typedef std::vector<Texture*>          TextureVector;
        typedef TextureVector::iterator        TextureVectorIterator;

        typedef std::vector<Renderable*>       RenderableVector;
        typedef RenderableVector::iterator     RenderableVectorIterator;

        RenderableVector                       m_renderables;
        TextureVector                          m_textures;
        ShaderVector                           m_shaders;

        float                                  m_frustumParameters[NUM_PARAMS];

        Matrix4                                m_viewMatrix;
        Matrix4                                m_projectionMatrix;

        void            Draw(Renderable* pRenderable);
public:
        explicit Renderer(android_app* pState, const unsigned int priority);
        virtual ~Renderer();
        void Init();
        void Destroy();

        void AddRenderable(Renderable* pRenderable);
        void AddShader(Shader* pShader);
        void RemoveShader(Shader* pShader);

        void AddTexture(Texture* pTexture);
        void RemoveTexture(Texture* pTexture);

        // From Task
        virtual bool  Start();
        virtual void  OnSuspend();
        virtual void  Update();
        virtual void  OnResume();
        virtual void  Stop();

        virtual void HandleEvent(Event* event);
        bool          IsInitialized() { return m_initialized; }

        void                SetViewMatrix(const Matrix4& viewMatrix)
        {
              m_viewMatrix = viewMatrix;
        }
        const Matrix4&      GetViewMatrix() const      { return m_viewMatrix; }

        void                SetFrustum(const float frustumParameters[]);
        const Matrix4&      GetProjectionMatrix() const { return m_projectionMatrix; }

        int                 GetWidth() const           { return m_width; }
        int                 GetHeight() const          { return m_height; }
};
```

You should initialize m_paused to false in the constructor of Renderer. Listings 8-15 and 8-16 show that we attach and detach from PAUSEAPP_EVENT and RESUMEAPP_EVENT in Renderer's Start and Stop methods.

*Listing 8-15. Attaching PAUSEAPP_EVENT and RESUMEAPP_EVENT in Renderer::Start. Renderer.cpp*

```
bool Renderer::Start()
{
        AttachEvent(PAUSEAPP_EVENT, *this);
        AttachEvent(RESUMEAPP_EVENT, *this);

        return true;
}
```

*Listing 8-16. Detaching from PAUSEAPP_EVENT and RESUMEAPP_EVENT in Renderer::Stop. Renderer.cpp*

```
void Renderer::Stop()
{
        DetachEvent(RESUMEAPP_EVENT, *this);
        DetachEvent(PAUSEAPP_EVENT, *this);
}
```

Once we are attached to the events, we must watch for them in HandleEvent, shown in Listing 8-17.

*Listing 8-17. Renderer::HandleEvent. Renderer.cpp*

```
void Renderer::HandleEvent(Event* pEvent)
{
        if (pEvent->GetID() == PAUSEAPP_EVENT)
        {
                m_paused = true;
        }
        else if (pEvent->GetID() == RESUMEAPP_EVENT)
        {
                m_paused = false;
        }
}
```

When we receive these events, we set the m_paused field to true or false respectively. Now we update the Renderer::Update method to prevent rendering while the app is paused. Listing 8-18 shows this.

*Listing 8-18. Pausing Rendering in Renderer::Update. Renderer.cpp*

```
void Renderer::Update()
{
        if (m_initialized && !m_paused)
        {
                glEnable(GL_DEPTH_TEST);
                glClearColor(0.95f, 0.95f, 0.95f, 1);

                glClear(GL_COLOR_BUFFER_BIT | GL_DEPTH_BUFFER_BIT);
                for (RenderableVectorIterator iter = m_renderables.begin();
```

```
        iter != m_renderables.end();
        ++iter)
    {
        Renderable* pRenderable = *iter;
        if (pRenderable)
        {
                Draw(pRenderable);
        }
    }

    eglSwapBuffers(m_display, m_surface);
    m_renderables.clear();
    }
}
```

You should no longer see error messages related to a missing OpenGL context and Surface once this code has been added to the Renderer. As stated earlier, the app would not have crashed without this, but it is generally better for our app to behave as Android expects to ensure that we are fully compatible with all past, present, and future Android versions and device drivers.

After our little detour, it's time to get back into working with cameras. This next section will use the information which we have in our camera related to its position and what it can see to optimize our rendering process. The specific technique which we will implement is called view frustum culling.

# View Frustum Culling

A modern GPU is a very efficient co-processor and can carry out calculations on the data which we supply it much, much faster than the CPU. The reason for this is that GPUs are designed to be massively parallel and are specifically designed to do nothing but churn through streams of data. Our game logic code is written for the much more flexible CPU in the phone. The benefit of the CPU is that it can carry out a much wider set of tasks which also are not necessarily suited to be broken up into small chunks. The implications of this are that the code which executes on the CPU has access to much more information about our game world than the GPU ever could. This includes our camera object and the other objects in our scene.

We can use this to our advantage. Our camera object can be represented by a frustum. Figure 8-5 shows the shape of a camera frustum in 3D space.

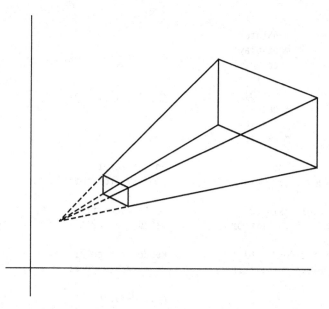

*Figure 8-5. A camera frustum when using perspective projection*

Figure 8-5 shows the shape of the perspective camera frustum. The frustum is a truncated pyramid. When we loop over the vector of Renderables in our scene, we can do a test to determine if part of the object is within the camera frustum; if it is, then we draw the object. If we can detect that the whole of the object is outside the frustum, we can discard this object and never send it to the GPU. The point where the lines meet in Figure 8-5 is the position of the camera, and the frustum is oriented to point along the z axis of the camera's transform matrix.

The first task we must complete to implement frustum culling in our Renderer is to store the camera matrix and frustum parameters each frame. Listing 8-19 shows the updates we must make to Renderer.

*Listing 8-19. Adding Frustum Culling Support to the Renderer. Renderer.h*

```
class Renderer
        :       public Task
        ,       public EventHandler
        ,       public Singleton<Renderer>
{
public:
        enum FrustumParameters
        {
                TOP,
                BOTTOM,
                RIGHT,
                LEFT,
                NEAR,
                FAR,
                NUM_PARAMS
        };
```

```
private:
        android_app*        m_pState;
        EGLDisplay          m_display;
        EGLContext          m_context;
        EGLSurface          m_surface;
        int                 m_width;
        int                 m_height;
        bool                m_initialized;
        bool                m_paused;

        typedef std::vector<Shader*>                ShaderVector;
        typedef ShaderVector::iterator              ShaderVectorIterator;

        typedef std::vector<Texture*>               TextureVector;
        typedef TextureVector::iterator             TextureVectorIterator;

        typedef std::vector<Renderable*>            RenderableVector;
        typedef RenderableVector::iterator          RenderableVectorIterator;

        RenderableVector                            m_renderables;
        TextureVector                               m_textures;
        ShaderVector                                m_shaders;

        float                                       m_frustumParameters[NUM_PARAMS];

    Matrix4 m_cameraMatrix;
        Matrix4                                     m_viewMatrix;
        Matrix4                                     m_projectionMatrix;

        void            Draw(Renderable* pRenderable);
    void BuildFrustumPlanes(Plane frustumPlanes[]);
    bool ShouldDraw(Renderable* pRenderable, Plane frustumPlanes[]) const;

public:
        explicit Renderer(android_app* pState, const unsigned int priority);
        virtual ~Renderer();
        void Init();
        void Destroy();

        void AddRenderable(Renderable* pRenderable);
        void AddShader(Shader* pShader);
        void RemoveShader(Shader* pShader);

        void AddTexture(Texture* pTexture);
        void RemoveTexture(Texture* pTexture);

        // From Task
        virtual bool  Start();
        virtual void  OnSuspend();
        virtual void  Update();
        virtual void  OnResume();
        virtual void  Stop();
```

```
        virtual void  HandleEvent(Event* event);
        bool          IsInitialized() { return m_initialized; }

void SetCameraMatrix(const Matrix4& cameraMatrix)
{
m_cameraMatrix = cameraMatrix;
}
const Matrix4& GetCameraMatrix() const { return m_cameraMatrix; }

        void    SetViewMatrix(const Matrix4& viewMatrix)  { m_viewMatrix = viewMatrix; }
        const Matrix4&   GetViewMatrix() const            { return m_viewMatrix; }

        void            SetFrustum(const float frustumParameters[]);
        const Matrix4&  GetProjectionMatrix() const { return m_projectionMatrix; }

        int             GetWidth() const           { return m_width; }
        int             GetHeight() const
        {
            return m_height;
        }
};
```

Our Renderer now has another Matrix4 to store the current camera's matrix. We also have two new methods, BuildFrustumPlanes and ShouldDraw.

Frustum culling takes advantage of a property of a geometric plane. A plane can be used to split a 3D space into two halves. We can then use a simple dot product to determine if the point we are testing is in front of the plane or behind. Don't worry if you don't understand the math behind this right now; there is code supplied with this book at http://www.apress.com/9781430258308, and Appendix D covers the math classes which are included with the code samples. I recommend that you read through the appendix and the source code until it becomes clear how the planes work.

BuildFrustumPlanes will be used to construct six planes (one for the near clip plane, one for the far clip plane, and one to represent each of the four sides of the frustum: top, bottom, left, and right). We will want each of these planes to have a positive half space which points toward the center of the frustum. The positive half space of the plane is the side to which the normal of the plane points. Listing 8-20 shows the code for BuildFrustumPlanes.

*Listing 8-20. Renderer::BuildFrustumPlanes. Renderer.cpp*

```
void Renderer::BuildFrustumPlanes(Plane frustumPlanes[])
{
        // Get the camera orientation vectors and position as Vector3
        Vector3 cameraRight(
                m_cameraMatrix.m_m[0],
                m_cameraMatrix.m_m[1],
                m_cameraMatrix.m_m[2]);
        Vector3 cameraUp(
                m_cameraMatrix.m_m[4],
                m_cameraMatrix.m_m[5],
                m_cameraMatrix.m_m[6]);
```

```
Vector3 cameraForward(
        m_cameraMatrix.m_m[8],
        m_cameraMatrix.m_m[9],
        m_cameraMatrix.m_m[10]);
Vector3 cameraPosition(
        m_cameraMatrix.m_m[12],
        m_cameraMatrix.m_m[13],
        m_cameraMatrix.m_m[14]);

// Calculate the center of the near plane
Vector3 nearCenter = cameraForward;
nearCenter.Multiply(m_frustumParameters[NEAR]);
nearCenter.Add(cameraPosition);

// Calculate the center of the far plane
Vector3 farCenter = cameraForward;
farCenter.Multiply(m_frustumParameters[FAR]);
farCenter.Add(cameraPosition);

// Calculate the normal for the top plane
Vector3 towardsTop = cameraUp;
towardsTop.Multiply(m_frustumParameters[TOP]);
towardsTop.Add(nearCenter);
towardsTop.Subtract(cameraPosition);
towardsTop.Normalize();
towardsTop = cameraRight.Cross(towardsTop);
frustumPlanes[TOP].BuildPlane(cameraPosition, towardsTop);

// Calculate the normal for the bottom plane
Vector3 towardsBottom = cameraUp;
towardsBottom.Multiply(m_frustumParameters[BOTTOM]);
towardsBottom.Add(nearCenter);
towardsBottom.Subtract(cameraPosition);
towardsBottom.Normalize();
towardsBottom = towardsBottom.Cross(cameraRight);
frustumPlanes[BOTTOM].BuildPlane(cameraPosition, towardsBottom);

// Calculate the normal for the right plane
Vector3 towardsRight = cameraRight;
towardsRight.Multiply(m_frustumParameters[RIGHT]);
towardsRight.Add(nearCenter);
towardsRight.Subtract(cameraPosition);
towardsRight.Normalize();
towardsRight = towardsRight.Cross(cameraUp);
frustumPlanes[RIGHT].BuildPlane(cameraPosition, towardsRight);

// Calculate the normal for the left plane
Vector3 towardsLeft = cameraRight;
towardsLeft.Multiply(m_frustumParameters[LEFT]);
towardsLeft.Add(nearCenter);
towardsLeft.Subtract(cameraPosition);
towardsLeft.Normalize();
towardsLeft = cameraUp.Cross(towardsLeft);
frustumPlanes[LEFT].BuildPlane(cameraPosition, towardsLeft);
```

```
    Vector3 towardsNear = cameraForward;
    frustumPlanes[NEAR].BuildPlane(nearCenter, towardsNear);
    Vector3 towardsFar = cameraForward;
    towardsFar.Negate();
    frustumPlanes[FAR].BuildPlane(farCenter, towardsFar);
}
```

As we can see, there's a section of code in the `BuildFrustumPlanes` method for each side of the camera frustum. The near and far planes can be optimized, and this means that there is less code required to calculate those.

Going through the method in order will show how we arrive at six planes representing the frustum. First off, we deconstruct the camera matrix. If you recall, in Chapter 6 we discussed that a rotation matrix is an orthogonal matrix. This means that each row of the matrix represents an axis in 3D space. The first row of a 3x3 matrix represents the right vector (x axis), the second row represents the up vector (y axis), and the third row represents the at vector (z axis). The first section of code extracts the three normal vectors for each axis from the matrix and also the translation component of the matrix. Each is converted into a `Vector3`.

We then calculate the center points of the near and far planes. The at vector of the camera matrix is a unit normal, so multiplying this by distance to the near plane gives us the center point of the near plane relative to the origin (the point at 0, 0, 0). We then add the position of the camera to get the center of the near plane relative to the camera's position. We repeat this process for the far plane but use the distance to the far plane.

We should now recap how we calculated the frustum parameters in Listing 8-2. The top parameter was calculated by multiplying the distance to the near plane by the half angle of the vertical field of view. This is actually taking advantage of right-angled triangles and trigonometry. Figure 8-6 shows the side view of the two right-angled triangles formed by splitting the field of view in half.

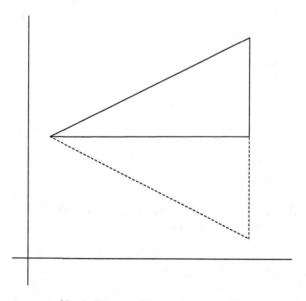

*Figure 8-6. A side profile of the camera position to the near plane*

By using trigonometry, we were able to calculate the vertical height of the top half of the near plane by using the tan function. We can use this value again along with the up vector from the camera's transformation matrix to calculate the normal of the plane which represents the top of the frustum.

Listing 8-21 is a snippet of code taken from the `BuildFrustumPlanes` function already shown in Listing 8-20.

*Listing 8-21. Calculating the Top Plane of the Frustum. Renderer.cpp*

```
// Calculate the normal for the top plane
Vector3 towardsTop = cameraUp;
towardsTop.Multiply(m_frustumParameters[TOP]);
towardsTop.Add(nearCenter);
towardsTop.Subtract(cameraPosition);
towardsTop.Normalize();
towardsTop = cameraRight.Cross(towardsTop);
frustumPlanes[TOP].BuildPlane(cameraPosition, towardsTop);
```

We start by assigning the camera's up vector to `Vector3`, `towardsTop`. Figure 8-7 shows this vector at the origin: the dotted lines show the y and z axes in profile, with y pointing up and z pointing to the right. The x axis is pointing away from you into the page. We are going to step through this process; in each stage, the dotted lines will show the previous steps.

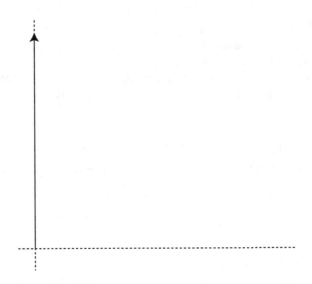

*Figure 8-7. Step one of creating the top frustum plane*

We then multiply this vector by the height of the top half of the near plane, which is stored in `m_frustumParameters[TOP]`, shown in Figure 8-8.

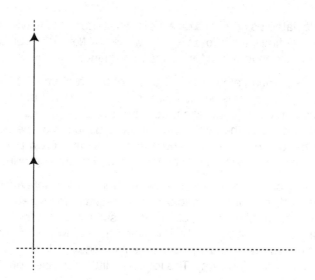

*Figure 8-8. The camera up vector multiplied by the height of the top half of the frustum*

Figure 8-9 shows the next step, which involves adding this vector to the nearCenter position.

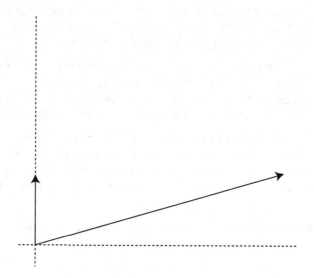

*Figure 8-9. Adding the nearCenter position to our vector in process*

The next two steps are hard to represent with figures, so we will just talk through them. Vector subtraction is useful, as it allows us to move a vector around in 3D space. At this moment in the process, we have managed to get ourselves a vector which represents the line pointing from the camera's position to the top of the near plane.

We now want to convert our vector into a unit normal pointing in this direction. To achieve this, we need to move the vector to the origin by subtracting the camera position. Remember that we added the nearCenter vector to our new up vector at the beginning of this process, and the nearCenter vector was originally calculated using the `cameraPosition` vector. This is why we can shift the vector back to the origin by subtracting `cameraPosition`. Now we call `Normalize` on the vector to create a unit normal pointing in the direction of the top of the near plane.

The vector we now have is pointing along the top plane of the frustum. The camera's right vector also lies on this plane. What we want is a unit vector pointing into the frustum, and we can obtain one of these using a cross product. The cross product of two unit vectors is another unit vector perpendicular to the plane in which the two vectors lie. The direction of the resulting vector is determined by the right-hand rule. The right-hand rule can be hard to wrap your head around, so I use the analogy of a screwdriver to work out which direction my cross product will give me.

If you have used a screwdriver before, you will know that turning the screw clockwise results in the screw moving into the object. Turning anticlockwise results in the screw coming back out. The cross product is the opposite of this: turning clockwise results in a vector coming toward you and anticlockwise away from you. I visualize this by imagining the screw pointing toward me with the head at the other end. If the screw is turning clockwise it means it will get closer to me, and if it's turning anticlockwise it will be moving away. The logic is a little confused but it has always served me well.

You can see how we achieve a vector pointing into the frustum by positioning your left hand with the palm down, thumb pointing right, the index finger pointing forward, and your middle finger pointing down. Your thumb represents the `cameraRight` vector and your index finger the `towardsTop` vector. Now rotate your hand so that your thumb moves to where your index finger was. This is what we are doing with the operation `cameraRight.Cross(towardsTop)`, and the resulting vector is our plane normal. We now construct our plane using the `BuildPlane` method.

The process is now repeated for each of the other planes using their respective frustum parameters and the appropriate cross product direction. It's interesting to note here that the cross product for the bottom plane is the opposite of the cross product for the top. This is how we achieve vectors pointing into the frustum for both sides. The same is true for the right and left planes.

The process for calculating the near and far planes is much more straightforward. Those planes already point along the existing camera at vector. The near plane points in the same direction as the camera, and the far plane points in the opposite direction. The points on the plane which we use in the `BuildPlane` method are the `nearCenter` and `farCenter` points, respectively, rather than the `cameraPosition` vector.

Now that we have constructed our frustum planes, we can detect if an object lies within the frustum before calling `Draw`.

# The View Frustum Culling Test

To be able to test our objects against the frustum, we must first know where in space their bounds are. Luckily, we can reuse our data from the `CollisionComponent` for this task. We begin by adding the min and max bounds vectors to the `Renderable` class in Listing 8-22.

*Listing 8-22. Adding Bounds to Renderable. Renderable.h*

```
class Renderable
{
private:
        Geometry*       m_pGeometry;
        Shader*         m_pShader;
        Transform       m_transform;
        Vector4         m_color;

  Vector3 m_min;
  Vector3 m_max;
  bool m_useBounds;

public:
        Renderable();
        ~Renderable();

        void                    SetGeometry(Geometry* pGeometry);
        Geometry*               GetGeometry();

        void                    SetShader(Shader* pShader);
        Shader*                 GetShader();

        Transform&              GetTransform()                          { return m_transform; }
        Vector4&                GetColor()                              { return m_color; }

  void SetBoundMin(const Vector3& min) { m_min = min; }
  const Vector3& GetBoundMin() const       { return m_min; }

  void SetBoundMax(const Vector3& max) { m_max = max; }
  const Vector3& GetBoundMax() const { return m_max; }

  void SetUseBounds(bool enabled) { m_useBounds = enabled; }
  bool GetUseBounds() const { return m_useBounds; }

        bool                    IsInitialized() const
        {
                return m_pGeometry && m_pShader;
        }
};
```

In Listing 8-23, we update the method RenderableComponent::HandleEvent to set the bounds when we add the object to the render list.

*Listing 8-23. Updating RenderableComponent::HandleEvent. RenderableComponent.cpp*

```
void RenderableComponent::HandleEvent(Event* pEvent)
{
        assert(pEvent);
        if (pEvent->GetID() == RENDER_EVENT)
        {
```

```
                TransformComponent* pTransformComponent = component_cast<TransformComponent>(GetOwner());
                if (pTransformComponent)
                {
                        m_renderable.GetTransform().Clone(pTransformComponent->GetTransform());
                }

CollisionComponent* pCollisionComponent = component_cast<CollisionComponent>(GetOwner());
if (pCollisionComponent)
{
m_renderable.SetBoundMin(pCollisionComponent->GetMin());
m_renderable.SetBoundMax(pCollisionComponent->GetMax());
m_renderable.SetUseBounds(true);
}
else
{
m_renderable.SetUseBounds(false);
}

                assert(Renderer::GetSingletonPtr());
                Renderer::GetSingleton().AddRenderable(&m_renderable);
        }
}
```

HandleEvent now sets the bounds on the Renderable if the object being rendered has a CollisionComponent object.

Now we can add the code to Renderer::Update to determine if the object is within the frustum. Listing 8-24 shows this update.

*Listing 8-24. Updating Renderer::Update. Renderer.cpp*

```
void Renderer::Update()
{
        if (m_initialized && !m_paused)
        {
Plane   frustumPlanes[NUM_PARAMS];
BuildFrustumPlanes(frustumPlanes);

                glEnable(GL_DEPTH_TEST);
                glClearColor(0.95f, 0.95f, 0.95f, 1);

                glClear(GL_COLOR_BUFFER_BIT | GL_DEPTH_BUFFER_BIT);
                for (RenderableVectorIterator iter = m_renderables.begin();
                        iter != m_renderables.end();
                        ++iter)
                {
                        Renderable* pRenderable = *iter;
                        if (pRenderable)
                        {
bool bDraw = ShouldDraw(pRenderable, frustumPlanes);
if (bDraw)
```

```
{
Draw(pRenderable);
}
                }
            }

            eglSwapBuffers(m_display, m_surface);
            m_renderables.clear();
        }
}
```

Now the Renderer's Update method builds new frustum planes each time it is called. This is due to the fact that the camera will have moved each frame and we must build new planes to represent this.

We also now determine if an object should be rendered using the ShouldDraw method. Listing 8-25 shows the contents of this method.

*Listing 8-25. Renderer::ShouldDraw. Renderer.cpp*

```cpp
bool Renderer::ShouldDraw(Renderable* pRenderable, Plane frustumPlanes[]) const
{
        bool shouldDraw = true;
        if (pRenderable && pRenderable->GetUseBounds())
        {
                shouldDraw = false;
                Vector3 min = pRenderable->GetBoundMin();
                min.Add(pRenderable->GetTransform().GetTranslation());
                Vector3 max = pRenderable->GetBoundMax();
                max.Add(pRenderable->GetTransform().GetTranslation());
                static const unsigned int NUM_POINTS = 8;
                Vector3 points[NUM_POINTS];
                points[0] = min;
                points[1] = max;

                points[2].m_x = min.m_x;
                points[2].m_y = min.m_y;
                points[2].m_z = max.m_z;

                points[3].m_x = min.m_x;
                points[3].m_y = max.m_y;
                points[3].m_z = max.m_z;

                points[4].m_x = max.m_x;
                points[4].m_y = min.m_y;
                points[4].m_z = max.m_z;

                points[5].m_x = max.m_x;
                points[5].m_y = max.m_y;
                points[5].m_z = min.m_z;

                points[6].m_x = min.m_x;
                points[6].m_y = max.m_y;
                points[6].m_z = min.m_z;
```

```
            points[7].m_x = max.m_x;
            points[7].m_y = min.m_y;
            points[7].m_z = min.m_z;

            for (unsigned int j=0; j<NUM_POINTS; ++j)
            {
                    unsigned int numPlanesInFront = 0;
                    for (unsigned int i=0; i<6; ++i)
                    {
                            if (!frustumPlanes[i].IsInFront(points[j]))
                            {
                                    break;
                            }

                            ++numPlanesInFront;
                    }

                    if (numPlanesInFront == 6)
                    {
                            shouldDraw = true;
                            break;
                    }
            }
    }

    return shouldDraw;
}
```

ShouldDraw begins by checking whether the Renderable pointer is valid and if the object has bounds which we can test against. If this is true, we set shouldDraw to false; this object will now be rendered only if it passes our tests. We then get the min and max bounds with the object's translation added so that we position the bounds in world space. The min and max positions represent two extreme corners of a cuboid; we use the elements of min and max to create the other six corners and store all eight into the points array.

The first for loop iterates over the points in turn. An inner loop then tests the point against each of the six frustum planes. For a given point to be inside the frustum, all six tests against the frustum planes must pass. Remember that a plane divides the world into two halves, positive space in front of the plane and negative space behind. If a point falls behind any plane, it is not inside the camera frustum. We break as soon as we detect that the point is not within the frustum to ensure that we are not wasting time testing against more planes than necessary.

Once an object has passed the test against all six planes, the shouldDraw boolean is set back to true and the function returns.

We have now successfully implemented an optimization strategy, and only objects which are actually going to contribute to the final rendering of the scene will be processed by the GPU. This would allow us to achieve a higher frame rate or render a more detailed scene in a commercial title.

# Summary

This chapter has seen us take a quick tour through what we can achieve with in-game cameras. You should now understand how essential a virtual camera is to any game. Being able to move around in 3D space is an integral feature to every modern game. We have only scratched the surface here in terms of camera development. Commercial titles today use complex physics and AI to control their cameras, especially in third-person titles, and even then many gamers can become frustrated with the way the camera in a given game behaves. Creating good cameras is a complex but rewarding endeavor, and hopefully this chapter has given you a good introduction to the topic.

We've also seen how to use the information the camera provides to accelerate our rendering process. Frustum culling becomes an invaluable acceleration algorithm once we want to create levels and worlds of any significant size. Open world games such as *Oblivion* would not be possible on today's hardware if it was to try to render every object in the world at any given time. A large part of a game team's job is to find ways to create as detailed worlds as possible with the limited resources at their disposal. These techniques are especially important on mobile devices, as there is a limited amount of memory bandwidth available for transferring data from the CPU to the GPU. We can use this bandwidth more efficiently by never transferring objects which will not be seen in the current frame to our GPU.

Now that we have our basic game up and running, it's time to make it look more appealing. So far, everything in our world has been colored with a flat color. In the next chapter, we are going to look at simulating lighting and materials to make our scene much more interesting and make it begin to look like a 3D game.

# Chapter 9

# Lighting and Materials

The programming team can help the art team achieve the look they desire for a game through the application of lighting and material models. Many techniques over the years have been developed to give games a specific style; *Jet Grind Radio* (*Jet Set Radio* outside North America), which was published in the year 2000, was one such game. *Jet Grind Radio* was famous for its cell-shaded graphical style which set it apart from the competition at the time.

The style of *Jet Grind Radio* was all the more impressive given that it was developed on a platform which did not have vertex and fragment shaders. Special lighting and material effects have become much more prevalent in video games over the last ten years as consumer hardware has advanced to a point which has made real-time shaders a possibility. These features are now also prevalent on mobile devices, and flexibility of shaders has opened up the use of advanced graphical techniques to game developers.

In this chapter, we're going to be looking at the basic lighting and material techniques which are used as a foundation for the more advanced effects. The basic lights and materials in this chapter are a recreation of the fixed function lights and materials from OpenGL ES 1.0.

> **Note** OpenGL ES 2.0 does not have any inbuilt support for lighting; it is up to the programmer to implement the model they desire using shaders.

To begin, we'll take a look at what how light is defined to a programmer and how light interacts with our game entities via materials.

## A Basic Lighting and Material Model

Light in the natural world is a complex phenomenon. Fortunately, as game developers we do not have to model light with physical reality; we instead use a model which approximates what light does and how it interacts with the objects in our scene.

At the most basic level, whether we are dealing with lights in a vertex or fragment shader, our light sources will eventually boil down to having a direction and a color which affect the output color of our object using some form of equation.

The light's properties make up one set of inputs for our lighting equations; another set of inputs will be the properties of the object itself. We refer to these object properties as materials. When discussing materials, we say that we are applying materials to objects.

A material definition in a modern game engine includes the shader program to be used to shade the model, the textures to be applied, as well as any other special effects and render states which are necessary for proper rendering of the object.

This is the brief overview of lighting, and you won't be surprised to learn that the actual implementation of the model is slightly more complex. Our lights and materials are going to be used to calculate three different components of light: ambient, diffuse, and specular. In this chapter, we are going to cover each of these components and look at the effects of each.

Once we have looked at the components of the lighting equation, we will look at three different representations of light sources in our engine. These will be directional lights, positional lights, and spotlights.

# Per-Vertex or Per-Fragment Shading

The shading model which was used in OpenGL ES 1.0 is called the Blinn-Phong shading model. It is named after Jim Blinn and Bui Tuong Phong. Phong described his lighting model in 1973, and this was later modified by Blinn, giving rise to the name.

The model itself describes the equations we will use in this chapter to calculate the ambient, diffuse, and specular components of the color to be applied to the object. Another aspect of the model which we must consider is how accurate we would like the computations to be. If we calculate the color of the result of the interactions among the light, the surface, and the material in the vertex shader, the color will be stored in a varying and then interpolated across the rest of the polygon. This form of interpolating color is known as Gouraud shading, again named after the author of the technique, Henri Gouraud.

This technique can give acceptable results, but it is often possible to easily see the edges of polygons. An alternative form of interpolation is the Phong shading model, which was described by Bui Tuong Phong, along with the rest of his shading model technique. This form of interpolation involves interpolating the normal of the vertex across the surface of the fragment and calculating lighting color for each individual pixel in the fragment shader. This gives much better results but is obviously much more computationally expensive.

Fortunately for us, the equations of lighting are the same in both cases, and as we have a very simple scene in comparison to commercial games, we will be using the Blinn-Phong lighting model and Phong shading to give us the best results.

Before we get on with the task of implementing the lighting in our scene, we have to create a class which can represent a material.

# Representing Materials

The Material class will be used to store all of the information which is relevant to the final appearance of the surfaces of the objects present in our scene. This includes any shaders, textures, and the colors which we will use to represent the separate sections of the lighting equation. Listing 9-1 describes the Material class. We haven't yet covered what the fields of this class will be used for, so don't worry about them for now.

*Listing 9-1. The Material Class Declaration. Material.h*

```
class Material
{
        private:
                Shader*         m_pShader;
                Texture*        m_pTexture;

                Vector4         m_ambientColor;
                Vector4         m_diffuseColor;
                Vector4         m_specularColor;
                float           m_specularExponent;

public:
        Material()
                :       m_pShader(NULL)
                ,       m_pTexture(NULL)
                ,       m_specularExponent(0.0f)
        {

        }

        ~Material()
        {

        }

        void SetShader(Shader* pShader)
        {
                m_pShader = pShader;
        }

        Shader* GetShader() const
        {
                return m_pShader;
        }

        void SetTexture(Texture* pTexture)
        {
                m_pTexture = pTexture;
        }
```

```cpp
Texture* GetTexture() const
{
        return m_pTexture;
}

void SetAmbientColor(Vector4 ambientColor)
{
        m_ambientColor = ambientColor;
}

const Vector4& GetAmbientColor() const
{
        return m_ambientColor;
}

void SetDiffuseColor(Vector4 diffuseColor)
{
        m_diffuseColor = diffuseColor;
}

const Vector4& GetDiffuseColor() const
{
        return m_diffuseColor;
}

void SetSpecularColor(Vector4 specularColor)
{
        m_specularColor = specularColor;
}

const Vector4& GetSpecularColor() const
{
        return m_specularColor;
}

void SetSpecularExponent(float specularExponent)
{
        m_specularExponent = specularExponent;
}

const float GetSpecularExponent() const
{
        return m_specularExponent;
}
};
```

As you can see, our Material class is just a container to store some data which we can associate with an object. We do this by adding it to our Renderable class. Listing 9-2 shows our new Renderable class with a Material in place of the Shader pointer and color Vector4 field which were there previously.

*Listing 9-2. Adding a Material to Renderable. Renderable.h*

```cpp
class Renderable
{
private:
        Geometry*       m_pGeometry;
 Material* m_pMaterial;
        Transform       m_transform;

        Vector3         m_min;
        Vector3         m_max;
        bool            m_useBounds;

public:
        Renderable();
        ~Renderable();

        void            SetGeometry(Geometry* pGeometry);
        Geometry*       GetGeometry();

 void SetMaterial(Material* pMaterial);
 Material* GetMaterial();

        Transform&   GetTransform()      { return m_transform; }

        void                SetBoundMin(const Vector3& min)   { m_min = min; }
        const Vector3&      GetBoundMin() const               { return m_min; }

        void                SetBoundMax(const Vector3& max)   { m_max = max; }
        const Vector3&      GetBoundMax() const               { return m_max; }

        void                SetUseBounds(bool enabled)  { m_useBounds = enabled; }
        bool                GetUseBounds() const        { return m_useBounds; }

        bool                IsInitialized() const
        {
 return m_pGeometry && m_pMaterial;
        }
};

inline Renderable::Renderable()
        :       m_pGeometry(NULL)
, m_pMaterial(NULL)
{

}

inline Renderable::~Renderable()
{

}
```

```
inline void Renderable::SetGeometry(Geometry* pGeometry)
{
        m_pGeometry = pGeometry;
}

inline Geometry* Renderable::GetGeometry()
{
        return m_pGeometry;
}

inline void Renderable::SetMaterial(Material* pMaterial)
{
 m_pMaterial = pMaterial;
}

inline Material* Renderable::GetMaterial()
{
 return m_pMaterial;
}
```

Now that we have a class which can store material properties for our Renderables, we will look at how we can use these in Shaders which add light to our scene.

# Ambient Lighting

The ambient component of the lighting model is used to approximate the background light which will be present in our scene. You can think of this much like daylight in a room with windows.

Nothing in the room is being lit directly by a light source; however, everything has light bouncing off of it. This is because the light from the sun is powerful enough that it can bounce off of many objects yet still carry on and light many more. Once the sun goes down, everything is much darker, as there is much less ambient light bouncing around.

In this sense, ambient light is treated much like a base level of lighting to ensure that objects in the scene do not appear to be completely black. The equation for the ambient lighting component is very straightforward.

*final color = ambient light color × ambient color*

The current rendering we have been using in TransformShader so far has effectively been the equivalent of having an ambient light value of (1, 1, 1, 1), which specifies that our object should be lit fully by ambient lighting; Figure 9-1 shows how the game currently renders with no lighting present.

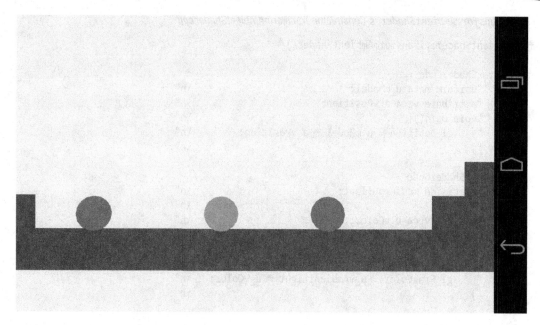

*Figure 9-1. An unlit scene from Droid Runner*

We'll change this now by adding a new shader. Listing 9-3 shows the TransformAmbientShader class.

*Listing 9-3. The TransformAmbientShader Class Declaration. TransformAmbientShader.h*

```
class TransformAmbientShader
        :       public Shader
{
private:
        GLint   m_transformUniformHandle;
        GLint   m_positionAttributeHandle;
        GLint   m_colorUniformHandle;
        GLint   m_ambientLightUniformHandle;

public:
        TransformAmbientShader();
        virtual ~TransformAmbientShader();

        virtual void Link();
        virtual void Setup(Renderable& renderable);
};
```

Our TransformAmbientShader class is almost identical to our TransformShader; the only addition is a new field to store the handle to the ambient light uniform.

The constructor for TransformAmbientShader contains the new GLSL code for our new shader. The fragment shader contains a new uniform, u_vAmbientLight. This uniform is a vec4 and contains the ambient light constant. This constant is multiplied with the fragment color to determine the ambient color for the fragment which is stored into gl_FragColor. Listing 9-4 shows the new GLSL code.

*Listing 9-4. TransformAmbientShader's Constructor. TransformAmbientShader.cpp*

```
TransformAmbientShader::TransformAmbientShader()
{
        m_vertexShaderCode =
                "uniform mat4 u_mModel;                          \n"
                "attribute vec4 a_vPosition;                     \n"
                "void main(){                                    \n"
                "    gl_Position = u_mModel * a_vPosition;       \n"
                "}                                               \n";

        m_fragmentShaderCode =
                "precision mediump float;                        \n"
                "                                                \n"
                "uniform vec4 u_vColor;                          \n"
                "uniform vec4 u_vAmbientLight;                   \n"
                "                                                \n"
                "void main(){                                    \n"
                "    gl_FragColor = u_vAmbientLight * u_vColor;  \n"
                "}                                               \n";
}
```

We need to obtain the handle to the new uniform, and we do this in TransformAmbientShader::Link, shown in Listing 9-5.

*Listing 9-5. TransformAmbientShader::Link. TransformAmbientShader.cpp*

```
void TransformAmbientShader::Link()
{
        Shader::Link();
        m_transformUniformHandle       = glGetUniformLocation(m_programId, "u_mModel");
        m_positionAttributeHandle      = glGetAttribLocation(m_programId, "a_vPosition");
        m_colorUniformHandle           = glGetUniformLocation(m_programId, "u_vColor");
        m_ambientLightUniformHandle    = glGetUniformLocation(m_programId, "u_vAmbientLight");
}
```

This new Shader's Setup method is also similar to that of TransformShader. Only the lines required to set up the ambient light color are new. Listing 9-6 highlights the changes.

*Listing 9-6. TransformAmbientShader::Setup. TransformAmbientShader.cpp*

```
void TransformAmbientShader::Setup(Renderable& renderable)
{
        Geometry* pGeometry = renderable.GetGeometry();
        if (pGeometry)
        {
                Shader::Setup(renderable);
                Renderer& renderer = Renderer::GetSingleton();
                const Matrix4& viewMatrix = renderer.GetViewMatrix();
                const Matrix4& projectionMatrix = renderer.GetProjectionMatrix();
                Matrix4 modelViewMatrix;
                renderable.GetTransform().GetMatrix().Multiply(viewMatrix, modelViewMatrix);
                Matrix4 modelViewProjectionMatrix;
```

```
                modelViewMatrix.Multiply(projectionMatrix, modelViewProjectionMatrix);
                glUniformMatrix4fv(m_transformUniformHandle, 1, false, modelViewProjectionMatrix.m_m);
                glVertexAttribPointer(
                        m_positionAttributeHandle,
                        pGeometry->GetNumVertexPositionElements(),
                        GL_FLOAT,
                        GL_FALSE,
                        pGeometry->GetVertexStride(),
                        pGeometry->GetVertexBuffer());
                glEnableVertexAttribArray(m_positionAttributeHandle);
                const Vector4& color = renderable.GetMaterial()->GetAmbientColor();
                glUniform4f(m_colorUniformHandle, color.m_x, color.m_y, color.m_z, color.m_w);
        const Vector4& ambientLightColor = renderer.GetAmbientLightColor();
        glUniform4f(m_ambientLightUniformHandle,
        ambientLightColor.m_x,
        ambientLightColor.m_y,
        ambientLightColor.m_z,
        ambientLightColor.m_w);
        }
}
```

This listing shows that we must also add some new methods to our Renderer. Listing 9-7 shows this minor addition; simply add a new private Vector4 field to the Renderer class and also add methods to set and get the values.

*Listing 9-7. Adding m_ambientLightColor to Renderer. Renderer.h*

```
class Renderer
        :       public Task
        ,       public EventHandler
        ,       public Singleton<Renderer>
{
public:
        enum FrustumParameters
        {
                TOP,
                BOTTOM,
                RIGHT,
                LEFT,
                NEAR,
                FAR,
                NUM_PARAMS
        };

private:
        android_app*        m_pState;
        EGLDisplay          m_display;
        EGLContext          m_context;
        EGLSurface          m_surface;
        int                 m_width;
        int                 m_height;
        bool                m_initialized;
        bool                m_paused;
```

```
        typedef std::vector<Shader*>           ShaderVector;
        typedef ShaderVector::iterator         ShaderVectorIterator;

        typedef std::vector<Texture*>          TextureVector;
        typedef TextureVector::iterator        TextureVectorIterator;

        typedef std::vector<Renderable*>       RenderableVector;
        typedef RenderableVector::iterator     RenderableVectorIterator;

        RenderableVector      m_renderables;
        TextureVector         m_textures;
        ShaderVector          m_shaders;

        float                 m_frustumParameters[NUM_PARAMS];

        Matrix4               m_cameraMatrix;
        Matrix4               m_viewMatrix;
        Matrix4               m_projectionMatrix;

        void Draw(Renderable* pRenderable);
        void BuildFrustumPlanes(Plane frustumPlanes[]);
        bool ShouldDraw(Renderable* pRenderable, Plane frustumPlanes[]) const;

    Vector4 m_ambientLightColor;
public:
        explicit Renderer(android_app* pState, const unsigned int priority);
        virtual ~Renderer();
        void Init();
        void Destroy();

        void AddRenderable(Renderable* pRenderable);
        void AddShader(Shader* pShader);
        void RemoveShader(Shader* pShader);

        void AddTexture(Texture* pTexture);
        void RemoveTexture(Texture* pTexture);

        // From Task
        virtual bool  Start();
        virtual void  OnSuspend();
        virtual void  Update();
        virtual void  OnResume();
        virtual void  Stop();

        virtual void  HandleEvent(Event* event);
        bool IsInitialized() { return m_initialized; }
        void                  SetCameraMatrix(const Matrix4& cameraMatrix)
        {
              m_cameraMatrix = cameraMatrix;
        }

        const Matrix4&        GetCameraMatrix() const     { return m_cameraMatrix; }
```

```
void                    SetViewMatrix(const Matrix4& viewMatrix)
{
        m_viewMatrix = viewMatrix;
}
const Matrix4&          GetViewMatrix() const        { return m_viewMatrix; }

void                    SetFrustum(const float frustumParameters[]);
const Matrix4&          GetProjectionMatrix() const { return m_projectionMatrix; }

int                     GetWidth() const             { return m_width; }
int                     GetHeight() const            { return m_height; }

void SetAmbientLightColor(const Vector4& ambientLightColor)
{
m_ambientLightColor = ambientLightColor;
}
const Vector4& GetAmbientLightColor() const
{
return m_ambientLightColor;
}
};
```

Figure 9-2 shows the state of the game with the ambient lighting being applied to the Renderables.

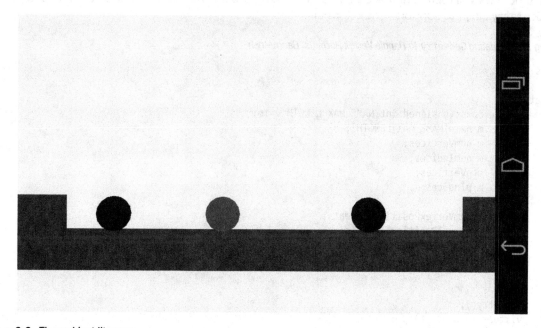

**Figure 9-2.** *The ambient lit scene*

As Figure 9-2 shows, an ambient light level of 0.2f for each color component means that our objects are almost black. It's almost impossible to make out any shade of red on the AI enemies, but the player does have a slight shade of green. The crates are also very slightly blue. This is ideal for our scene, as we will see when we add more color.

Before we move onto the next element in the lighting equation, we must update our Geometry. The diffuse and specular components of the lighting equation need to know in which direction the polygons in our models are facing. We can do this by supplying a normal vector into our shader along with each vertex.

# Vertex Normals

We have come across normal vectors a few times so far in this book. If you recall, a normal vector is a vector which is a single unit long and is used to show a direction rather than represent a displacement.

We can work out the normal for a polygon using the plane equation. Since we are always dealing with flat triangles when developing OpenGL ES 2.0 games for Android, we can use the three points of the triangle to generate the surface normal for the triangle. The math for this process is covered in Appendix D, along with the listing of the Plane class and its methods.

Fortunately, all of our models are generally exported from 3D modeling packages. These 3D modeling packages are usually more than capable of generating and exporting the surface normals for any models which we are creating. For this book I have been using the free modeling package, Blender, which you can obtain from www.blender.org.

Given that we will be exporting the vertex normals for our meshes from a 3D package, we should look at how we will represent this data in code. Listing 9-8 shows the updates which are needed in the Geometry class to support vertex normals.

*Listing 9-8. Updating Geometry to Handle Vertex Normals. Geometry.h*

```
class Geometry
{
private:
        static const unsigned int NAME_MAX_LENGTH = 16;
        char    m_name[NAME_MAX_LENGTH];
        int     m_numVertices;
        int     m_numIndices;
        void*   m_pVertices;
        void*   m_pIndices;

        int     m_numVertexPositionElements;
        int m_numNormalPositionElements;
        int     m_numTexCoordElements;
        int     m_vertexStride;

public:
        Geometry();
        virtual ~Geometry();

        void    SetName(const char* name)                   { strcpy(m_name, name); }
        void    SetNumVertices(const int numVertices)       { m_numVertices = numVertices; }
        void    SetNumIndices(const int numIndices)         { m_numIndices = numIndices; }

        const char*    GetName() const                      { return m_name; }
```

```
        const int      GetNumVertices() const              { return m_numVertices; }
        const int      GetNumIndices() const               { return m_numIndices; }

        void*          GetVertexBuffer() const             { return m_pVertices; }
        void*          GetIndexBuffer() const              { return m_pIndices; }

        void           SetVertexBuffer(void* pVertices)    { m_pVertices = pVertices; }
        void           SetIndexBuffer(void* pIndices)      { m_pIndices = pIndices; }

        void           SetNumVertexPositionElements(const int numVertexPositionElements)
        {
            m_numVertexPositionElements = numVertexPositionElements;
        }

        int            GetNumVertexPositionElements() const
        {
            return m_numVertexPositionElements;
        }

void SetNumNormalPositionElements(const int numNormalPositionElements)
{
m_numNormalPositionElements = numNormalPositionElements;
}

int GetNumNormalPositionElements() const
{
return m_numNormalPositionElements;
}

        void           SetNumTexCoordElements(const int numTexCoordElements)
        {
            m_numTexCoordElements = numTexCoordElements;
        }

        int            GetNumTexCoordElements() const
        {
            return m_numTexCoordElements;
        }

        void           SetVertexStride(const int vertexStride)
        {
            m_vertexStride = vertexStride;
        }

        int            GetVertexStride() const
        {
            return m_vertexStride;
        }
};
```

We have added fields to store the number of normals to our Geometry class. This further extends our storage of vertex data in our array of structures format. This is the most optimal method for streaming geometry data to current mobile GPUs.

With the `Geometry` class now able to handle models which contain vertex normal data, let's move on to look at how the diffuse lighting shader will utilize them.

# Diffuse Lighting

The lighting equation which we are attempting to implement with our shaders in this chapter is an additive equation. This means that our lighting components add together to make the final result. In this section on diffuse lighting, we are going to look at the second part of the following equation:

*final color = ambient color + diffuse color + specular color*

We've already seen how the ambient color sets the base light value of our objects. On its own, however, the ambient light still leaves our objects looking flat. This is because the ambient light function does not take into account the angle between the light source and the direction which the surface is facing.

For now, we are going to implement the simplest version of a light source for a game, a directional light. A directional light is used to simulate a light source which is an extreme distance away. If you imagine the sun, we could simplify the light which is given off by thinking of it in terms of a sphere of equal intensity in all directions. By the time the light from the sun reaches earth, the light rays from the sphere are coming from a very small fragment of the overall sphere. In a game situation, we simplify this down to a model where we suggest that all light from this source is traveling in parallel and hits all of our objects from exactly the same direction.

The words "direction" and "directional" have been used several times in the last paragraph, and you might have guessed that we will be using another normal vector to represent the direction of our light. However, we will not be storing the direction in which our light is traveling; we will actually be storing the opposite. The reason for this will become clear when you look at the equation for the diffuse lighting component of our color:

*diffuse color = max(L.N, 0) × diffuse light color × diffuse material color*

The term L.N in the preceding equation represents the dot product between our directional light vector and the current vertex normal. The dot product gives us the following result:

*L.N = |L||N|cos(alpha)*

The lines surrounding L and N represent the length (or magnitude) of those vectors. Our vectors in the lighting equation are normals; therefore, their length is 1. This means that the result of the dot product between two normal vectors is the cosine of the angle between the two. The cosine of 0 degrees is 1, the cosine of 90 degrees is 0, and the cosine of 180 degrees is −1. As our fragment color values are output in the range from 0 to 1, we will use the higher of either the dot product result or 0. For any angle between 0 and 90 degrees, we will add a diffuse color component to this fragment.

## Diffuse Component Vertex Shader

Before we can look at the fragment shader code for the diffuse component, we will examine the vertex shader necessary to set up the vertex position and normal. Listing 9-9 contains the code for `TransformAmbientDiffuseShader`'s vertex shader.

*Listing 9-9. TransformAmbientDiffuseShader's Vertex Shader Source. TransformAmbientDiffuseShader.cpp*

```
m_vertexShaderCode =
        "uniform mat4 u_mModelViewProj;                          \n"
        "uniform mat3 u_mModelIT;                                \n"
        "attribute vec4 a_vPosition;                             \n"
        "attribute vec3 a_vNormal;                               \n"
        "varying   vec3 v_vNormal;                               \n"
        "void main(){                                            \n"
        "    gl_Position = u_mModelViewProj * a_vPosition;       \n"
        "    v_vNormal = normalize(u_mModelIT * a_vNormal);      \n"
        "}                                                       \n";
```

Our vertex shader is straightforward to read. We have a matrix, u_mModelViewProj, which we use to transform our vertex's position attribute into normalized device coordinates as usual.

We now also have an attribute for our vertex normal and a varying variable to store the output. Varyings in GLSL are used to interpolate values between the three vertices which make up a triangle. As we are now specifying a normal vector per vertex, we must store each into a varying to be interpolated for each fragment to be shaded.

When we store our normal into v_vNormal, we are also multiplying it by the matrix u_mModelIT. This matrix is responsible for transforming the matrix from the model's local space into world space. As a normal vector does not require any translation, the matrix itself is only a 3x3 rotation and scaling matrix. Unfortunately, we cannot simply transform normals with the model's transform matrix directly. Any scaling which could be applied to the model will cause the normal to change direction relative to its surface. Instead, we must transform normals using the inverse transpose of the model's matrix.

If you recall, a rotation matrix is an orthogonal matrix. This type of matrix is special in that its inverse is also its transpose; therefore, the inverse transpose of the rotation part of the model's transform will remain unchanged. A scaling matrix is a diagonal matrix, and as such the transpose of a scaling matrix is no different from the standard matrix. The inverse scale elements contain one divided by the original scales, giving us the inverse. Multiplying normals by this inverse transpose of the model matrix allows us to rotate our normals into world space in the same manner as our model but also to preserve the direction of the original normal relative to the surface it represents.

# Diffuse Component Fragment Shader

With the vertex shader out of the way, we can look at the fragment shader. We do this in Listing 9-10.

*Listing 9-10. TransformAmbientDiffuseShader's Fragment Shader Source. TransformAmbientDiffuseShader.cpp*

```
m_fragmentShaderCode =
        "precision mediump float;                    \n"
        "varying vec3 v_vNormal;                     \n"
        "                                            \n"
        "uniform vec4 u_vAmbientColor;               \n"
        "uniform vec4 u_vDiffuseColor;               \n"
        "uniform vec4 u_vAmbientLight;               \n"
        "uniform vec4 u_vDiffuseLight;               \n"
```

```
"uniform vec3 u_vLightDirection;                                    \n"
"                                                                   \n"
"const float c_zero = 0.0;                                          \n"
"const float c_one  = 1.0;                                          \n"
"                                                                   \n"
"void main(){                                                       \n"
"    gl_FragColor = vec4(c_zero, c_zero, c_zero, c_zero);           \n"
"                                                                   \n"
"    float ndotl = dot(u_vLightDirection, v_vNormal);               \n"
"    ndotl = max(ndotl, c_zero);                                    \n"
"    gl_FragColor += ndotl * u_vDiffuseLight * u_vDiffuseColor;     \n"
"                                                                   \n"
"    gl_FragColor += u_vAmbientLight * u_vAmbientColor;             \n"
"                                                                   \n"
"    gl_FragColor.a = c_one;                                        \n"
"}                                                                  \n";
```

The fragment shader for the diffuse lighting component begins by declaring the default precision of the floating-point operations for this shader program. Shader precision qualifiers can be a complicated topic when looking into the specific details. For the purposes of this book, it's sufficient to know that the precision affects the range of values available to a given data type.

There are three precision qualifiers available, `lowp`, `mediump`, and `highp`. For the purposes of a lighting equation, `lowp` usually does not provide enough precision and `highp` usually provides more than we require. The increase in precision at each level results in a shader taking longer to execute; therefore, it is important to select a level of precision which is suitable for any given shader. I've used `mediump` here; however, I can't actually see any difference when changing the setting to `lowp`.

It's also worth remembering that some platforms may not support all of the precision qualifiers. The OpenGL ES 2.0 standard states that the minimum required precision qualifier is `mediump` for fragment shaders and `highp` for vertex shaders.

> **Note**    At this time, Nvidia's Tegra 3 platform is the only chipset which does not support the `highp` qualifier in fragment shaders. If you do use `highp`, however, the Tegra 3 shader compiler will automatically use `mediump`, but it is worth bearing this in mind.

Next, we declare the varying which will contain our interpolated normal vector. Remember that the vertex shader will compute a transformed normal for each vertex, and the GPU will use linear interpolation to calculate the normal position at each fragment. Linear interpolation is calculated by using the values 0 and 1 at each extreme. A linear interpolation of halfway between the digits 5 and 10 would look like the following equation.

$$((10 - 5) * 0.5) + 5 = 7.5$$

Here we calculate the difference between our two extremes, which in this case is covered by the sum $10 - 5$. We then multiply the range by the interpolation factor, which is 0.5 to represent halfway between the extremes. The last step involves adding the first extreme to calculate the point which rests between the first and second points.

We then have our uniform values. The uniforms are variables which are supplied to all instances of the fragment shader from the game code. In our diffuse shader, we are supplying uniforms which represent the ambient and diffuse color of the object's material, the ambient and diffuse colors of the light, and the direction of the light. We have also specified constants to represent the values 0.0 and 1.0; these are c_zero and c_one, respectively.

Our main method is defined after all of our variables are declared. We begin by initializing gl_FragColor to a vec4 containing c_zero at each element.

The dot method is then used to calculate the dot product of the vectors v_vLightDirection and v_vNormal. We have achieved the technique known as per-pixel lighting by carrying out this calculation in our fragment shader. We would be implementing per-vertex lighting if we had calculated the dot product in our vertex shader. Calculating the lighting equation in the vertex shader is much faster but does not give as nice results. If you were implementing a full game, having key objects lit with a per-fragment shader and other less important objects lit with a per-vertex shader could be one technique used to optimize your game.

The next line in the shader uses max to limit the lowest possible value of the dot product to 0. We then multiply the three elements needed to calculate the diffuse color, ndotl, u_vDiffuseLight, and u_vDiffuseColor.

With our diffuse color component computed, we then add the result of the ambient component. This is calculated in the same way as in Listing 9-4 by multiplying the ambient light vector with the ambient color vector.

# Initializing the Shader Using OpenGL ES 2.0

Listing 9-11 contains the Link method needed to acquire the handles to our uniforms and attributes.

*Listing 9-11. TransformAmbientDiffuseShader::Link. TransformAmbientDiffuseShader.cpp*

```
void TransformAmbientDiffuseShader::Link()
{
        Shader::Link();
        m_modelViewProjUniformHandle     = glGetUniformLocation(m_programId, "u_mModelViewProj");
        m_modelITMatrixUniformHandle     = glGetUniformLocation(m_programId, "u_mModelIT");
        m_positionAttributeHandle        = glGetAttribLocation(m_programId,  "a_vPosition");
        m_normalAttributeHandle          = glGetAttribLocation(m_programId,  "a_vNormal");
        m_ambientColorUniformHandle      = glGetUniformLocation(m_programId, "u_vAmbientColor");
        m_diffuseColorUniformHandle      = glGetUniformLocation(m_programId, "u_vDiffuseColor");
        m_ambientLightUniformHandle      = glGetUniformLocation(m_programId, "u_vAmbientLight");
        m_diffuseLightUniformHandle      = glGetUniformLocation(m_programId, "u_vDiffuseLight");
        m_lightDirectionUniformHandle    = glGetUniformLocation(m_programId, "u_vLightDirection");
}
```

Recall from Listing 9-9 that we had to provide the model's inverse transpose Transform matrix to the vertex shader to transform the vertex normal. Listing 9-12 shows the TransformAmbientDiffuseShader::Setup method, which contains the code to calculate this matrix.

*Listing 9-12. TransformAmbientDiffuseShader::Setup. TransformAmbientDiffuseShader.cpp*

```cpp
void TransformAmbientDiffuseShader::Setup(Renderable& renderable)
{
        Geometry* pGeometry = renderable.GetGeometry();
        if (pGeometry)
        {
                Shader::Setup(renderable);
                Renderer& renderer = Renderer::GetSingleton();
                const Matrix4& viewMatrix = renderer.GetViewMatrix();
                const Matrix4& projectionMatrix = renderer.GetProjectionMatrix();
                const Matrix4& modelMatrix = renderable.GetTransform().GetMatrix();
                Matrix4 modelViewMatrix;
                modelMatrix.Multiply(viewMatrix, modelViewMatrix);
                Matrix4 modelViewProjectionMatrix;
                modelViewMatrix.Multiply(projectionMatrix, modelViewProjectionMatrix);
                glUniformMatrix4fv(
                        m_modelViewProjUniformHandle,
                        1,
                        false,
                        modelViewProjectionMatrix.m_m);

                Matrix3 modelIT;
                renderable.GetTransform().GetInverseTransposeMatrix(modelIT);
                glUniformMatrix3fv(m_modelITMatrixUniformHandle, 1, false, modelIT.m_m);
                glVertexAttribPointer(
                        m_positionAttributeHandle,
                        pGeometry->GetNumVertexPositionElements(),
                        GL_FLOAT,
                        GL_FALSE,
                        pGeometry->GetVertexStride(),
                        pGeometry->GetVertexBuffer());
                glEnableVertexAttribArray(m_positionAttributeHandle);
                glVertexAttribPointer(
                        m_normalAttributeHandle,
                        pGeometry->GetNumNormalPositionElements(),
                        GL_FLOAT,
                        GL_FALSE,
                        pGeometry->GetVertexStride(),
                        static_cast<float*>(pGeometry->GetVertexBuffer()) +
                                pGeometry->GetNumVertexPositionElements());
                glEnableVertexAttribArray(m_normalAttributeHandle);
                const Vector4& ambientColor = renderable.GetMaterial()->GetAmbientColor();
                glUniform4f(
                        m_ambientColorUniformHandle,
                        ambientColor.m_x,
                        ambientColor.m_y,
                        ambientColor.m_z,
                        ambientColor.m_w);
```

```
        const Vector4& diffuseColor = renderable.GetMaterial()->GetDiffuseColor();
        glUniform4f(
                m_diffuseColorUniformHandle,
                diffuseColor.m_x,
                diffuseColor.m_y,
                diffuseColor.m_z,
                diffuseColor.m_w);

        const Vector4& ambientLightColor = renderer.GetAmbientLightColor();
        glUniform4f(
                m_ambientLightUniformHandle,
                ambientLightColor.m_x,
                ambientLightColor.m_y,
                ambientLightColor.m_z,
                ambientLightColor.m_w);

        const Vector4& diffuseLightColor = renderer.GetDiffuseLightColor();
        glUniform4f(
                m_diffuseLightUniformHandle,
                diffuseLightColor.m_x,
                diffuseLightColor.m_y,
                diffuseLightColor.m_z,
                diffuseLightColor.m_w);

        const Vector3& lightDirection = renderer.GetLightDirection();
        glUniform3f(
                m_lightDirectionUniformHandle,
                lightDirection.m_x,
                lightDirection.m_y,
                lightDirection.m_z);
    }
}
```

We begin this method by obtaining references to the current view matrix, projection matrix, and model matrix. modelMatrix is then multiplied with viewMatrix to obtain modelViewMatrix. modelViewMatrix is then multiplied with projectionMatrix. This gives us modelViewProjection matrix, which is necessary to transform our model's vertices into the canonical view volume. We use glUniformMatrix4fv to upload this matrix to the GPU to be used with the uniform u_mModelViewProj in our vertex shader.

The next step in the method is to get the inverse transpose of the model's transform matrix. We do this using Transform::GetInverseTransposeMatrix. The class declaration for Transform was shown in Listing 6-21; we describe the code for GetInverseTransposeMatrix in Listing 9-13.

*Listing 9-13. Transform::GetInverseTransposeMatrix. Transform.cpp*

```
void Transform::GetInverseTransposeMatrix(Matrix4& out) const
{
        float invScale = 1.0f / m_scale;
        out.m_m[0] = m_rotation.m_m[0] * invScale;
        out.m_m[1] = m_rotation.m_m[1];
        out.m_m[2] = m_rotation.m_m[2];
```

```
        out.m_m[3] = 0.0f;
        out.m_m[4] = m_rotation.m_m[3];
        out.m_m[5] = m_rotation.m_m[4] * invScale;
        out.m_m[6] = m_rotation.m_m[5];
        out.m_m[7] = 0.0f;
        out.m_m[8] = m_rotation.m_m[6];
        out.m_m[9] = m_rotation.m_m[7];
        out.m_m[10] = m_rotation.m_m[8] * invScale;
        out.m_m[11] = 0.0f;
        out.m_m[12] = -m_translation.m_x;
        out.m_m[13] = -m_translation.m_y;
        out.m_m[14] = -m_translation.m_z;
        out.m_m[15] = 1.0f;
}

void Transform::GetInverseTransposeMatrix(Matrix3& out) const
{
        float invScale = 1.0f / m_scale;
        out.m_m[0] = m_rotation.m_m[0] * invScale;
        out.m_m[1] = m_rotation.m_m[1];
        out.m_m[2] = m_rotation.m_m[2];
        out.m_m[3] = m_rotation.m_m[3];
        out.m_m[4] = m_rotation.m_m[4] * invScale;
        out.m_m[5] = m_rotation.m_m[5];
        out.m_m[6] = m_rotation.m_m[6];
        out.m_m[7] = m_rotation.m_m[7];
        out.m_m[8] = m_rotation.m_m[8] * invScale;
}
```

Listing 9-13 contains two versions of the method to obtain the inverse transpose matrix from a Transform. As we already know, the inverse transpose of a rotation matrix is the original matrix, so we copy the rotation matrix in the normal order. The transpose of the scale matrix doesn't change anything and we can calculate the inverse of the scale components very easily by dividing the scale into 1. Our code in Listing 9-12 is using the version of this method, which obtains a 3x3 matrix, as our normals do not require the translation component to be present.

Our vertex attributes are then set up. The m_positionAttributeHandle is initialized with the proper parameters from the geometry class and is enabled with glEnableVertexAttribArray. We then do the same for the normals. The address of the first normal is calculated by casting the vertex buffer pointer to a float pointer and adding the number of vertex position elements.

The vectors containing the material and light color properties are then initialized using glUniform4f and glUniform3f.

Our code should now be complete, and we will see some diffuse lighting in our game. This is the first time where we can actually see some depth in our scene and be able to tell that we have successfully created a three-dimensional game. Figure 9-3 shows a screenshot of the scene with diffuse lighting enabled.

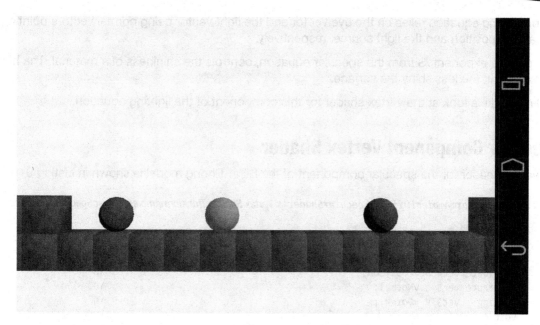

*Figure 9-3. Diffuse lighting*

As is evident from the preceding screenshot, we have set up our diffuse light source to be situated above and to the right of our objects. The light shines most brightly in those areas and becomes darker on the bottom left of the objects. We can also see the spherical shape of the player and AI objects, as well as the depth of our cubes.

The remaining component of the Blinn-Phong lighting model is the specular component. We look at this next.

# Specular Lighting

The specular component of the lighting equation is responsible for the apparent shininess of a given object. So far, the ambient component has given a base level of light to show color in the darkest areas of our objects. The diffuse component has added the majority of lighting to the object, which helps determine the color and shape of the object in our scene. The specular component is now added to these to make an object appear more or less reflective. Just as with the diffuse component, the specular component has an equation which we will implement in our fragment shader. That equation is as follows:

*specular color = max(H.N, 0)^S × specular light color × specular material color*

The preceding equation contains the modification to the Phong shading model made by Blinn. The original model contained the vector R instead of H. R represented a reflected light vector which had to be calculated for every vertex in a given model. The vector H represents a half vector and can be calculated once for each model:

*half vector = normalize(eye vector + light vector)*

The preceding equation relies on the eye vector and the light vector being normal vectors pointing to the camera position and the light source, respectively.

The specular exponent, S from the specular equation, controls the shininess of a material. The higher this exponent, the less shiny the surface.

We'll now take a look at the vertex shader for this component of the lighting equation.

# Specular Component Vertex Shader

The vertex shader for the specular component of the Blinn-Phong model is shown in Listing 9-14.

*Listing 9-14. TransformAmbientDiffuseSpecularShader's Vertex Shader. TransformAmbientDiffuseSpecularShader.cpp*

```
m_vertexShaderCode =
        "uniform mat4 u_mModelViewProj;                              \n"
        "uniform mat3 u_mModelIT;                                    \n"
        "attribute vec4 a_vPosition;                                 \n"
        "attribute vec3 a_vNormal;                                   \n"
        "varying    vec3 v_vNormal;                                  \n"
        "void main(){                                                \n"
        "    gl_Position = u_mModelViewProj * a_vPosition;           \n"
        "    v_vNormal = normalize(u_mModelIT * a_vNormal);          \n"
        "}                                                           \n";
```

Hopefully, it comes as no surprise that our vertex shader does not differ from the vertex shader used in TransformAmbientDiffuseShader. We are using Phong shading to calculate our lighting values at a per-pixel level. We'll move straight on to the fragment shader.

# Specular Component Fragment Shader

Our fragment shader will add the next additive component of the Blinn-Phong model, the specular component. We have already looked at the equation for this component, so Listing 9-15 gets straight into the fragment shader source code.

*Listing 9-15. TransformAmbientDiffuseSpecularShader's Fragment Shader. TransformAmbientDiffuseSpecularShader.cpp*

```
m_fragmentShaderCode =
        "precision mediump float;                                    \n"
        "varying    vec3 v_vNormal;                                  \n"
        "                                                            \n"
        "uniform vec4 u_vAmbientColor;                               \n"
        "uniform vec4 u_vDiffuseColor;                               \n"
        "uniform vec4 u_vSpecularColor;                              \n"
        "uniform float u_fSpecularExponent;                          \n"
        "uniform vec4 u_vAmbientLight;                               \n"
        "uniform vec4 u_vDiffuseLight;                               \n"
        "uniform vec4 u_vSpecularLight;                              \n"
        "uniform vec3 u_vLightDirection;                             \n"
        "uniform vec3 u_vLightHalfVector;                            \n"
        "                                                            \n"
```

```
"const float c_zero = 0.0;                                             \n"
"const float c_one  = 1.0;                                             \n"
"                                                                      \n"
"void main(){                                                          \n"
"    gl_FragColor = vec4(c_zero, c_zero, c_zero, c_zero);              \n"
"                                                                      \n"
"    float ndoth =  dot(u_vLightHalfVector, v_vNormal);               \n"
"    ndoth = max(ndoth, c_zero);                                       \n"
"    float dotPow = pow(ndoth, u_fSpecularExponent);                  \n"
"    gl_FragColor += dotPow * u_vSpecularColor * u_vSpecularLight;     \n"
"                                                                      \n"
"    float ndotl = dot(u_vLightDirection, v_vNormal);                 \n"
"    ndotl = max(ndotl, c_zero);                                       \n"
"    gl_FragColor += ndotl * u_vDiffuseLight * u_vDiffuseColor;        \n"
"                                                                      \n"
"    gl_FragColor += u_vAmbientLight * u_vAmbientColor;                \n"
"                                                                      \n"
"    gl_FragColor.a = c_one;                                           \n"
"}                                                                     \n";
```

As our new shader contains both the ambient and diffuse components, it retains all of the uniforms necessary for those calculations. Our newly introduced uniforms are u_vSpecularColor, u_fSpecularExponent, u_vSpecularLight, and u_vLightHalfVector.

There are four new lines in the shader which calculate the specular component. The first calculates the dot product between u_vLightHalfVector and v_vNormal. This gives us the angle between the half vector and the fragment's normal vector. We then take the higher of either the dot product or zero. The result of the previous steps is then raised to the power of the specular component, and finally the dot product raised to the specular exponent is multiplied by the specular material and light colors.

As the equation is an additive process, we add the diffuse component and then the ambient component to get to the final fragment color.

With our shader code complete, the last step is to look at the OpenGL ES 2.0 code we require to put the shader into use.

# Initializing TransformAmbientDiffuseSpecularShader

Like all of our shaders, we must override the Link and Setup methods to be able to use this specific shader.

We look at TransformAmbientDiffuseSpecularShader::Link in Listing 9-16.

*Listing 9-16. TransformAmbientDiffuseSpecularShader::Link. TransformAmbientDiffuseSpecularShader.cpp*

```
void TransformAmbientDiffuseSpecularShader::Link()
{
    Shader::Link();
    m_modelViewProjUniformHandle    = glGetUniformLocation(m_programId, "u_mModelViewProj");
    m_modelITMatrixUniformHandle    = glGetUniformLocation(m_programId, "u_mModelIT");
    m_positionAttributeHandle       = glGetAttribLocation(m_programId,  "a_vPosition");
```

```
m_normalAttributeHandle             = glGetAttribLocation(m_programId,  "a_vNormal");
m_ambientColorUniformHandle         = glGetUniformLocation(m_programId, "u_vAmbientColor");
m_diffuseColorUniformHandle         = glGetUniformLocation(m_programId, "u_vDiffuseColor");
m_specularColorUniformHandle        = glGetUniformLocation(m_programId, "u_vSpecularColor");
m_specularExponentUniformHandle     = glGetUniformLocation(m_programId, "u_fSpecularExponent");
m_ambientLightUniformHandle         = glGetUniformLocation(m_programId, "u_vAmbientLight");
m_diffuseLightUniformHandle         = glGetUniformLocation(m_programId, "u_vDiffuseLight");
m_specularLightUniformHandle        = glGetUniformLocation(m_programId, "u_vSpecularLight");
m_lightDirectionUniformHandle       = glGetUniformLocation(m_programId, "u_vLightDirection");
m_lightHalfVectorUniformHandle      = glGetUniformLocation(m_programId, "u_vLightHalfVector");
}
```

In Link, we obtain all of the handles required for setting the uniforms and attributes using the
OpenGL ES 2.0 methods glGetUniformLocation and glGetAttribLocation. We put these handles to
use in TransformAmbientDiffuseSpecularShader::Setup, shown in Listing 9-17.

*Listing 9-17. TransformAmbientDiffuseSpecularShader::Setup. TransformAmbientDiffuseSpecularShader.cpp*

```cpp
void TransformAmbientDiffuseSpecularShader::Setup(Renderable& renderable)
{
        Geometry* pGeometry = renderable.GetGeometry();
        if (pGeometry)
        {
                Shader::Setup(renderable);
                Renderer& renderer = Renderer::GetSingleton();
                const Matrix4& viewMatrix = renderer.GetViewMatrix();
                const Matrix4& projectionMatrix = renderer.GetProjectionMatrix();
                const Matrix4& modelMatrix = renderable.GetTransform().GetMatrix();
                Matrix4 modelViewMatrix;
                modelMatrix.Multiply(viewMatrix, modelViewMatrix);
                Matrix4 modelViewProjectionMatrix;
                modelViewMatrix.Multiply(projectionMatrix, modelViewProjectionMatrix);
                glUniformMatrix4fv(
                        m_modelViewProjUniformHandle,
                        1,
                        false,
                        modelViewProjectionMatrix.m_m);

                Matrix3 modelIT;
                renderable.GetTransform().GetInverseTransposeMatrix(modelIT);
                glUniformMatrix3fv(m_modelITMatrixUniformHandle, 1, false, modelIT.m_m);
                glVertexAttribPointer(
                        m_positionAttributeHandle,
                        pGeometry->GetNumVertexPositionElements(),
                        GL_FLOAT,
                        GL_FALSE,
                        pGeometry->GetVertexStride(),
                        pGeometry->GetVertexBuffer());
                glEnableVertexAttribArray(m_positionAttributeHandle);
                glVertexAttribPointer(
                        m_normalAttributeHandle,
                        pGeometry->GetNumNormalPositionElements(),
```

```
                GL_FLOAT,
                GL_FALSE,
                pGeometry->GetVertexStride(),
                static_cast<float*>(pGeometry->GetVertexBuffer()) +
                        pGeometry->GetNumVertexPositionElements());
        glEnableVertexAttribArray(m_normalAttributeHandle);
        const Vector4& ambientColor = renderable.GetMaterial()->GetAmbientColor();
        glUniform4f(
                m_ambientColorUniformHandle,
                ambientColor.m_x,
                ambientColor.m_y,
                ambientColor.m_z,
                ambientColor.m_w);

        const Vector4& diffuseColor = renderable.GetMaterial()->GetDiffuseColor();
        glUniform4f(
                m_diffuseColorUniformHandle,
                diffuseColor.m_x,
                diffuseColor.m_y,
                diffuseColor.m_z,
                diffuseColor.m_w);

const Vector4& specularColor = renderable.GetMaterial()->GetSpecularColor();
glUniform4f(
m_specularColorUniformHandle,
specularColor.m_x,
specularColor.m_y,
specularColor.m_z,
specularColor.m_w);

glUniform1f(
m_specularExponentUniformHandle,
renderable.GetMaterial()->GetSpecularExponent());
        const Vector4& ambientLightColor = renderer.GetAmbientLightColor();
        glUniform4f(
                m_ambientLightUniformHandle,
                ambientLightColor.m_x,
                ambientLightColor.m_y,
                ambientLightColor.m_z,
                ambientLightColor.m_w);

        const Vector4& diffuseLightColor = renderer.GetDiffuseLightColor();
        glUniform4f(
                m_diffuseLightUniformHandle,
                diffuseLightColor.m_x,
                diffuseLightColor.m_y,
                diffuseLightColor.m_z,
                diffuseLightColor.m_w);
```

```
const Vector4& specularLightColor = renderer.GetSpecularLightColor();
glUniform4f(
m_specularLightUniformHandle,
specularLightColor.m_x,
specularLightColor.m_y,
specularLightColor.m_z,
specularLightColor.m_w);

        const Vector3& lightDirection = renderer.GetLightDirection();
        glUniform3f(
            m_lightDirectionUniformHandle,
            lightDirection.m_x,
            lightDirection.m_y,
            lightDirection.m_z);

Vector3 lightHalfVector = renderer.GetCameraTransform().GetTranslation();
lightHalfVector.Subtract(
Vector3(modelMatrix.m_m[12], modelMatrix.m_m[13], modelMatrix.m_m[14]));
lightHalfVector.Normalize();
lightHalfVector.Add(lightDirection);
lightHalfVector.Normalize();
glUniform3f(
m_lightHalfVectorUniformHandle,
lightHalfVector.m_x,
lightHalfVector.m_y,
lightHalfVector.m_z);
    }
}
```

The lines of code which are in bold in the preceding listing are the lines which differ between `TransformAmbientDiffuseSpecularShader::Setup` and `TransformAmbientDiffuseShader::Setup`.

The first block is responsible for uploading the specular color and exponent of the object's material to the GPU. The second identified section uploads the light's specular color to the GPU.

The last section is responsible for calculating the light's half vector. We begin by getting the position of the camera object in world space. By subtracting the model's position, we obtain a vector which points in the direction of the camera from the model. We then turn this into a unit normal by calling the `Normalize` method. Now we find the vector halfway between the eye vector and the light vector by adding them together. Once we have this vector, we would like to be a unit normal once again, so we call `Normalize` for a second time. Calculating this vector once for each model is the optimization which Blinn made to the original Phong lighting model.

With the specular component now added to the shader, we can see the results of the complete lighting equation. Figure 9-4 shows a screenshot containing the final result.

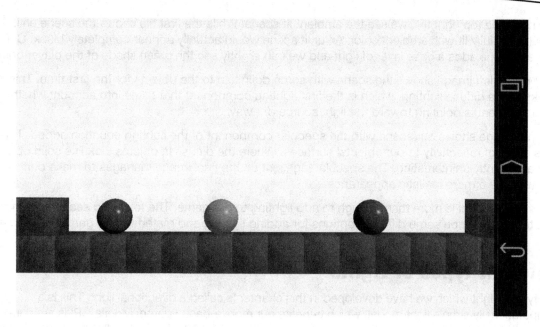

*Figure 9-4. The complete Blinn-Phong lighting model*

Figure 9-5 shows each of the figures from this chapter together.

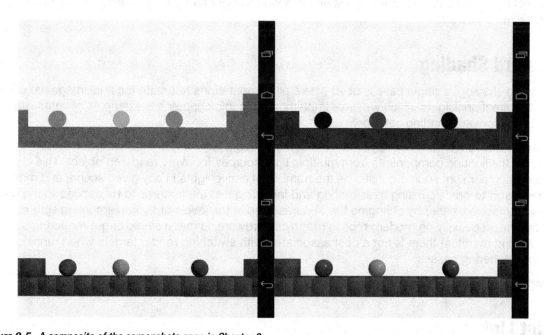

*Figure 9-5. A composite of the screenshots seen in Chapter 9*

Starting in the top left corner, we have the unlit scene. The colors are fully saturated and the objects in the scene all look completely flat.

Moving to the top right tile, we see the ambient lit scene. While the first tile shows the scene unlit, in reality it's fully lit with ambient color. An unlit scene would actually appear completely black. Our ambient scene adds a base layer of light and we can slightly see the green shade of the player object.

The bottom left image shows the scene with some definition to the objects for the first time. This is thanks to the diffuse lighting, which is the first lighting component that takes into account whether a given fragment is pointing toward the light source or away.

The last image shows our scene with the specular component of the lighting equation added. This adds a hint of reflectivity to our objects' surfaces. Where the diffuse lit objects look like solid objects, they are slightly uninteresting. The specular highlight on the final image manages to make our spheres take a more realistic appearance.

This simple model is more than enough to add lighting to our game. The following sections of this chapter will describe some different options for adding lighting and materials to a game via shaders.

# Different Types of Lights

The type of light which we have developed in this chapter is called a directional light. This is a computationally simple light model, which benefits our mobile-based game. Mobile GPUs are currently not as powerful as those available in game consoles or desktop PCs. Undoubtedly, the next few years will see a vast increase in the processing power of GPUs in mobile phones and tablets, but for now, games targeting these devices cannot use overly complicated lighting models in their shaders.

This section will discuss two other types of lights which might find greater use as mobile GPUs become more powerful.

## Forward Shading

In forward shading, a single pass is used where all computations to create the final image are carried out. The directional lights which we have implemented in this chapter are examples of lights which fall into the forward shading category.

The major drawback from this approach is that it requires a large amount of computation to calculate the lighting components from multiple light sources for every rendered object. This cost of computation per light source constrains the number of active lights in any given scene, and many games resort to precalculating their lighting and including it in the textures to be applied to the game levels themselves, either by changing the textures used in the levels or by implementing light maps. The benefit, especially on modern mobile graphics hardware, is that a single target rendering surface is used, and therefore there is not a cost associated with switching render targets when running multiple rendering passes.

Other types of lights which are useful in forward shading are point lights and spotlights.

## Point Lights

A point light is different from the directional light which we have described in our shaders, in that it has a position in the world. This means that the light can be placed inside the world and light objects from different directions.

A point light affects all objects by calculating the light direction at each vertex by subtracting the vertex's position from the light position. Doing this creates a spherical shape for the light source.

Point lights are usually also implemented with an attenuation algorithm. The attenuation of a light causes it to have less of an effect on an object the further away from the light that object becomes. Directional lights are used to simulate lights which are infinitely far away, such as a simple sunlight model, so the attenuation factor makes little sense for them.

The addition of the calculation of the light vector and the attenuation factor increases the computational complexity of the vertex shader. If your game is very simple, this type of light may be feasible, but in most games multiple lights of this type are needed to create the desired effects. This usually puts this technique out of the reach of most low-end mobile GPUs for scenes which have some geometric complexity.

## Spotlights

Spotlights are another type of light which are even more complex than point lights. Spotlights have a position and a direction. When spotlights are implemented, they resemble the effects of a torch. Spotlights contain an attenuation factor like point lights but they also have a spotlight cutoff parameter.

This cutoff parameter defines the half angle of the cone of the spotlight. This determines how wide the spotlight is. Anything outside of the cone created by the direction and angle will not be lit by the spotlight. Spotlights also have another attenuation factor which determines the brightness of the light from the center of the cone out to the sides. This allows the spotlight to be brighter in the middle and gradually fade toward the edges of the cone.

Point lights and spotlights were the types of lights which were supplied by OpenGL ES 1.0, and their implementation in the traditional manner is known as forward shading. A modern technique for compositing a scene in modern games is known as deferred rendering.

## Deferred Rendering

An alternative technique which has been put to use in many games on the Xbox 360 and Playstation 3 is deferred rendering.

Deferred rendering is usually implemented in two passes. The first pass renders into several buffers. The diffuse color of objects is stored in the diffuse color G buffer. This is different from the diffuse color as we implemented it in the Blinn-Phong model. The stored color is simply the single diffuse material color of the object. No ambient light is used in deferred rendering, and any specular lighting is calculated later. Along with the diffuse G buffer, a normal G buffer stores the normal vectors for each fragment, and the z buffer stores the depth of each fragment at each location.

The second pass then renders a geometric shape for each light. The lighting equation is calculated at each location using the light's information along with the color, normal, and depth read from the buffers written in the first pass.

The benefit of this model is that hundreds of lights can be rendered in a scene, as they are calculated only for pixels in the frame which will actually make it into the final image. The downside is that it can't handle transparent objects, so you still need a traditional rendering pass for these.

Another advanced topic which can be implemented with shaders is different types of materials. This is done using different lighting equations in the shaders. These equations are known as bidirectional reflectance distribution functions (BRDFs).

## Bidirectional Reflectance Distribution Functions

BRDFs are a group of equations which describe methods for calculating reflected vectors. The Blinn-Phong equation which we have implemented in this chapter is just one example of this set of equations.

The Blinn-Phong model is very good for approximating materials which have a look similar to plastic. Fixed-function graphics pipelines such as those found in OpenGL ES 1.0 have exposed only this model to game developers, but with OpenGL ES 2.0 programmers are free to implement more types of BRDFs thanks to shaders.

Entire books have been written on the subject of lighting in computer graphics, and if you are interested in learning more about BRDFs, the major models to begin with are the Torrance-Sparrow model, the Oren-Nayer diffuse reflection model, and Ward's reflection model.

These different lighting equations are better suited to recreating the look of different materials such as metals, paper, velvet, sand, and wood.

## Summary

In this chapter, we have finally added a sense of depth to our scene. We have achieved this by adding new shader programs which implement a directional light.

We've learned that directional lights are used in games to create a simple model of light sources which are very far from our game objects. A real-world example of a directional light source is the sun. We all know that the sun does not emit parallel rays of light, and this shows how we can use simplifications to simulate simple models of real-world phenomenon. This ability to simplify the physical world is a key skill for a game programmer who is working on real-time games which rely on completing the computations for an entire frame in 33 milliseconds or less.

The Blinn-Phong shading model was covered and implemented in GLSL shaders. The sample code provided at `http://www.apress.com/9781430258308` to accompany this chapter contains implementations of all of the shader stages described in this chapter. You can switch between them to see how each lighting component behaves, and you can alter the material and light colors as well as the specular exponent to get a feeling for how this lighting model behaves with different parameters.

You should now also be aware that the Blinn-Phong model consists of three different components which make up the final color in a fragment shader. The ambient color is a base level of light applied to an object. The diffuse color determines the main aspect of the objects color and takes into account the intensity of the reflected light based on the angle between the vertex normal and the light vector. The last component is the specular component. This component adds an element of reflectivity to the surface and is also the component of the Phong model which was adapted by Blinn to create the Blinn-Phong model.

We finished the section by covering some details of further topics in the area of lighting and materials. While this is a beginner-level text, it's important to know that the lighting and material properties of a game engine constitute a deep and very interesting topic. Vertex and fragment shaders have opened up the possibilities of photo-realistic material rendering to game developers, and shader programming will be an ever-evolving and interesting topic as GPUs become capable of implementing ever-more-complex lighting models.

In the next chapter, we are going to move on from the player's sense of sight and engage their sense of sound. Audio is an exceptionally important aspect of modern video games, and while audio used to be an overlooked part of the development process, this is no longer the case. Successful titles plan their audio early in production, and audio designers and engineers are hired for these specialized roles.

Chapter **10**

# Game Audio

Audio is a key component to making a compelling modern video game. Sound and music design in AAA games has begun to reach a level of quality comparable to some Hollywood movies with high-quality effects and orchestral scores.

Unfortunately this level of production is very expensive, in terms of both costs of production and processing power required to apply all of the required effects, stream multiple audio sources, and mix all of the results into the final output.

In this chapter, we're going to look at adding sound effects to our game which are more in line with the types of effects you used to hear on the 16-bit consoles. These sounds were created by manipulating sound waves and noise using digital filters to create the desired effects. Modern games tend to use Foley artists to recreate and record sounds using a wide variety of techniques. A classic rumored example is the melee attack in the *Halo* series. It is said that the sound effect for this maneuver was created by wrapping a watermelon in tin foil and hitting it with a baseball bat while recording in a studio. If you have the time, equipment, and inclination to give this sort of thing a go it could be a fun and interesting avenue to explore.

Before we can begin the process of creating effects, it would be beneficial to know a little about how audio works in the physical world.

## The Physics of Sound

The physics involved when dealing with sound is a complicated mathematical topic. Fortunately, we do not need to much more than the basics of audio physics to recreate some suitable sound effects.

Sound travels through a medium. Typically for us, that medium is air but it can also travel through solid objects and substances such as water. The tag line for the movie *Alien*, "In space no one can hear you scream," is completely accurate. Space is a vacuum and the lack of a medium for sound to travel through would mean that there is actually no sound present in space. Despite this, many movies and games set in space have sound effects; the scenes of a space battle would be quite dull without laser beams and explosions.

Sound travels through mediums as a set of areas of high compression and low compression. We visualize this phenomenon using graphs representing sound waves. Figure 10-1 shows the graph of a sine wave created using Audacity.

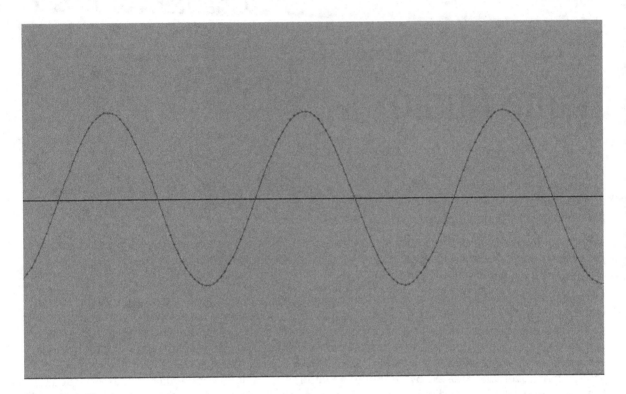

*Figure 10-1.* *The sine wave graph*

The peaks of this graph represent the areas of high compression in the sound wave and the troughs represent the areas of low compression.

There are two main properties of this sound graph which we are interested in manipulating. The first is its amplitude.

## Amplitude

The amplitude of a sound wave represents the intensity of the energy stored by the wave. The higher the amplitude, the louder the perceived volume of that sound to the listener. Figure 10-2 shows another sine wave created in Audacity but this time with a much lower amplitude.

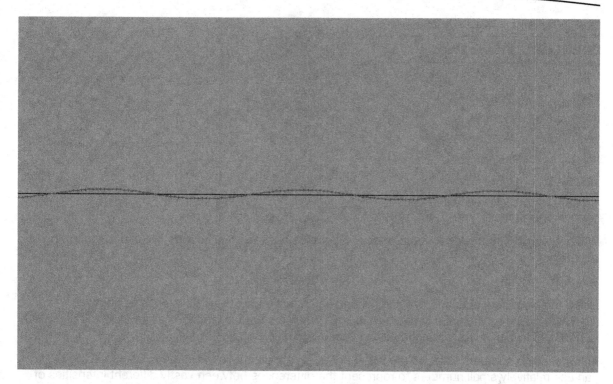

*Figure 10-2. A low-amplitude sound wave*

A direct comparison between Figures 10-1 and 10-2 shows that the sound wave has exactly the same number of peaks and troughs. The only difference is the distance of the peaks and troughs from the black center line. The graph in Figure 10-2 represents the same sound wave as Figure 10-1 but with much less energy and intensity. The difference between the two waves to a listener is simply in the volume. The first wave will sound much louder than the second when both are heard from the same distance.

When dealing with sounds at different intensities, we can order them on a scale. This scale is defined using decibels (dB). Decibels are a relative unit of measurement and therefore are used to describe the difference in intensity between two levels of sound.

If we take a human's perception of sound, we can say that the level of sound at which we hear nothing represents 0dB. Table 10-1 contains some common sounds with their decibel levels relative to perceived silence (source: `http://articles.washingtonpost.com/2009-03-10/news/36815953_1_ db-temporary-threshold-shift-subway-train`).

*Table 10-1. Sounds at Different Decibel Levels*

| Decibel Level | Example Sound |
| --- | --- |
| 0dB | No perceived sounds |
| 20dB | Ticking watch |
| 50dB | Rainfall |
| 70dB | Washing machine |
| 80dB | An alarm clock at two feet |
| 105dB | Lawn mower |
| 130dB | Jet plane at 100 feet |

When we are trying to work out the decibel difference between two sounds, we use the following equation:

$$10 \log (P2/P1) = dB$$

Using the preceding equation, we can tell that when a sound is twice as intense as another (so *P2/P1* is 2) the difference in decibels is 3dB. When a sound is ten times as intense, the difference is 10dB, and when it is a million times as intense, the difference is 60dB.

The preceding numbers show us the benefit of using a logarithmic scale to represent decibels. We can use relatively small numbers to represent the differences between vastly different intensities of sound waves. Unfortunately, this isn't immediately intuitive when comparing sounds at 3dB, 10dB, and 60dB.

The second property of the sound wave which interests us is its frequency.

# Frequency

The frequency of a sound wave affects its pitch. Different pitches of sounds are perceived by people to be higher or lower notes in music. When dealing with sound effects, altering the frequency of sound effects can give us subtle variations of the same effects for variety. It's also important to know which level of pitch is most likely to be effective when designing a particular sound. A quick example is that high-frequency sounds would be better suited to laser gun effects and low-frequency sounds for explosions.

Frequency also plays an important role in human hearing. The average person's ears are sensitive to only a narrow range of frequencies between 20Hz and 20,000Hz. The symbol Hz denotes the unit of measurement hertz. Hertz is used to measure repetition. If you recall from Figure 10-1, our sound wave consisted of three peaks and two troughs. Increasing the frequency of the sound wave will give us a higher-sounding effect and is visualized on the graph by having a larger number of peaks and troughs in the same amount of time. Figure 10-3 shows the sound wave with increased frequency.

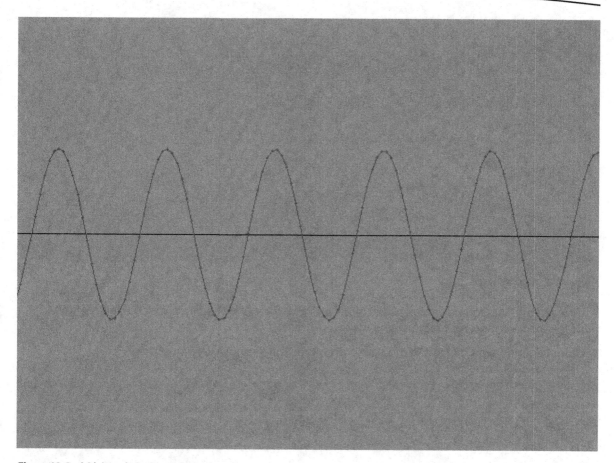

*Figure 10-3. A higher-pitched sound wave*

## Other Types of Sound Waves

The graphs shown in Figures 10-1 through 10-3 show the waveform of the sine wave. The waveform represents a graphical representation of how the sound travels through a given medium. Under normal circumstances for human hearing, that medium is air; however, the medium could also be water, concrete, or metal.

The sine wave oscillates smoothly between its peaks and troughs; other types of sound waves can be represented by different-looking waveforms.

Figure 10-4 shows the waveform for a square wave.

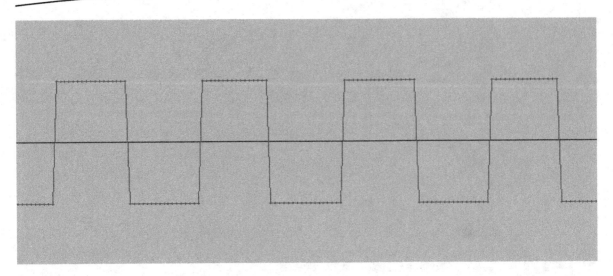

*Figure 10-4. A square wave*

As Figure 10-4, the square wave has flat high- and low-frequency sections which alternate and produce a different sound from the sine wave.

Another common type of wave is the sawtooth wave. This is shown in Figure 10-5.

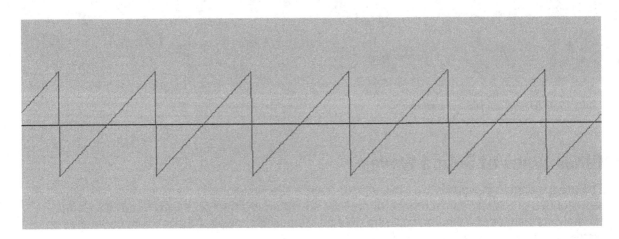

*Figure 10-5. The sawtooth wave*

The sawtooth wave creates a sound which is distinct from the sine and square waves. Each of these waves can be used as the base for a sound effect, and combinations of waves and filters are used to generate different types of sound.

# Aliasing

Aliasing is an undesired effect caused when using digital sampling techniques. Games programmers are more likely to have heard the term anti-aliasing used with respect to jagged edges seen in game screenshots. Anti-aliasing in this respect is used to remove jagged edges which appear in rendered graphics. The same "jaggies" can appear in sampled audio.

Digital audio works by taking discrete samples of audio at certain points in time, but digital audio also applies certain other constraints such as the maximum and minimum amplitudes which it can store. If there are audio frequencies above and below these frequencies, the sampled amplitude might be above or below the point it should be. This leads to the audio sounding different from the original sound when the digital representation is recreated through a digital-to-analog converter. We are not going to be concerned with audio aliasing in this chapter but you should be aware of its existence.

Now that we have covered the basics of a sound wave, we'll look at the software package which we will use to generate our sound effects.

# Audacity

Audacity is a free sound editing suite and is available for Windows, Mac OSX, and Linux. The version of Audacity which I have used during the writing of this chapter is 2.0.2. Figure 10-6 shows the main window which is presented when Audacity is opened.

*Figure 10-6. Audacity's main window*

In Figure 10-6, the main recording controls can be seen in the top left. The next panel to the right contains the selection tools for modifying sound waves. We then have the output and input meters followed by another panel of controls which contains volumes, copy/paste, trim, zoom, and so on. The bar below this contains the input and output source selectors.

Of the menu bars which run along the top of the Windows, we will be using the Generate and Effect panels.

# The Chirp Generator

A chirp signal is one which increases or decreases in amplitude over time. It should therefore not be a surprise to learn that Audacity's Chirp Generator can be used to create sound waves which behave in exactly this way. This section contains the exact details on how we will use this type of wave to begin the creation of our sound effect.

Figure 10-7 shows the Generate Menu.

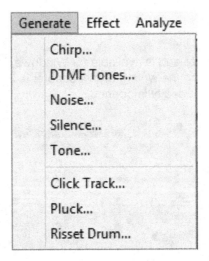

*Figure 10-7. Audacity's Generate Menu*

The Generate Menu is used to generate basic sound waves. The specific option which we will be using is the Chirp Generator. When clicking on Chirp, we are presented with the dialog box shown in Figure 10-8.

*Figure 10-8. The Chirp Generator dialog*

The Chirp Generator allows us to specify a waveform to be generated. The options presented are Sine, Square, Sawtooth, and Square, no alias. Each of these produces a slightly different basic sound wave.

The Chirp Generator is useful as it allows us to specify a beginning and ending frequency and amplitude. The selections shown begin with a low-frequency sound which increases by the end of the wave. The generated wave will also decrease in amplitude as it reaches the end.

The Interpolation type allows us to select Linear or Logarithmic. Linear interpolation will allow us to create effects change from the start state to the end state evenly. The Logarithmic option creates waves which change more smoothly. The last variable is the required duration of sound to be generated.

Once we have a basic sound wave, we can modify it using the filters available in the Effect Menu.

# Effects

Audacity supplies some preconfigured filters which can manipulate sound waves. These filters can be found in the Effect Menu. Effects can be used to increase the frequency or amplitude of a sound wave. They can also be used to remove high- or low-frequency sounds from a wave or even remove noise.

This section will look at how we can use some of the supplied effects to shape our sound wave into a specific effect.

Figure 10-9 shows the Effect Menu from Audacity.

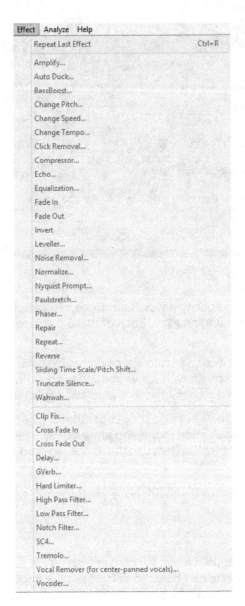

*Figure 10-9. The Audacity Effect Menu*

The effects from this menu which we will be interested in for our sound effects are the Amplify Effect, Change Pitch, Change Speed, Change Tempo, Fade In, Fade Out, High Pass Filter, and Low Pass Filter. These effects can be applied to whole sound waves or just selections within waves and combinations of these effects can create some interesting sounds.

- The Amplify Effect does exactly what you think it might do. It allows us to change the amplitude, and thus the volume, of a sound wave. We can either increase or decrease the amplitude using this tool.

- The Change Speed Effect allows us to alter the duration of a sound effect. Shortening the effect's play time has the effect of increasing the sound wave's frequency, making it appear to be played at a higher pitch. Lengthening a sound reduces the frequency and makes the effect sound lower.

- Change Pitch allows us to alter the frequency of the sound wave without affecting its duration.

- Change Tempo allows us to alter the length of the effect without altering its frequency.

> **Note** These last two effects can add some noticeable clicks to the sound wave due to the way they process the sound wave.

- Fade In and Fade Out work exactly as they are named; they will linearly fade in or fade out a selection of a sound effect. This is useful for effects which sound too harsh at the beginning or which we would like to get louder or quieter over time. They affect the amplitude of the selected section of the sound wave.

- The Low Pass Filter allows us to decrease the amplitude of frequencies above a certain specified frequency. This effect takes a rolloff value and a frequency as its parameter. The cutoff frequency allows us to specify which frequencies will not be affected by the filter. For example, if we specified 1000Hz as the cutoff, no frequencies below 1000Hz would be reduced in amplitude. The rolloff allows us to specify how aggressive the filter is. The options we can choose are between 6dB and 48dB. The rolloff dB value is applied as a multiple based on how far above the cutoff frequency the sound is. The higher the rolloff value, the more the amplitude of high-frequency sounds is reduced.

- The High Pass Filter works in exactly the opposite manner to the Low Pass Filter. We can specify a frequency above which no sound waves are affected and a rolloff value to specify how aggressively the filter is applied.

With our whirlwind tour of Audacity over, we can use these tools to create a basic jump sound effect.

# Creating a Jump Sound Effect with Audacity

The only interaction our player will have with *Droid Runner* will be to make the character jump, so this action is an ideal candidate for our first sound effect. This section is going to be a step-by-step walk through the process of creating a sound which we can use to represent jumping.

1. From the Generate menu, select Chirp. In the Chirp Generator dialog box, generate a Square Waveform with the parameters set as shown in Figure 10-10.

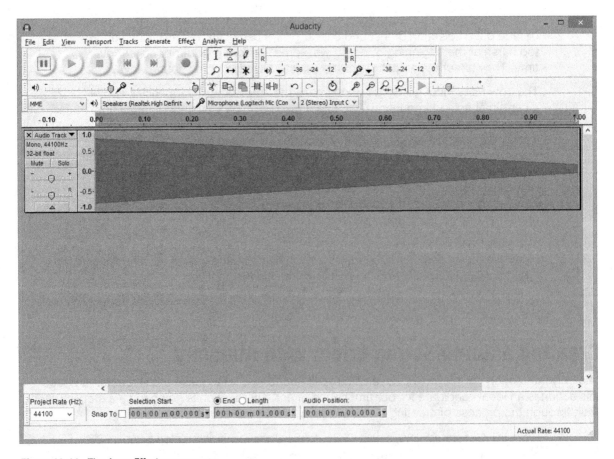

*Figure 10-10. The Square Chirp Generator Dialog for the jump sound effect*

The resulting sound wave should resemble the one in Figure 10-11.

*Figure 10-11. The Jump Effect square wave*

2.  In the Effect Menu, select High Pass Filter to run a high-pass filter over the entire wave with the parameters from Figure 10-12.

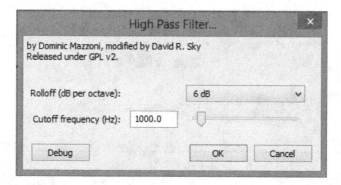

*Figure 10-12.  Jump High Pass Filter dialog*

3.  Next, we select Amplify from the Effect Menu and amplify the sound wave by -2.8dB, as shown in Figure 10-13.

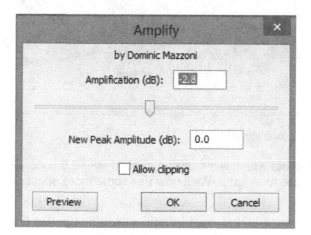

*Figure 10-13.  Jump Amplify dialog*

4.  Again, select High Pass Filter from the Effect menu and use the same parameters as in Figure 10-11, that is, 6db rolloff and 1000Hz cutoff frequency.

5.  Select Effect ➤ Amplify and run another Amplify Filter with the amplification parameter set to 1.2.

6.  Run the Fade Out Filter by selecting Effect ➤ Fade Out; then run Effect ➤ Change Speed with the parameter set to 60. At this point, your sound wave should resemble the one shown in Figure 10-14.

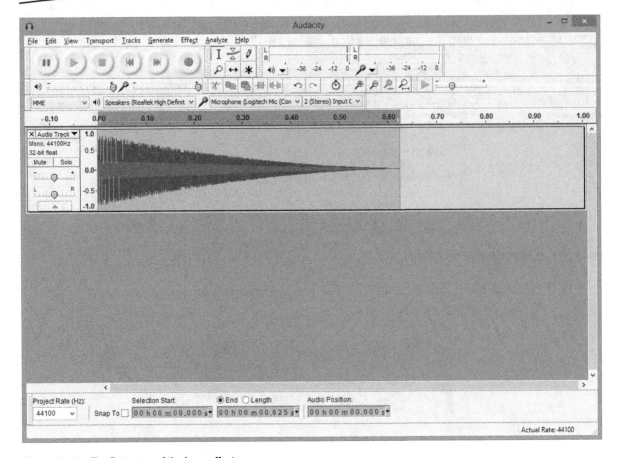

*Figure 10-14. The first stage of the jump effect*

At this point, we have an effect which is increasing in pitch over 0.6 seconds and sounds like an effect which we could use for a jump. We'll now use some more effects to embellish the sound a little.

1.  First off, duplicate the sound wave using the Duplicate option from the Edit menu. Audacity should now resemble Figure 10-15.

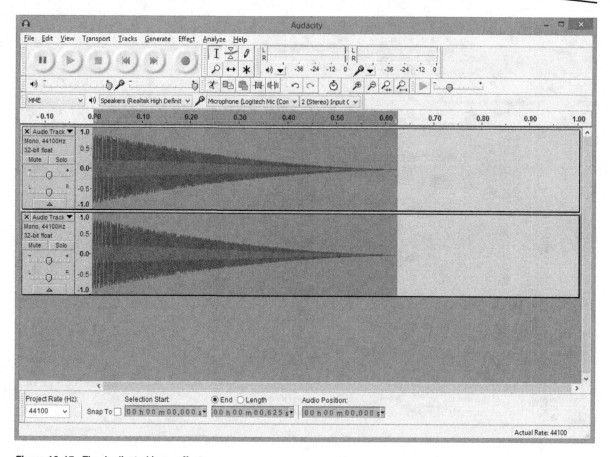

*Figure 10-15. The duplicated jump effect*

2.  Now use the Time Shift Tool from the Tools toolbar to move the second sound wave over to the right. Drag it over until the selection start time reads 0.025s. The result of this step is shown in Figure 10-16.

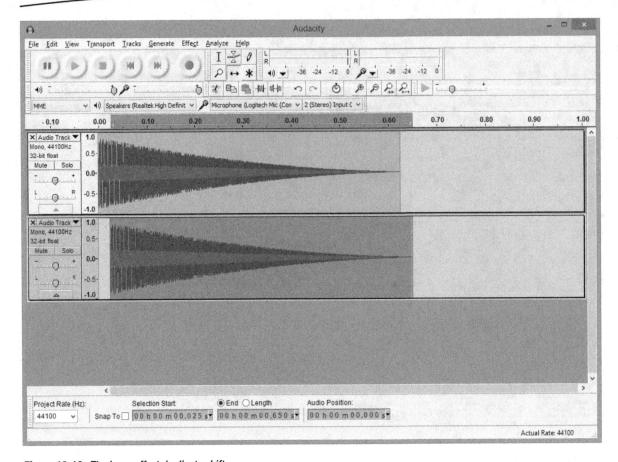

*Figure 10-16. The jump effect duplicate shift*

3. Now, with both tracks selected, use the menu option Tracks ➤ Mix and Render.

4. This duplicate, shift, and mix step has added a little bit of an echo to our sound effect but has left the beginning of the sound a little sharp and the effect as a whole a little harsh and pitchy. We'll reduce the high-pitched tones using Low Pass Filter from the Effect Menu with the parameters rolloff 6dB and frequency 1200Hz. Once this has been done, run Effect ➤ Amplify with 7.3dB to boost the volume.

5. We'll now boost the low end once more by applying Effect ➤ Bass Boost with the parameters 600Hz and 12dB. We'll now run Effect ➤ Low Pass Filter with 6dB and 1200Hz parameters. After the last Low Pass Filter, the amplitude is a little low, so we'll boost it again by running Effect ➤ Amplify with the parameter 3.2dB.

6.  Our effect now has a harsh double pop at the beginning left over from our duplicate and shift, so we'll use Effect ➤ Fade In to smooth it out a little. Select the first 0.025s of the track using the Selection Tool from the Tools toolbar, then select Effect ➤ Fade In. With the amplitude of the beginning of the track fading in, we now boost the amplitude of the whole track using Effect ➤ Amplify with the parameters 2.5dB and the Allow Clipping check box ticked.

7.  The final step is to use Effect ➤ Fade In on the first 0.75 seconds of the track. The finished effect in Audacity should resemble the track shown in Figure 10-17.

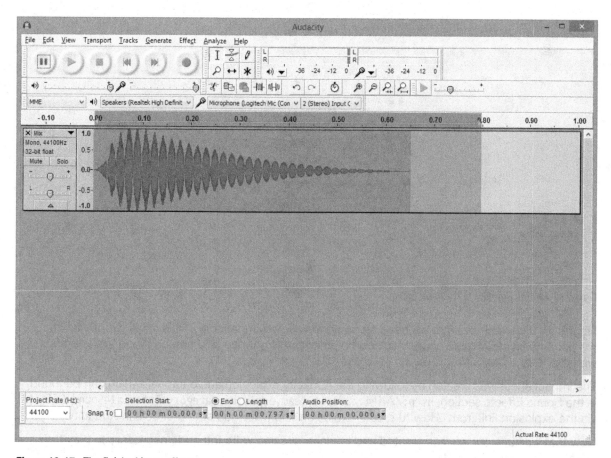

*Figure 10-17. The finished jump effect*

We are now ready to export our sound file. We will be using the Ogg Vorbis audio format for our sounds. OpenSL on Android supports loading and playing Ogg files without any real effort on our part and they are compressed, so they are an ideal option for Android game development.

The Ogg Vorbis audio format consists of two components. The Vorbis component specifies the compression algorithm for the audio. This is a lossy compression format created by the Xiph.Org foundation. The Ogg component specifies a container which dictates how the data is stored into files for saving. Combined, these components create the Ogg Vorbis format.

The sound files should be placed in the Assets folder of your project. Use the File ➤ Export option to export the audio into jump.ogg under assets/sounds as shown in Figure 10-18.

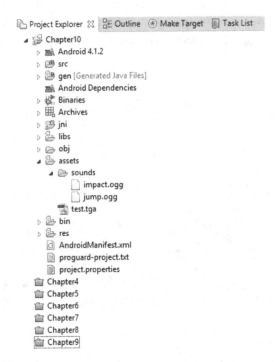

*Figure 10-18. The Ogg files in the Asset folder*

Figure 10-18 also shows that we need an audio file named impact.ogg. This file is supplied with the accompanying sample code which complements this chapter and can be found at the book's website, http://www.apress.com/9781430258308.

The impact effect was created by following the Audacity explosion audio tutorial, which can be found in the Sound Effects section, http://wiki.audacityteam.org/wiki/Category:Tutorial#Sound_Effects, via the explosion link from "How to create explosion and laser-gun sound effects in Audacity."

Now that we have our sounds created and in place, we can write the code necessary to play the effects from our native code.

# Playing Audio Using OpenSL ES

So far in this book, we have been using the Android NDK to create a game without using any Java code whatsoever. We have used EGL to interact with Android's windowing system, OpenGL, to submit data to the GPU for rendering, and now we will use the native OpenSL ES API to submit audio data for playback.

When we are displaying graphics, we have created the Renderer class to encapsulate the code and separate our OpenGL code from our gameplay logic. We will be doing the same with our audio code. The AudioManager class will be created to encapsulate the OpenSL code and simplify our gameplay logic code going forward. This helps us to make a game engine and promote code reuse across multiple projects.

## Creating the AudioManager

The AudioManager class will be used to create an interface between the game logic and the OpenSL ES API. Listing 10-1 shows the class declaration for the AudioManager class.

*Listing 10-1. The AudioManager Class Declaration*

```
class AudioManager
        :       public Singleton<AudioManager>
{
public:
        typedef unsigned int        AudioHandle;
        static const AudioHandle   INVALID_HANDLE = 0xFFFFFFFF;

private:
        AAssetManager*              m_pAssetManager;

public:
        explicit AudioManager(AAssetManager* pAssetManager);
        virtual ~AudioManager();

        bool        Initialize();
        void        Destroy();

        AudioHandle CreateSFX(std::string& filename);
        void        PlaySFX(AudioHandle handle);
        void        DestroySFX(AudioHandle handle);
};
```

This simple interface will allow us to initialize and destroy OpenSL ES as well as create, play, and destroy individual sound effects. We are using a typedef of an unsigned int to store handles to specific audio events once they have been created.

The constructor to AudioManager takes a pointer to the Android NDK's AAssetManager class and is used to access the files which we added to the project previously. Listing 10-2 shows the code for the constructor.

*Listing 10-2. AudioManager's Constructor*

```
AudioManager::AudioManager(AAssetManager* pAssetManager)
        :       m_pAssetManager(pAssetManager)
{
        Initialize();
}
```

The constructor simply calls the `Initialize` method. The destructor is shown in Listing 10-3.

*Listing 10-3. AudioManager's Destructor*

```
AudioManager::~AudioManager()
{
        Destroy();
}
```

As you may have expected, the destructor calls `Destroy`.

This covers the interface of the `AudioManager` class and the constructor and destructor. Now we will look at the code necessary to initialize OpenSL.

# An Introduction to OpenSL ES

OpenSL ES is another API provided by Khronos. Where OpenGL ES is their graphics library API for embedded systems, OpenSL ES is their sound library API for embedded systems. The philosophies between the two APIs are completely different due to the way that these APIs have developed. OpenGL has a more C-like interface where we call functions; there are no objects involved in the API itself. OpenSL, on the other hand, is an object-based API.

The main structure of the API involves creating instances of objects and instances of interface objects which interact with those objects. The very first object which we must interact with is the Engine object. The Engine object is used to create the other objects which we need for our sound system. We need to add some fields to the `AudioManager` class before we can work with OpenSL. These fields are added in Listing 10-4.

*Listing 10-4. Adding OpenSL Objects to AudioManager*

```
class AudioManager
        :       public Singleton<AudioManager>
{
public:
        typedef unsigned int        AudioHandle;
        static const AudioHandle    INVALID_HANDLE = 0xFFFFFFFF;

private:
        SLObjectItf                 m_engineObject;
        SLEngineItf                 m_engine;
        SLObjectItf                 m_outputMixObject;

        AAssetManager*              m_pAssetManager;
```

```
public:
        explicit AudioManager(AAssetManager* pAssetManager);
        virtual ~AudioManager();

        bool        Initialize();
        void        Destroy();

        AudioHandle CreateSFX(std::string& filename);
        void        PlaySFX(AudioHandle handle);
        void        DestroySFX(AudioHandle handle);
};
```

We have added two SLObjectItf fields and a SLEngineItf and to AudioManager in Listing 10-4. We look at how these are used in the Initialize method in Listing 10-5.

*Listing 10-5. AudioManager::Initialize*

```
bool AudioManager::Initialize()
{
        SLresult result;

        result = slCreateEngine( &m_engineObject, 0, NULL, 0, NULL, NULL );
        assert(result == SL_RESULT_SUCCESS);

        result = (*m_engineObject)->Realize(m_engineObject, SL_BOOLEAN_FALSE);
        assert(result == SL_RESULT_SUCCESS);

        result = (*m_engineObject)->GetInterface(m_engineObject, SL_IID_ENGINE, &m_engine);
        assert(result == SL_RESULT_SUCCESS);

        result = (*m_engine)->CreateOutputMix(m_engine, &m_outputMixObject, 0, NULL, NULL);
        assert(result == SL_RESULT_SUCCESS);

        result = (*m_outputMixObject)->Realize(m_outputMixObject, SL_BOOLEAN_FALSE);
        assert(result == SL_RESULT_SUCCESS);

        return result == SL_RESULT_SUCCESS;
}
```

There aren't many lines of code involved in initializing OpenSL for basic use in the Android NDK. First off, we call slCreateEngine. This method is passed the address of m_engineObject as its first parameter. The remaining parameters are all default values, as we do not require any specific functionality from the engine object.

OpenSL objects are created in two steps. The first step is to tell the OpenSL object which features you would like it to support. Once this has been done, we then instruct OpenSL to formally create the object; this is called realization and is done with the Realize method. After calling slCreateEngine, we instruct OpenSL to realize the engine.

Once the engine has been created and realized, we can get the engine interface. You can see this being done with a call to GetInterface on m_engineObject. We pass the object as the first parameter.

The second parameter, SL_IID_ENGINE, tells OpenSL which interface we would like to retrieve for the object, and the last parameter is the field where we would like to store the interface.

We now use the engine interface to create an output mix object. The output mix is exactly what its name suggests. It is the object responsible for receiving the audio, mixing it, and playing it out through the operating system and eventually the device's speakers. Again, once the output mix object is created it must be realized.

That's all there is to initializing a basic setup for OpenSL ES on Android. We have an engine object, an engine interface, and an output mix object. Now we will look at the code required to create sounds from our Ogg files.

# Creating OpenSL ES Player Objects for Files

At the beginning of this chapter, we walked through the process of creating sound effects and saving them in the Ogg Vorbis audio format. In this section, we are going to take a look at how we can use these sound effects in our game.

Before we can play a sound effect, we must create an audio player object which can reference the file containing the sound and retrieve a play interface from the object.

We are likely to want to create multiple player objects, so we begin by adding a PlayInstance struct and an unorderer_map to the AudioManager class in Listing 10-6.

*Listing 10-6. Adding PlayInstance to AudioManager*

```
class AudioManager
    :       public Singleton<AudioManager>
{
public:
        typedef unsigned int AudioHandle;
        static const AudioHandle INVALID_HANDLE  = 0xFFFFFFFF;

private:
        SLObjectItf                 m_engineObject;
        SLEngineItf                 m_engine;
        SLObjectItf                 m_outputMixObject;

        AAssetManager*              m_pAssetManager;

        struct PlayInstance
        {
                SLObjectItf         m_playerObject;
                SLPlayItf           m_playerPlay;
        };
        typedef std::tr1::unordered_map<AudioHandle, PlayInstance*>        PlayInstanceMap;
        typedef PlayInstanceMap::iterator                                  PlayInstanceMapIterator;

        PlayInstanceMap                                    m_playInstances;
```

```
public:
        explicit AudioManager(AAssetManager* pAssetManager);
        virtual ~AudioManager();

        bool      Initialize();
        void      Destroy();

        AudioHandle        CreateSFX(std::string& filename);
        void               PlaySFX(AudioHandle handle);
        void               DestroySFX(AudioHandle handle);
};
```

Our sound effect instances will be stored in the structure represented by PlayInstance. To facilitate having multiple sound effects, we store instances of PlayInstance in an unordered_map with a pair consisting of AudioHandle and a pointer to a PlayInstance object. We also define a type for the iterator to the map and create an instance of the map in m_playInstances.

Listing 10-7 shows the code for AudioManager::CreateSFX which creates a new instance of a sound effect.

*Listing 10-7. AudioManager::CreateSFX*

```
AudioManager::AudioHandle AudioManager::CreateSFX(std::string& filename)
{
        AudioHandle handle = INVALID_HANDLE;

        AAsset* asset = AAssetManager_open(
                m_pAssetManager,
                filename.c_str(),
                AASSET_MODE_UNKNOWN);

        if (asset != NULL)
        {
                handle = Hash(filename.c_str());

                PlayInstanceMapIterator iter = m_playInstances.find(handle);
                if (iter == m_playInstances.end())
                {
                        PlayInstance* pNewInstance = new PlayInstance();

                        if (pNewInstance)
                        {
                                std::pair<AudioHandle, PlayInstance*> newInstance(handle, pNewInstance);
                                std::pair<PlayInstanceMapIterator, bool> addedIter =
                                        m_playInstances.insert(newInstance);
                        }

                        off_t start;
                        off_t length;
                        int fd = AAsset_openFileDescriptor(asset, &start, &length);
                        assert(0 <= fd);
                        AAsset_close(asset);
```

```
// configure audio source
SLDataLocator_AndroidFD loc_fd = {
      SL_DATALOCATOR_ANDROIDFD,
      fd,
      start,
      length};

SLDataFormat_MIME format_mime = {
      SL_DATAFORMAT_MIME,
      NULL,
      SL_CONTAINERTYPE_UNSPECIFIED};

SLDataSource audioSrc = {&loc_fd, &format_mime};

// configure audio sink
SLDataLocator_OutputMix loc_outmix = {
      SL_DATALOCATOR_OUTPUTMIX,
      m_outputMixObject};

SLDataSink audioSnk = {&loc_outmix, NULL};

// create audio player
const unsigned int NUM_INTERFACES = 1;
const SLInterfaceID ids[NUM_INTERFACES]    = {SL_IID_PLAY};
const SLboolean req[NUM_INTERFACES]        = {SL_BOOLEAN_TRUE };
SLresult result = (*m_engine)->CreateAudioPlayer(
      m_engine,
      &pNewInstance->m_playerObject,
      &audioSrc,
      &audioSnk,
      NUM_INTERFACES,
      ids,
      req);
assert(SL_RESULT_SUCCESS == result);

// realize the player
result = (*pNewInstance->m_playerObject)->Realize(
      pNewInstance->m_playerObject,
      SL_BOOLEAN_FALSE);
assert(SL_RESULT_SUCCESS == result);

// get the play interface
result = (*pNewInstance->m_playerObject)->GetInterface(
      pNewInstance->m_playerObject,
      SL_IID_PLAY,
      &pNewInstance->m_playerPlay);
assert(SL_RESULT_SUCCESS == result);
(*pNewInstance->m_playerPlay)->RegisterCallback(
      pNewInstance->m_playerPlay,
      play_callback,
      NULL);
```

```
                    (*pNewInstance->m_playerPlay)->SetCallbackEventsMask(
                        pNewInstance->m_playerPlay,
                        SL_PLAYEVENT_HEADATEND);
                }
            }

        return handle;
}
```

We begin the `CreateSFX` method by using the Android NDK's `AAssetManager` to attempt to open the file supplied in the filename method parameter. `AAssetManager_open` will return a pointer to an `Asset` if the file exists.

We then create a hash of the filename using the method `Hash`. `Hash` returns an SDBM hash of the filename. The code for the `Hash` method is covered in Listing 10-9.

After creating the hash, `CreateSFX` tries to find if this sound effect has already been added to the map by calling the `find` method on `m_playInstances`. This means that any sound effect we would like to use in the game must have a unique filename.

If this is a new sound effect, we create a new instance of `PlayInstance` and create a pair with the hash handle and the pointer, `pNewInstance`. This new pair is added to `m_playInstances`.

The next step required is to get a file descriptor for the opened `Asset`. We do this by calling `AAsset_openFileDescriptor`. This method also supplies an offset to the start of the file and the length of the file. Once we have our file descriptor, we call `AAsset_close` on `asset`.

We now have all of our dependencies in check to be able to create an audio player object using OpenSL. The first dependency required by the audio player is the source of the audio data. We inform OpenSL where it can find the data for this sound effect by creating a `SLDataLocator_AndroidFD` object. This object stores the `fd`, `start`, and `length` variables we obtained when we called `AAsset_openFileDescriptor`.

We must also supply OpenSL with a MIME type for the file. MIME types traditionally are used when creating websites to determine the type of file which has been transferred from the server. Luckily for us, we can pass `SL_CONTAINERTYPE_UNSPECIFIED` and OpenSL will determine the type from the file. We could have specified `SL_CONTAINERTYPE_OGG` if we knew we would only ever use Ogg files, but you may choose to use MP3 files or some other supported media format. Both `loc_fd` and `format_mime` are then bundled into the structure `audioSrc`, which is of type `SLDataSource`.

While `SLDataSource` specifies the input for our sound effect, we need to create a `SLDataSink` object to specify the output. Our output object will be represented by `SLDataSink` and it takes a single element of type `SLDataLocator_OutputMix`. The second field is left empty. The variable `loc_outmix` is used to specify our `m_outputMixObject` as the output receiver.

We're now ready to create the player object for this effect. OpenSL supports multiple types of interfaces for player objects but we are interested only in the Play interface. `NUM_INTERFACES` is used to specify that we want a single interface. `ids` stores the identifier for the Play interface, and `SL_IID_PLAY` and `req` store `SL_BOOLEAN_TRUE`. `req` is used to inform OpenSL that the Play interface is not optional.

The engine interface is then used to create the player object. This is done using the method `CreateAudioPlayer`. If this call is successful, we will then have a reference to a player object stored in pNewInstance->m_playerObject. As with all of our OpenSL objects, we then call Realize to finalize the creation process.

With our player object realized, we can obtain the interface to allow us to play our sound effect. We do this by calling GetInterface with SL_IID_PLAY as the second parameter.

We're not quite finished with CreateSFX. We also want to know when the sound effect has finished playing and to specify a function to be called when this event takes place. We register the callback method play_callback using RegisterCallback called on m_playerPlay. Callbacks can also have masks specified to ensure that the callbacks are triggered only for events which we are interested in. In this case, we mask for the SL_PLAYEREVENT_HEADATEND. This will cause the play_callback function to be called whenever the sound effect reaches the end of its playback. There is more code here for creating a new instance of a player object than for setting up OpenSL itself, but we are finally done with CreateSFX. Listing 10-8 looks at the play_callback function.

Listing 10-8. play_callback

```
void SLAPIENTRY play_callback( SLPlayItf player, void *context, SLuint32 event )
{
        if( event & SL_PLAYEVENT_HEADATEND )
        {
                (*player)->SetPlayState(player, SL_PLAYSTATE_STOPPED);
        }
}
```

There isn't much to play_callback. SLPlayItf interfaces do not automatically stop themselves when they finish playing and this prevents them from being replayed later. To ensure this does not happen, we use the SetPlayState method to set our player to the SL_PLAYSTATE_STOPPED state.

Now we'll go back and look at the Hash method we used in this section.

# SDBM Hashes

Our unordered_map requires unique keys to be used to identify objects stored in the map. The SDBM hash function allows us to turn the filenames of the sound effects into unique identifiers. The code which achieves this is described in Listing 10-9.

Listing 10-9. The SDBM Hash Function

```
inline unsigned int Hash(const std::string& key)
{
        unsigned int result = 0;

        for (unsigned int i=0; i<key.length(); ++i)
        {
                int c = key[i];
                result = c + (result << 6) + (result << 16) - result;
        }

        return result;
}
```

Hashing is a fast operation on small strings and it creates unsigned integer results which are very fast to compare in our game loop; this is why we hash once when we create new sound effects then use the hashed values for lookups. The key to the hashes generating unique values for a string is in the line where the current character is used in the result. The hash is built iteratively with each character being used to calculate the current value of the hash. It is possible to have clashes (where two strings create the same hash) but very rare, especially for short strings such as filenames.

We've now covered all of the code which was necessary to create a new instance of a sound effect; we will now look at how to play sounds.

# Playing Sounds Using OpenSL

Playing sounds with OpenSL is very straightforward once the player object has been created and the play interface obtained.

The PlaySFX method is simple. It gets the PlayInstance object from m_playInstances and then calls SetPlayState twice: once to stop the sound if it is already playing and once again to set the state to SL_PLAYSTATE_PLAYING.

Listing 10-10 shows the code for PlaySFX.

*Listing 10-10. AudioManager::PlaySFX*

```
void AudioManager::PlaySFX(AudioHandle handle)
{
        PlayInstanceMapIterator iter = m_playInstances.find(handle);
        if (iter != m_playInstances.end())
        {
                SLPlayItf pPlayInstance = iter->second->m_playerPlay;
                if (pPlayInstance != NULL)
                {
                        // set the player's state
                        (*pPlayInstance)->SetPlayState(pPlayInstance, SL_PLAYSTATE_STOPPED);
                        (*pPlayInstance)->SetPlayState(pPlayInstance, SL_PLAYSTATE_PLAYING);
                }
        }
}
```

The last task for the AudioManager is to clean up unused sounds and shut down the system.

# Cleaning Up Sounds

Once we are finished with a sound effect, it's a good idea to destroy the resources which it takes up. We do this for sound effects by calling DestroySFX. The code for this is shown in listing 10-11.

*Listing 10-11. AudioManager::DestroySFX*

```
void AudioManager::DestroySFX(AudioHandle handle)
{
        PlayInstanceMapIterator iter = m_playInstances.find(handle);
        if (iter != m_playInstances.end())
```

```
        {
                PlayInstance* pInstance = iter->second;
                if (pInstance && pInstance->m_playerObject)
                {
                        (*pInstance->m_playerObject)->Destroy(pInstance->m_playerObject);
                        pInstance->m_playerObject   = NULL;
                        pInstance->m_playerPlay     = NULL;
                }

                m_playInstances.erase(iter);
        }
}
```

In DestroySFX, we retrieve the PlayInstance object for the supplied handle, verify that the object and m_playerObject are valid, and then call Destroy on m_playerObject.

We also free our resources in the Destroy method which is called from the destructor. Listing 10-12 shows this code.

*Listing 10-12. AudioManager::Destroy*

```
void AudioManager::Destroy()
{
        for (PlayInstanceMapIterator iter = m_playInstances.begin();
             iter != m_playInstances.end();
             ++iter)
        {
                PlayInstance* pInstance = iter->second;
                if (pInstance && pInstance->m_playerObject)
                {
                        (*pInstance->m_playerObject)->Destroy(pInstance->m_playerObject);
                        pInstance->m_playerObject = NULL;
                        pInstance->m_playerPlay = NULL;
                }
        }
        m_playInstances.clear();

        if (m_outputMixObject != NULL)
        {
                (*m_outputMixObject)->Destroy(m_outputMixObject);
                m_outputMixObject = NULL;
        }

        if (m_engineObject != NULL)
        {
                (*m_engineObject)->Destroy(m_engineObject);
                m_engineObject = NULL;
                m_engine = NULL;
        }
}
```

AudioManager::Destroy cleans up all of our OpenSL resources. We first iterate over all of our sound effects in m_playInstances and call Destroy on each. We then also free up m_outputMixObject and m_engineObject.

With all of our AudioManager code complete, we can now add some sound effects to our game logic.

# Adding Sound Effects to *Droid Runner*

Our first sound effect is a jump sound, so we need to add a new event for when the player jumps. We register this new event in the DroidRunnerLevel constructor shown in Listing 10-13.

*Listing 10-13. Registering PLAYERJUMP_EVENT in DroidRunnerLevel Constructor*

```
DroidRunnerLevel::DroidRunnerLevel()
        :       m_pPlayerMovementComponent(NULL)
        ,       m_pPlayerTransformComponent(NULL)
        ,       m_pPlayerCollisionComponent(NULL)
        ,       m_levelEnd(0.0f)
        ,       m_initialized(false)
        ,       m_levelBuilt(false)
{
        m_levelObjects.reserve(64);

        RegisterEvent(PLAYERJUMP_EVENT);
}
```

With our event registered, we now create our sound effects and attach the messages in DroidRunnerLevel::Initialize. Listing 10-14 shows how to create two sound effects: a jump effect and an explosion effect that represents the impact of a player hitting a wall or an AI character.

*Listing 10-14. DroidRunnerLevel::Initialize*

```
        .
        .
        .

        CollisionManager::GetSingleton().AddCollisionBin();

        BuildLevelData();

        Renderer* pRenderer = Renderer::GetSingletonPtr();
        if (pRenderer)
        {
                pRenderer->AddShader(&m_shader);
        }

        AudioManager& audioManager = AudioManager::GetSingleton();
        std::string jumpEffectName("sounds/jump.ogg");
        m_jumpHandle = audioManager.CreateSFX(jumpEffectName);
        AttachEvent(PLAYERJUMP_EVENT, *this);
```

```
        std::string explosionEffectName("sounds/impact.ogg");
        m_explosionHandle = audioManager.CreateSFX(explosionEffectName);

    m_initialized = true;
}
```

We look at where we play both of these sound effects in Listing 10-15 and the method
DroidRunnerLevel::HandleEvent.

*Listing 10-15. Playing Sounds in DroidRunnerLevel::HandleEvent*

```
void DroidRunnerLevel::HandleEvent(Event* pEvent)
{
    if (pEvent->GetID() == POSTUPDATE_EVENT)
    {
        bool endLevel = false;

        if (m_pPlayerTransformComponent)
        {
            if (m_pPlayerTransformComponent->GetTransform().GetTranslation().m_x >
                m_levelEnd)
            {
                endLevel = true;
            }
        }

        if (m_pPlayerMovementComponent && m_pPlayerMovementComponent->IsDead())
        {
            AudioManager* pAudioManager = AudioManager::GetSingletonPtr();
            if (pAudioManager)
            {
                pAudioManager->PlaySFX(m_explosionHandle);
            }
            endLevel = true;
        }

        if (endLevel)
        {
            CleanLevel();
            BuildLevelData();
        }

        if (m_pPlayerCollisionComponent)
        {
            CollisionManager::GetSingleton().TestAgainstBin(
                0,
                m_pPlayerCollisionComponent);
        }
    }
}
```

```
        else if (pEvent->GetID() == PLAYERJUMP_EVENT)
        {
                AudioManager* pAudioManager = AudioManager::GetSingletonPtr();
                if (pAudioManager)
                {
                        pAudioManager->PlaySFX(m_jumpHandle);
                }
        }
}
```

The new code in HandleEvent plays the two sound effects. The first plays m_explosionHandle when the player has died; the second plays the m_jumpHandle when the player jumps. Our new PLAYERJUMP_EVENT is sent from the method MovementComponent::HandleEvent. We look at this in Listing 10-16.

*Listing 10-16. Updating MovementComponent::HandleEvent*

```
void MovementComponent::HandleEvent(Event* pEvent)
{
        if (m_isDead)
        {
                return;
        }

        if (pEvent->GetID() == JUMP_EVENT)
        {
                TransformComponent* pTransformComponent =
                        component_cast<TransformComponent>(GetOwner());
                assert(pTransformComponent);
                if (pTransformComponent &&
                        m_isSupported)
                {
                        static const float JUMP_ACCELERATION = 220.0f;
                        m_acceleration.m_y = JUMP_ACCELERATION;
                        SendEvent(PLAYERJUMP_EVENT);
                }
        }
        else if (pEvent->GetID() == UPDATE_EVENT)
        .
        .
        .
```

Our one new line in this method is to call SendEvent on PLAYERJUMP_EVENT. Now every time this method is called, our jump effect will be triggered.

# Summary

We have now covered all of the basics required to create a game engine when using the Android NDK. This chapter covered adding audio to our engine using the OpenSL ES API.

We have looked at the basics of the physics of sound to try to understand how we can alter the frequency and amplitude of basic sound waves to create sound effects using Audacity. Audacity is an excellent free tool and has many different filters which can be applied to create all sorts of sound effects.

Once we had created some sound effects, we looked at the code for initializing OpenSL ES. While Android provides a Java interface for playing sound effects, OpenSL ES provides the native interface for doing the same.

This chapter has seen the completion of the core functionality of the game engine framework which we have been creating in this book. We now have a renderer which uses OpenGL ES 2.0 to create a 3D scene using geometry, shaders, textures, lighting, and perspective projection. The engine also has functionality to support audio playback and modern features such as a component-based system for creating game objects and an event-based system for communicating between different objects and systems.

This engine will give you a good foundation to create a shippable title for Android. The next chapter will look at how we can use the Google Developer Console to do just that.

# Chapter 11

# Self-Publishing 101

Once you have built your app and are happy with the contents and quality, it's time to publish your work on the Google Play Store. The Play Store is Google's official distribution network for Android developers. It's worth noting that it's not the only option but it is definitely the easiest and most visible option for distributing all types of apps on Android.

Distributing apps via the Play Store is not free; like any retailer, Google makes money from every app sold. Google's fee is 30% of the sales price after tax. It's worth bearing this in mind whenever you are doing any calculations with regards to working out how much to charge for your app.

Getting ready to sell your app is an exciting time but it can also be daunting. There are many tasks which need to be completed before your app can show up in the Play Store. The purpose of this chapter is to take a look at what those are.

## The Google Play Developer Console

Before you can get your app on the Google Play Store you must register as a developer. Google charges a one-time fee of $25 to register as a developer and obtain a Google Play Developer Console account. The page to sign up can be found here: https://support.google.com/googleplay/android-developer/answer/113468.

The Google Play Developer Console is a full-featured web app to control the distribution of your app. This is where you will upload your app, upload updates, set pricing, upload marketing material, and see your number of downloads and revenue.

Before we can upload any apps to the Developer Console we must create secure, signed versions of our app.

## Keys, Keystore, and Digital Signatures

The Play Store uses digital signatures to verify the authenticity of apps which are uploaded via the Google Play Developer Console. The basis of the signature process lies in the public-private key system which is also used in some forms of encryption.

Keys used for these purposes come in pairs: the public key and the private key. The private key is a file which you must keep secure. Private keys allow you to create encrypted messages or signatures which you can then share with others. The public key is a file which you can share with others to allow them to unecrypt this data. In the Android ecosystem, the APKs themselves are simple zip files which can be opened by any capable program. These are not encrypted but the application will have a digital signature included. This signature includes data which is encrypted with the private key you create and includes the public key so that others can read the signature. This two-step process allows the Android OS on a device to validate that an app is legitimate. If the signature cannot be read using the supplied public key, or if the data it contains cannot be recreated from the data contained within the APK, the OS can be sure that the app is not legitimate. The exact process which Google uses to create signatures for Android APKs is not available to the public; this in itself is an added layer of security.

Keystores are the files used to provide public-private key signatures for use with your APKs. A keystore may contain multiple aliases; each alias represents a public-private key pair. The entire keystore is also password encrypted. This configuration allows you to create different public-private key pairs for each app which you plan to release and to easily manage these keys by storing them within a single keystore.

At this point, you may be wondering why the applications need to be signed in this way. Essentially it is a method for securing your identity. By signing the applications with your private key, of which you have the only unique copy, Google can trust that any applications uploaded using this key are new versions of the same application and safe to upload to users. This prevents others from being able to hijack your applications and upload compromised APKs to the store.

Keys used to encrypt data being transmitted via the Internet are generally issued by an authorized certificate authority. Certificate authorities are organizations which provide third-party verification of public keys. Web browsers contain built-in lists of certificate authorities who are on trusted lists and are contacted by the program to verify that a key is legitimate and should to be used. Android does not require that APKs be signed by keys provided by a certificate authority. It is acceptable to create your own keys which you generate using the tools supplied with the Android SDK. You can only be sure that your APKs are safe, however, if you properly secure your own keys. Make sure that you keep them in a safe location and never share your keystore or your passwords.

# Signing an APK for the Play Store

When you create an app for the Play Store, you must package it into an Android application package file (APK), which is Google's distribution format. This format is Google's proprietary format but is essentially a zip file and can be opened using a utility such as 7-Zip.

Every time you have built an app during the process of reading through this book, the ADT plug-in for Eclipse has been automatically creating APKs and transferring them to your device. All Android apps must be signed, the ADT plug-in signs these debug APKs with a debug key. The Google Play Developer Console will show an error if you try to upload an APK signed with a debug key to the Play Store.

1.  To be able to upload an app to the Play Store, we must create a version which is signed with a unique key. The Android SDK contains methods for achieving this and the ADT plugin provides an easy-to-use wizard to aid in this process. The following instructions will walk you through the process of creating an APK signed with a unique key which you can use to upload to the Google Play Store. Run Eclipse and open your project in the Project Explorer window.

2.  Right-click your project folder and select the Export Signed Application Package… option under the Android Tools menu. The menu option is shown in Figure 11-1. Selecting this option will cause the Export wizard to begin to create your signed APK.

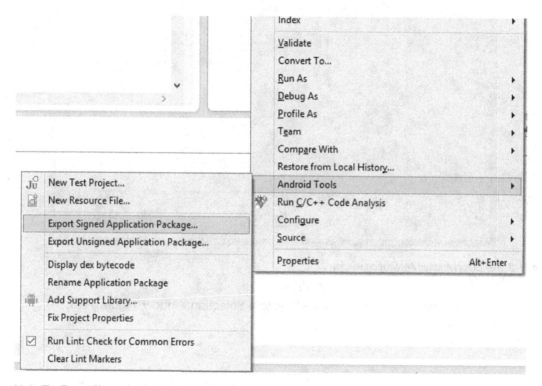

*Figure 11-1. The Export Signed Application Package option*

3.  In the wizard, select the project which you are going to use to export the APK. If you right-clicked the project you would like to export, the name should already be entered. Figure 11-2 shows the Export Android Application window.

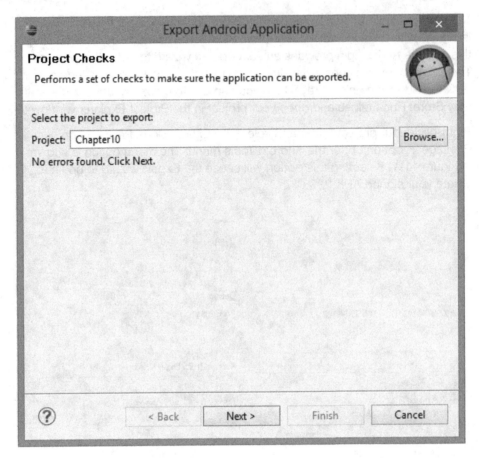

*Figure 11-2. The Export Android Application window*

4.  Click Next; you will be taken to the Keystore Selection window. Figure 11-3 shows this dialog.

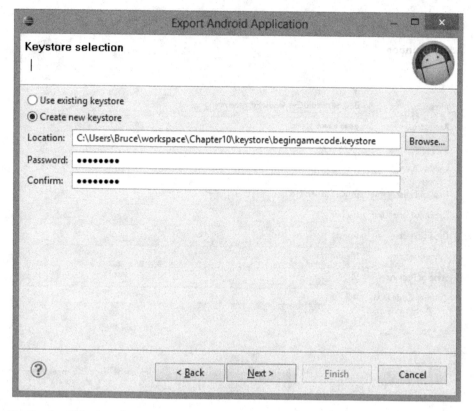

*Figure 11-3.* *The Keystore Selection window*

5.  Select the radio button for "Create new keystore" if this is the first time you have exported an Android application. Otherwise, you will want to select "Use existing keystore."

Figure 11-4 shows the Key Creation window. This window is used to enter the information used to identify the owner of the key.

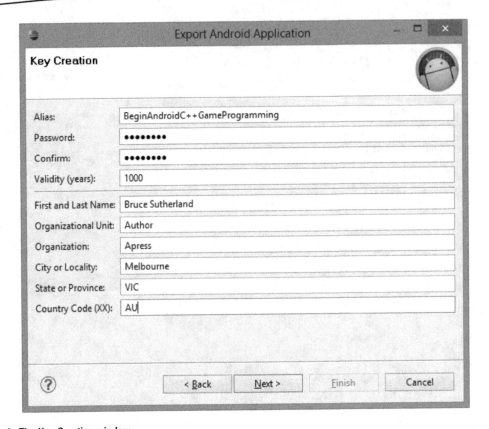

*Figure 11-4. The Key Creation window*

The Key Creation window requires that you supply some detailed information about the owner of the keystore.

The alias is most likely to be the name of the company or organization which is releasing the game.

A password is also required for the alias.

Keys expire; therefore, selecting a long-validity period is essential to ensure that your keystore's validity does not expire while you are likely to still be using it. Google recommends a minimum validity period of 25 years in its documentation, which can be found at `http://developer.android.com/tools/publishing/app-signing.html`. An expired key does not prevent your app from being used on user's devices but it does prevent you from issuing updates to your app. If your key were to expire, you would need to register a new app to issue updates.

Then, the personal details for an employee or company director should be entered. The candidate for this is an easy selection in a one-person operation.

Figure 11-5 shows the last step of the export process, which is to select an output location for your exported APK.

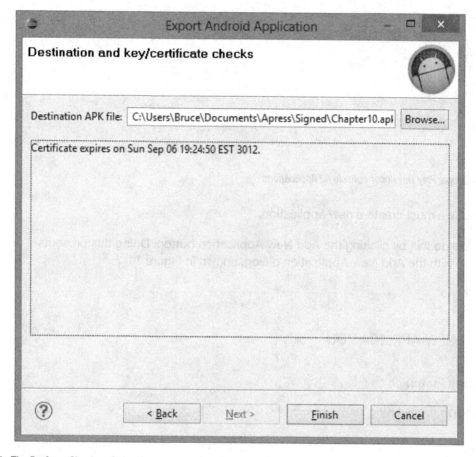

*Figure 11-5.  The Perform Checks window*

This last window performs some last-minute error checking on your keystore and will list any errors which are found. More often than not, there will be no errors, as in Figure 11-5.

Once you click Finish, your APK will be written to your selected location and will be ready for upload to the Play Store Developer Console.

# Uploading to the Google Play Developer Center

The Google Play Developer Console is your portal to the Play Store. This web app is provided by Google to allow developers easy access to their distribution channel without needing to form complicated publishing agreements. This is ideal for small developers, as it allows self-publishing without needing an external relationship with a publishing partner.

The first step in having your game appear on the Play Store is to create a new application in the Developer Console. The Developer Console can be found at the following URL: http://play.google.com/apps/publish.

When you first log in, your console will be empty and appear as it does in Figure 11-6.

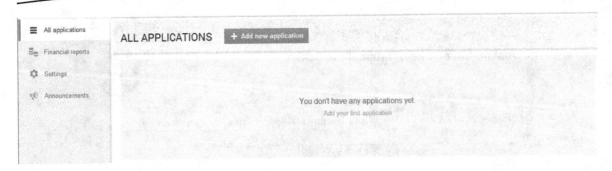

*Figure 11-6. Google Play Developer console All Applications*

At this point, we must create a new application.

1.  We do this by clicking the Add New Application button. Doing this presents us with the Add New Application dialog, shown in Figure 11-7.

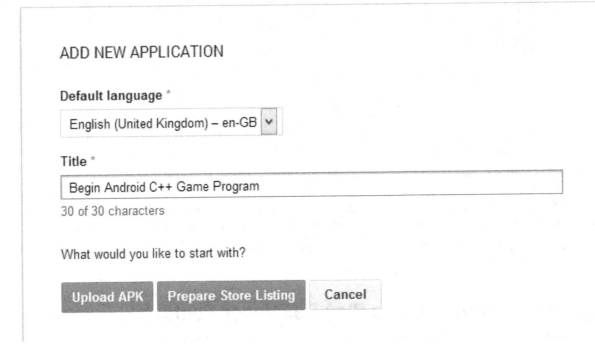

*Figure 11-7. The Add New Application dialog*

2.  This dialog allows us to select the default language for our application and the app's title. There are two options which we can now take: Upload APK and Prepare Store Listing. Figure 11-8 shows the screen which appears after selecting Upload APK. This screen now consists of the title for our app and screens which allow us to control our Store Listing, Pricing and Distribution, In-app products, and Services and APIs.

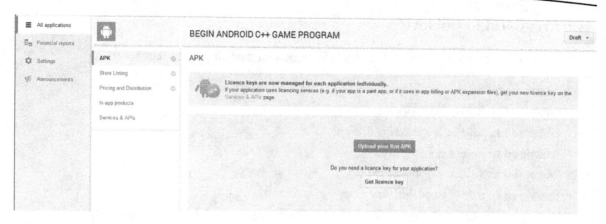

*Figure 11-8. The APK screen*

3. When you select Upload, the web application will present a dialog where you can drag and drop your APK file. Once you have done this, you will see the progress bar shown in Figure 11-9.

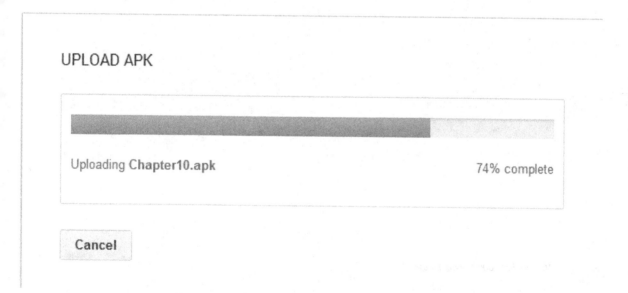

*Figure 11-9. Upload APK progress bar*

Once the APK has finished uploading, your app will be in the draft state. This means that it has been set up and configured on the Play Store but not yet "live."

Before you can make your app appear in the Play Store listings on users' devices, you must finishing configuring the details needed to list the app in the store. The Developer Console provides a list of this information in the Why Can't I Publish dialog box. We look at this list in Figure 11-10.

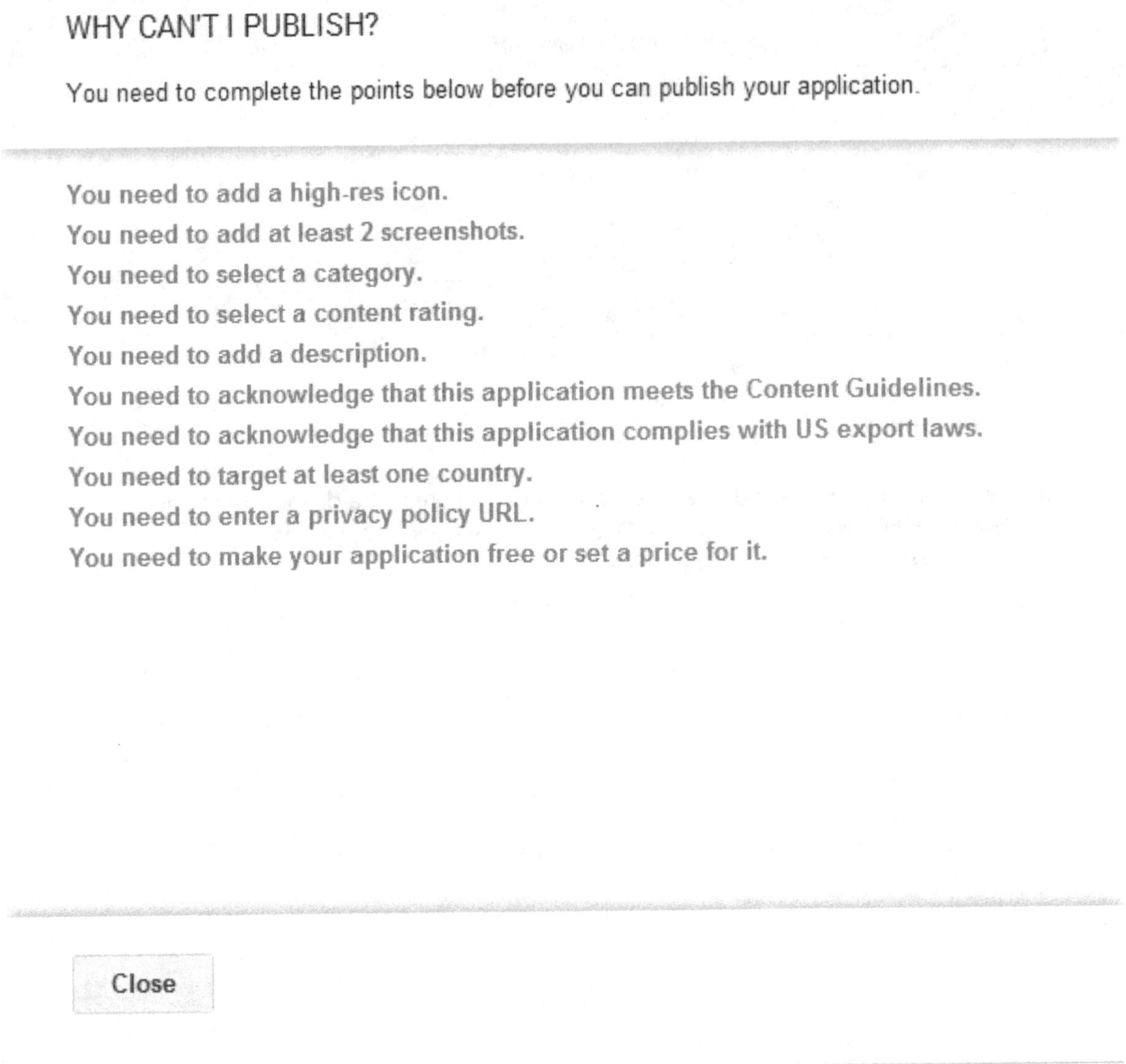

## WHY CAN'T I PUBLISH?

You need to complete the points below before you can publish your application.

You need to add a high-res icon.

You need to add at least 2 screenshots.

You need to select a category.

You need to select a content rating.

You need to add a description.

You need to acknowledge that this application meets the Content Guidelines.

You need to acknowledge that this application complies with US export laws.

You need to target at least one country.

You need to enter a privacy policy URL.

You need to make your application free or set a price for it.

Close

*Figure 11-10. The Why Can't I Publish dialog*

As you can see, there are quite a few steps which must still be completed before you can push your app into the live Play Store environment.

The icon and screenshots are essential to your listing. These attract customers and should be created with a purpose of showing your game in its best light. You should take a look at some of the listings of the most popular apps and games and try to determine if there are any particular trends which may be contributing to their success. It's also important to select the appropriate category for your app and a description which entices people to play your game.

These details are supplied via the Store Listing screen. The title of your app can be changed here and can consist of up to 30 characters. It's also possible to provide translations for different languages.

Your description can be up to 4,000 characters long. It's important to provide an enticing introduction to your app in the description. The description will convey the type of gameplay and experience the player can expect to have when downloading your app. It's also possible to provide a list of the latest updates which are included in your app if this is not the first release in the recent changes section.

The graphic assets are vitally important to the success of your app. While not all players will read the lengthy description of your app, almost all users will look at the screenshots which you provide. It's important to provide screenshots which show the graphics of your game in their best light and also some screenshots which show the gameplay of your app. Google has also provided a link to a Youtube video for your game. If you have created a trailer for the app, it would be a very good idea to upload this to Youtube and include the link with your store listing. The Google Play Store app will automatically embed the Youtube video you supply into your store listing. Providing all of the requested assets at any given time is important if you wish to be featured in the Play Store. It's important to periodically check the required assets, as Google is known to change and update these to suit different types of devices and resolutions. If the Play Store app or website changes, then you will be less likely to be featured if you have not provided the assets Google needs to show your app off on their new layout.

Selecting the appropriate category is important for your game. This category determines where in the Play Store your app will be listed. Selecting an accurate category will help people find your game when they are looking for apps of that type. You can expect your game to be more successful due to the category properly targeting your users.

It's likely that you will have a website to promote your company or your app. Google requires that you provide a URL to your privacy policy, so it's a good idea to think about what you would like this important declaration to contain. Sites such as `http://www.docracy.com/mobileprivacy/` can be used as a good starting point, but it's important that your privacy policy covers all of the ways in which you may be using your users data.

# Monetization

The Developer Console is also the place where you will set up the monetization strategy for your app. The traditional business model where apps are sold for a price is available, and you can set the price for your app in the Pricing and Distribution section of the Google Play Developer Console.

When setting a price, you initially set the default price for your application in your own local currency. This is the price for your app excluding local sales tax. You then have the choice to automatically convert the price of the app to all of the foreign markets which you choose to support. The Google Play Developer Console currently supports distribution in 135 different countries. It is also possible for you to set specific prices for some of these countries in their local currencies. Certain countries also support limiting distribution to specific mobile network operators.

> **Caution**   It's also entirely possible to set your app to be free. Make sure that this is something which you wish to do before finalizing the setting; changing your app's price to free cannot be reversed.

Another option for making money with your app is to support in-app purchases. There are two types of in-app purchases, permanent purchases and consumables. Downloadable content packs, which include levels, weapons, characters, or cars, can be considered as permanent purchases. With this type of purchase, a player pays once for the content and it permanently belongs to them. The other type of purchase is consumables. An example of this may be health potions. A user may buy a potion but once it is used they would be required to buy another. Getting the balance of cost and benefits of in-app purchases is a delicate and complicated topic but is one which can reap rewards for a developer who gets it right. The decisions you eventually make with regards to how much to charge will include factors such as the cost of development, your expected return, and also how much you believe customers will be willing to spend for the product you have produced. There are no easy methods to determine how you should make these decisions; however, an excellent starting point on the theory of pricing can be found at `http://book.personalmba.com/pricing-uncertainty-principle/`.

Last but not least are subscriptions. Google now offers subscription services and billing via the Play Store. This could allow developers to create massively multiplayer online (MMO)–type experiences on mobile platforms. If you believe your game could sustain players for a considerable period of time, then this may be a viable option.

Once you have released your game and begin having users make purchases, data will begin to appear in the Financial Reports sections of the Play Store. This allows you to track the revenue which your app is making. You can use this section to determine if new features, updates, or publicity is making any impact on the revenue generated by your app.

# App Quality

The Google Play Developer Console is also able to provide you with crash data from your application, data on App Not Responding notifications to users, and other recommendations for optimizing your store listing.

It's important to take any suggestions made by the Developer Console seriously. These recommendations and notices help indicate areas where your application may not meet the standards of other applications, thus reducing the rating of your app. High ratings and high quality listings are key to gaining traction among users and possibly even being featured in the Play Store. Being featured by Google in the Play Store will make a massive difference to the earning potential of your game.

The quality of your applications can be improved over time in a number of ways, and this can tie into an overall strategy for increasing your user base and revenues. In the past, it was common for game developers to develop every part of a game title before launch. This was especially true for cartridge-based games and disc-based games, which were distributed on physical media.

Today, the Internet has opened brand-new methods of game development for developers. The Internet has allowed developers to create games gradually by building minimum viable versions of their games and releasing them to the public. Feedback is then received from people who play the games and developers can follow paths of development which their users have found interesting.

A perfect current example of this is *Minecraft*. *Minecraft* was developed as a very minimal product in the initial stages. Each new release has added more and more content and gameplay elements to build the product up into something which is a modern phenomenon and a massively successful title. While it won't be possible for every game to reach the levels of success which *Minecraft* has achieved, it is a business model and development practice which smaller, independent studios should be looking to emulate as opposed to developing full titles with large budgets and lots of risk.

To support this type of development, I recommend using a three-part game versioning system which categorizes builds using the major, minor, and maintenance method. An example of such a version number would be 1.0.1.

The major version of the preceding build is 1.0 should be used for prerelease builds such as alpha and beta builds which are given to internal or external testers. Build 1 should be the first public release of a title.

The minor version here is 0. Minor versions are generally useful for updates which include new content. The mechanics and structure of the game are likely the same between minor versions, but new content has been added which denotes that the game is a reasonable update over the previous minor revision.

The maintenance number should be used to indicate versions which contain only bug fixes. It is common for titles to ship with bugs. Some of these bugs will be serious and some will be minor, but it is good for developers to issue updates to resolve bugs which are frustrating users. Players have taken to using the Google Play 5-star rating system to encourage developers to fix bugs in their games. If you take a look at the reviews for any top title in the Play Store, it won't be long before you come across some comments from users letting the developer know that they would score the game with a higher score if a certain bug which frustrates them could be fixed.

The last point is especially important to game developers. Google will feature apps which are popular, are of high quality, and receive good reviews. Any developer who would like to have their game featured in the Play Store by Google should absolutely be responding to the feedback supplied by Google in the Developer Console and to the reviews of users who may be unhappy with a certain aspect of your game.

# Summary

This chapter has covered the final step of taking an app from development to distribution. We have looked at the process of signing an APK for distribution and creating a keystore to uploading to the Developer Console. Lastly, we looked at the options available to developers to monetize their game products.

Shipping a product is not the end of the journey for a game title. For independent, small developers finishing the game code and putting the app on sale is just the end of the first stage of the game business cycle. At this point it's important to begin to learn what players of the game think and feel about the product and make changes and updates to the app on a regular basis to maintain interest and create a dedicated following.

Some of the biggest games on the Android platform do not follow the old style of game development, where the game is finished up front then put out for sale. It's more common now for successful games to ship and then grow to a large committed user base.

It's an exciting time to be an independent developer. Services such as the Play Store allow anyone with the skill and determination to create commercially successful games without necessarily having a large budget or team.

# Using the Android Development Environment

Google provides the Android SDK to developers to allow them to create apps for the Android platform. The SDK contains all of the tools and libraries necessary to create applications which can be deployed to Android devices. Google also provides the Android Native Development Kit (NDK). The NDK is used to create native code libraries which can execute much more efficiently than Java code. This is important for certain applications such as games. This appendix will walk through the process of setting up the Android SDK, the Eclipse IDE, and Android NDK and then building a sample app.

## Setting Up the Android SDK and Eclipse

Google provides their SDK and the Eclipse IDE in a single preconfigured download. At the time of writing this can be found at `http://developer.android.com/sdk/index.html`.

These bundles and software versions update reasonably frequently. You can find the latest installation instructions for the bundle at the following web address: `http://developer.android.com/sdk/installing/bundle.html`.

Once you have the bundle installed, it is time to try building a Java app. The process for building a Java app is the basis for building apps using the NDK. Google provides up-to=date instructions for building your first Android SDK based app here: `http://developer.android.com/training/basics/firstapp/index.html`.

## Installing the Android NDK

The Android NDK is a stand-alone suite of libraries and command-line tools which are downloaded separately from the Android SDK. The appropriate version of the NDK for your platform can be downloaded from `http://developer.android.com/tools/sdk/ndk/index.html`.

Once you have downloaded the compressed package for the NDK, you should extract it to a suitable folder on your computer.

Once we have installed the NDK, we need to let Eclipse know where the NDK folder has been placed on our computer. We can do this by launching the preferences dialog by selecting the Window (the Application on OS X) ➤ Preferences option. Once we have the Preferences dialog open, we can set the NDK location by browsing to Android ➤ NDK and then setting the NDK Location field.

# Building a Native App

Before we can build an example native app, we need to create a project in Eclipse to hold the code.

1.  When we first run Eclipse, we will be shown the welcome screen as in Figure A-1.

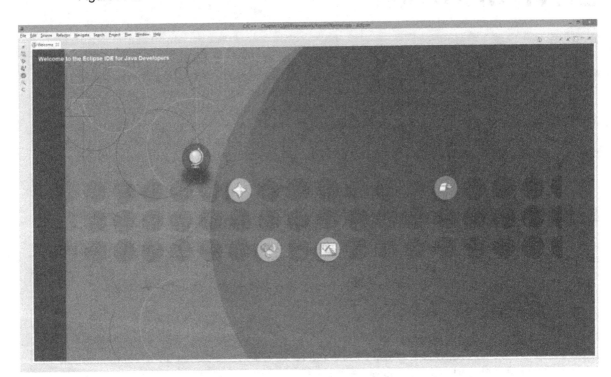

*Figure A-1. The Eclipse welcome screen*

2.  We then create a new project by Selecting File ➤ New ➤ Project. This will show the New Project dialog which we see in Figure A-2.

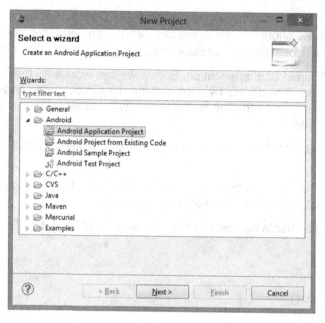

**Figure A-2.** *The New Project dialog*

3.  After clicking Next, we will be presented with the New Android Application dialog. Figure A-3 shows this dialog with the Application Name, Project Name, and Package Name fields all set. We also set the Minimum Required SDK field to API 9 and the Theme to None.

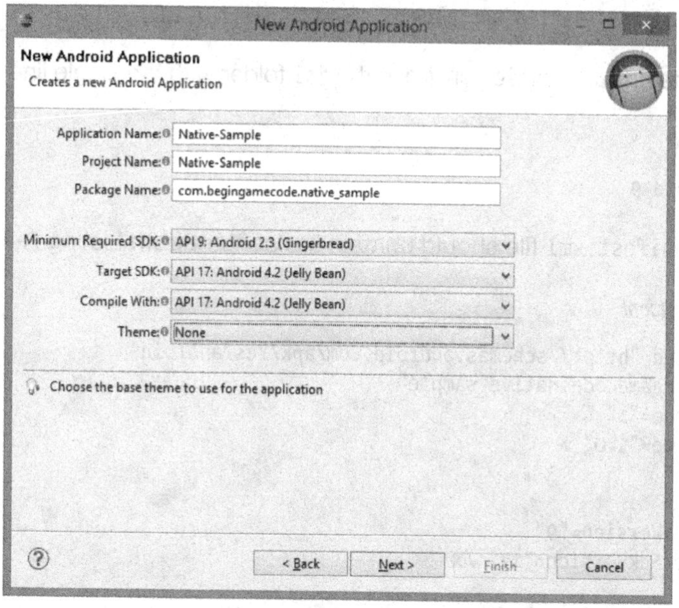

**Figure A-3.** *The New Android Application dialog*

4.  After clicking Next, we will be presented with the Configure Project dialog.
    In this dialog, we should uncheck the Create Custom Launcher icons and
    Create Activity icons. Finally, we click Finish.

We now have a basic Android SDK application. Before we can work with the NDK, we must add
NDK support to the project. You do this by right-clicking the project name and then selecting
Android Tools ➤ Add Native Support. The dialog shown will contain a library name: leave this
at the default value and click Finish.

At this point, we will be able to right-click the project name and select Build Project to have Android
build the default code.

At this point, let's copy the contents of `main.c` from the `native-activity` sample found in the
samples directory of the Android NDK into `Native-Sample.cpp`.

Listing A-1 contains the contents we need to place in your `Android.mk` file. This file can be found
in the `jni` folder.

*Listing A-1.  Android.mk*

```
LOCAL_PATH := $(call my-dir)

include $(CLEAR_VARS)

LOCAL_MODULE     := native-activity
LOCAL_SRC_FILES := Native-Sample.cpp
LOCAL_LDLIBS     := -llog -landroid -lEGL -lGLESv1_CM
LOCAL_STATIC_LIBRARIES := android_native_app_glue

include $(BUILD_SHARED_LIBRARY)

$(call import-module,android/native_app_glue)
```

You also need to create an `Application.mk` file in the `jni` folder with the single line shown in Listing A-2.

*Listing A-2.  Application.mk*

```
APP_PLATFORM := android-9
```

Finally, the `AndroidManifest.xml` file should contain the content from Listing A-3.

*Listing A-3.  AndroidManifest.xml*

```
<manifest xmlns:android="http://schemas.android.com/apk/res/android"
    package="com.begingamecode.native_sample"
    android:versionCode="1"
    android:versionName="1.0" >

    <uses-sdk
        android:minSdkVersion="9"
        android:targetSdkVersion="17" />
```

```
<application
    android:allowBackup="true"
    android:icon="@drawable/ic_launcher"
    android:label="@string/app_name"
    android:theme="@style/AppTheme" >

    <activity
        android:label="@string/app_name"
        android:configChanges="orientation|keyboardHidden"
        android:name="android.app.NativeActivity">
            <!-- Tell NativeActivity the name of or .so -->
            <meta-data
                android:name="android.app.lib_name"
                android:value="native-activity"/>
            <intent-filter>
                <action android:name="android.intent.action.MAIN"/>
                <category android:name="android.intent.category.LAUNCHER"/>
            </intent-filter>
    </activity>
</application>
</manifest>
```

With everything configured, we can now right-click the project and select Run As ➤ Android Application to have the application run on your chosen device or emulator.

# Android Hardware Overview

Unsurprisingly, the Android operating system runs on computer hardware. Developers for other mobile platforms can rely on supporting a single CPU architecture, instruction set, and GPU type. Android developers do not have this luxury if they would like to maximize the reach of their apps.

We take a look at the major CPU and GPU architectures in used on the Android platform in this appendix.

## CPU Architectures

There are currently three major CPU architectures in use on the Android platform today. These are based on the ARM, MIPS, and x86 instruction sets.

## ARM

ARM currently enjoys the position of being the dominant CPU architecture in the mobile space. The ARM architecture was originally created in the 1980s by Acorn for use in desktop computer systems. In recent years, ARM has been more commonly known as a designer of CPU instruction sets and architectures and has not manufactured its own CPUs.

There are currently two different types of ARM licensee. Companies can either license the design of an entire CPU which they can then fabricate for their devices or they can obtain a license to the architecture itself and then design their own CPUs.

ARM's most popular licensed CPUs at the moment are the Cortex-A9 and the Cortex-A15. The Cortex-A9 is an older and less flexible design which can be found in many modern smartphones and architectures today. The Tegra 3 platform from NVIDIA contained a quad-core Cortex-A9 CPU, and phones such as the Galaxy Nexus contained dual-core A9s.

The Cortex-A15 is a more powerful CPU which runs at higher temperatures and uses more power than the A9. To date, it has been used only in high-end products such as the Nexus 10, Samsung Galaxy S4 Octal-core variant, and the upcoming Tegra 4 chipset from NVIDIA.

Qualcomm creates their own CPUs based on an ARM architecture license. The Snapdragon system on chip (SoC) parts which the company manufactures are found in many modern devices. A high-profile example is the Nexus 4 smartphone.

## MIPS

There is not much to say on the MIPS front when it comes to Android, as there are not many devices which currently use this architecture. MIPS as a company, however, has a rich history in the games business. Consoles such as Playstation, Playstation 2, and Nintendo 64 all have CPUs created by MIPS.

More recently, MIPS was purchased by Imagination Technologies, the company behind the PowerVR GPUs. The Android NDK supports building for the MIPS architecture, and this is a CPU which may be used in more devices in the future.

## x86

The x86 architecture has a long-established role in desktop and laptop computers. To date, there has not been much of a presence for x86 on the mobile scene. This may be about to change, as Intel has been making massive strides in power efficiency and performance with their Atom range of processors. This year, their Haswell architectures will be even more power efficient, and in the coming years we may begin to see a convergence of Intel's desktop and mobile processors. At that point, ensuring that your games work on x86 will be important.

## GPU Architectures

Android supports the OpenGL ES APIs from Khronos, which allows our games to target graphics drivers as an external chip, which we do not need to concern ourselves with. This has been a perfectly fine approach for the purposes of learning the basics of creating games with the NDK in this book; however, creating high-performance games on Android requires a deeper understanding of the available GPU architectures.

## PowerVR

The most common PowerVR GPU chipset is currently the SGX range of chips. PowerVR GPUs have a unique architecture in the GPU world. The unique selling point of these chips is their tile-based deferred rendering engine. We'll break that phrase down to understand how the PowerVR SGX operates.

The first phrase to consider is tile based. The SGX works by splitting the screen up into a series of small tiles. When we submit a `glDrawElements` command to the driver, it carries out a process known as *binning*. Each draw command is binned into a tile. The tiles are then rendered in order with all of the draw commands which will affect that tile being executed. The benefit from this expensive step comes in the GPU itself. Rather than having to constantly access main memory to read depth values and write out pixel colors, the GPU contains a small amount of very fast on-chip memory. This memory is large enough to contain the data needed for reading and writing a single tile while processing this frame. The process of filling in the data needed to read from the tile (such as depth or stencil values) is known as a restore, and the process for writing out the data from the tile pass is known as a resolve.

The deferred part of the term involves PowerVR's unique Hidden Surface Removal (HSR) algorithm. When processing a tile, the GPU calculates the depth of the closest polygon to the camera before executing the fragment shaders. This completely eliminates overdraw for opaque objects and saves memory bandwidth by not having to sample textures for hidden polygons or write out their depth and colors as well as saving the fragment processing time associated with executing fragment shaders for pixels which will be overwritten.

The drawback to this approach is that it may limit performance on scenes with large numbers of vertices.

## Mali and Adreno

For the developer, the high-level architecture of the Mali and the Adreno are very similar. Both of these GPU architectures implement tile-based rendering. The draw commands are binned and executed per tile just like on PowerVR chips but they do not carry out the hidden surface removal step.

Instead, they execute the commands per tile in the order they were received. This is known as Immediate Mode Rendering (IMR). The GPU does, however, execute early-z rejection; therefore, the developer can improve performance in games where the GPU is a bottleneck by sorting geometry from the closest to the camera to the furthest away to reduce overdraw.

## Tegra

Last but not least is NVIDIA's Tegra architecture. Tegra works much more like a traditional desktop GPU compared to the others in that it does not use tiled rendering. It simply executes all rendering commands in the order in which they were received. It also contains the early-z rejection testing and would benefit from the front-to-back sorting of geometry.

# C++ Programming

C++ is a programming language which provides an almost infinite number of options for solving problems. This book uses some techniques which may not be familiar to beginner programmers. This appendix aims to cover some of the more advanced language features used.

## The Friend Keyword

C++ classes can contain fields and methods which are of different scopes. These available scopes are public, private, and protected.

- Public scope ensures that all fields and methods can be accessed from outside the class itself.

- Private fields and methods can be accessed only from methods which are also declared in the same class.

- Protected fields and methods are similar to private but can also be accessed by derived classes.

It is often desirable to be able to access private fields or methods from outside a class but only in restricted places. These restricted places may be other classes or functions. One method to achieve this would be to make the fields and methods public; however, this allows any class or function access. Another option is to use the `friend` keyword. Consider the class shown in Listing C-1.

*Listing C-1. A Simple Class*

```
class Simple
{
private:
        void Interact();
}
```

As you can see, the Interact method is private and therefore could be accessed only from other methods inside this same class. If we had another class with which we would like to be able to access this method, we could make it a friend, as in Listing C-2.

*Listing C-2. Simple Class' Friend*

```
class SimpleFriend
{
public:
        void Interact(Simple* pSimple)
        {
                pSimple->Interact();
        }
}

class Simple
{
        friend class SimpleFriend;

private:
        void Interact();
}
```

Listing C-2 shows how we can use the friend keyword to provide access to private fields and data to specific classes.

# Templates

C++ is a type safe language. This means that the compiler must know the expected types of all variables at compile time. Sometimes this rigid use of types can lead to lots of duplicate code just to provide the same functionality to work on different types of objects. Fortunately, C++ provides a solution to this in the form of templates.

Templates allow us to create generic code implementations and specify the specific types when we need them in the code.

Listing C-3 shows two methods to return the minimum value of two numbers.

*Listing C-3. min Functions*

```
inline int min(int a, int b)
{
        return (a<b) ? a : b;
}

inline float min(float a, float b)
{
        return (a<b) ? a : b;
}
```

If we were to continue down this path, we would have to supply different versions of min for every type supported by C++. Instead, Listing C-4 shows how we can implement min using a template.

*Listing C-4. Templatized min*

```
template<class T>
inline const T& min(const T& a, const T& b)
{
        return (a < b) ? a : b;
}
```

Here you can see that we do not specify multiple versions of the function and that the types have been replaced with T. The T comes from the first line, which tells the compiler that this method is a template and to use T in place of specific types. If you change T to be something different, you will also need to change it in the function itself. Another difference in this template is that the function parameters and the return value are passed by reference. The original int and float methods returned built-in types and therefore were simple four-byte copies. As this template may be used with classes, it's important to pass by reference to ensure that the copy constructor is not invoked on these objects.

Now to the code which uses the template in Listing C-5.

*Listing C-5. Using Templates*

```
min<int>(1, 2);
min<float>(1.0f, 2.0f);
```

The code here shows that we can now specify the type of min which we would like to use where and when we need it. C++ will create specific versions of min only for the types which we actually use in our code.

# The Singleton Pattern

The code samples supplied with this book make use of the singleton pattern. The specific implementation of the pattern can be seen in the sample code, which can be obtained from this book's accompanying web site at http://www.apress.com/9781430258308.

The singleton pattern is used to provide global access to a single instance of an object throughout the code. Many people disagree with the use of global objects; however, they can provide useful features in game development. Renderers and audio managers, for example, are objects which we often need only a single instance of in game development.

By using a singleton, we can ensure that we have a single instance of these objects which we can access from anywhere in the code. Implementing singletons in a manner where we still must call new and delete on the object also means that we are in control of how and where the memory is allocated for the objects. The only global aspect of the objects is the static pointer which we use to access our instance.

The original author of the singleton class used was Scott Bilas. Scott has full source code and detailed explanations of the technique on his web site at http://scottbilas.com/publications/gem-singleton/.

# Appendix D

# C++ Math

Video games cannot be created without at least a basic understanding of math, especially geometry.

This appendix covers the basic math classes provided with the samples on this book's web site at http://www.apress.com/9781430258308.

## Vectors

A vector is used for two purposes: to represent displacement and direction.

Vectors in games can come in three different varieties: two-dimensional (2D), 3D, and 4D homogenous vectors. This book only makes use of 3D and 4D vectors.

Listing D-1 shows the class declaration for the 3D Vector3 class.

*Listing D-1. The Vector3 Class Declaration*

```cpp
class Vector3
{
public:
        float m_x;
        float m_y;
        float m_z;

        Vector3();
        Vector3(const float x, const float y, const float z);
        virtual ~Vector3();

        void      Set(const Vector3& in);
        void      Multiply(const float scalar);
        void      Divide(const float scalar);
        void      Add(const Vector3& in);
        void      Subtract(const Vector3& in);
        void      Negate();
```

```
float        Length() const;
float        LengthSquared() const;
void         Normalize();
void         GetNormal(Vector3& normal);

Vector3& operator=(const Vector3& in);
Vector3& operator=(const Vector4& in);

float        Dot(const Vector3& in) const;
Vector3      Cross(const Vector3& in) const;
};
```

The data stored in the Vector3 class is represented by three floats, one for each of the three cardinal axes: x, y, and z.

We then have a set of methods which can be used to work with the Vector3 class. Listing D-2 contains the constructors and destructor for Vector3.

*Listing D-2. Vector3 Constructors and Destructor*

```
Vector3::Vector3()
        :        m_x(0.0f)
        ,        m_y(0.0f)
        ,        m_z(0.0f)
{
}

Vector3::Vector3(const float x, const float y, const float z)
        :        m_x(x)
        ,        m_y(y)
        ,        m_z(z)
{
}

Vector3::~Vector3()
{
}
```

We also have a method, Set (Listing D-3), which overwrites the values in the vector.

*Listing D-3. Vector3::Set*

```
void Vector3::Set(const Vector3& in) {
        m_x = in.m_x;
        m_y = in.m_y;
        m_z = in.m_z;
}
```

Vectors can be multiplied and divided by floating point numbers. This has the effect of lengthening or shortening a vector. Multiplying a vector by two, for example, doubles the length of the vector. Listing D-4 shows these methods.

*Listing D-4. Vector3 Multiply and Divide*

```
void Vector3::Multiply(const float scalar) {
      m_x *= scalar;
      m_y *= scalar;
      m_z *= scalar;
}

void Vector3::Divide(const float scalar) {
      float divisor = 1.0f / scalar;
      m_x *= divisor;
      m_y *= divisor;
      m_z *= divisor;
}
```

Vectors can also be added and subtracted from other vectors. Listing D-5 shows the Add and Subtract methods.

*Listing D-5. Vector3 Add and Subtract*

```
void Vector3::Add(const Vector3& in) {
      m_x += in.m_x;
      m_y += in.m_y;
      m_z += in.m_z;
}

void Vector3::Subtract(const Vector3& in) {
      m_x -= in.m_x;
      m_y -= in.m_y;
      m_z -= in.m_z;
}
```

Another common operation which we carry out on vectors is to negate them. Listing D-6 shows the method which achieves this.

*Listing D-6. Vector3::Negate*

```
void Vector3::Negate()
{
      m_x = -m_x;
      m_y = -m_y;
      m_z = -m_z;
}
```

We use Pythagoras' theorem to calculate the length of a vector. The function to calculate the length of a hypotenuse in a triangle is as follows:

$$length\ of\ hypotenuse = \sqrt{(x^2 + y^2 + z^2)}$$

The standard implementation of Pythagoras' theorem includes a square root. Calculating the square root can be an expensive operation; therefore, we also implement a method to calculate the squared length of a vector. We can use this to determine if a vector is longer or shorter than another by comparing the squared lengths of both vectors. Listing D-7 shows the Length and LengthSquared methods.

*Listing D-7. Vector3 Length and LengthSquared*

```
float Vector3::Length() const
{
        return sqrt((m_x*m_x) + (m_y*m_y) + (m_z*m_z));
}

float Vector3::LengthSquared() const
{
        return (m_x*m_x) + (m_y*m_y) + (m_z*m_z);
}
```

A common variant of vectors which we use in games programming is the unit normal vector. A unit normal is a vector which represents a direction and has a length of one. These are useful as we can then use the fact that the normal has unit length in other situations. Listing D-8 shows the code necessary to obtain normal vectors from a Vector3 object.

*Listing D-8. Vector3 Normalize and GetNormal*

```
void Vector3::Normalize()
{
        Divide(Length());
}

void Vector3::GetNormal(Vector3& normal)
{
        normal = *this;
        normal.Normalize();
}
```

The dot (or scalar) product is an operation which is performed on two vectors. One of the most common uses for the dot product is to calculate the angle between those vectors. The details of the dot product are covered in Chapter 9. Listing D-9 describes the Vector3::Dot method.

*Listing D-9. Vector3::Dot*

```
float Vector3::Dot(const Vector3& in) const
{
        return (m_x * in.m_x) + (m_y * in.m_y) + (m_z * in.m_z);
}
```

The cross product is used to calculate a new vector which is perpendicular to the two input vectors. This is also covered in more detail in Chapter 9; however, the code is shown in Listing D-10.

*Listing D-10.  Vector3::Cross*

```
Vector3 Vector3::Cross(const Vector3& in) const
{
        return Vector3(
                (m_y * in.m_z) - (m_z * in.m_y),
                (m_z * in.m_x) - (m_x * in.m_z),
                (m_x * in.m_y) - (m_y * in.m_x));
}
```

4D vectors cover largely the same operations as 3D vectors with one small addition, the w component. This component is used to determine the difference between a displacement vector and a normal vector. When the w component of a 4D vector is set to 1, we are signifying that this vector is a positional vector, and when it is 0 we are signifying that it is a directional vector.

The significance of this change comes when we are multiplying the vectors by 4×4 transformation matrices. When the w component is set to 0, the vector will not be translated by the position elements of the 4×4 matrix.

# Matrices

Matrices are used in 3D game programming to represent transform information. A matrix can contain information suitable to increase or decrease the size of an object, rotate an object, and translate an object in 3D space. Listing D-11 contains the class declaration of the Matrix4 class.

*Listing D-11.  The Matrix4 Class Declaration*

```
class Matrix4
{
public:
        enum Rows
        {
                X,
                Y,
                Z,
                W,
                NUM_ROWS
        };

        float m_m[16];

        Matrix4();
        virtual ~Matrix4();

        void Identify();
        Vector3 Transform(const Vector3& in) const;
        Vector3 TransformTranspose(const Vector3& in) const;
        Vector4 Multiply(const Vector4& in) const;
        void RotateAroundX(float radians);
        void RotateAroundY(float radians);
        void RotateAroundZ(float radians);
        void Multiply(const Matrix4& in, Matrix4& out) const;
```

```
Matrix4 Transpose() const;

Matrix4& operator=(const Matrix3& in);
Matrix4& operator=(const Matrix4& in);

Vector4  GetRow(const Rows row) const;
};
```

The listing shows that our matrix contains 16 floating point values which can be represented as a set of 4 vectors each containing 4 elements, which gives us our 4×4 matrix. We have defined an enum, Rows, to represent the rows of the matrix.

# Identity Matrix

A special type of matrix is a diagonal matrix. This is a matrix where only the diagonal values are set. Each of the diagonal values in the identity matrix is 1. The identity matrix represents the matrix which leaves another matrix or vector unchanged when they are multiplied together. Listing D-12 shows the method Identify, which we use to set a matrix to be the identity matrix.

*Listing D-12. Matrix4::Identify*

```
void Matrix4::Identify()
{
        m_m[0] = 1.0f;
        m_m[1] = 0.0f;
        m_m[2] = 0.0f;
        m_m[3] = 0.0f;
        m_m[4] = 0.0f;
        m_m[5] = 1.0f;
        m_m[6] = 0.0f;
        m_m[7] = 0.0f;
        m_m[8] = 0.0f;
        m_m[9] = 0.0f;
        m_m[10] = 1.0f;
        m_m[11] = 0.0f;
        m_m[12] = 0.0f;
        m_m[13] = 0.0f;
        m_m[14] = 0.0f;
        m_m[15] = 1.0f;
}
```

# Rotation Matrices

It is possible to create rotation matrices which rotate around each of the cardinal axes. Listing D-13 shows the necessary code to create matrices which rotate around the x, y, and z axes.

*Listing D-13. Matrix4 Rotation Matrix Creation Methods*

```
void Matrix4::RotateAroundX(float radians)
{
        m_m[0] = 1.0f; m_m[1] = 0.0f; m_m[2] = 0.0f;
        m_m[4] = 0.0f; m_m[5] = cos(radians); m_m[6] = sin(radians);
        m_m[8] = 0.0f; m_m[9] = -sin(radians); m_m[10] = cos(radians);
}

void Matrix4::RotateAroundY(float radians)
{
        m_m[0] = cos(radians); m_m[1] = 0.0f; m_m[2] = -sin(radians);
        m_m[4] = 0.0f; m_m[5] = 1.0f; m_m[6] = 0.0f;
        m_m[8] = sin(radians); m_m[9] = 0.0f; m_m[10] = cos(radians);
}

void Matrix4::RotateAroundZ(float radians)
{
        m_m[0] = cos(radians); m_m[1] = sin(radians); m_m[2] = 0.0f;
        m_m[4] = -sin(radians); m_m[5] = cos(radians); m_m[6] = 0.0f;
        m_m[8] = 0.0f; m_m[9] = 0.0f; m_m[10] = 1.0f;
}
```

# Multiplying Matrices

Matrix operations can be combined; this process is known as concatenation and is achieved by multiplying matrices together. It's important to note that the order of operations when concatenating matrices is important. Rotating an object then translating it will give you different results compared to translating an object then rotating. Matrix4::Multiply is described in Listing D-14.

*Listing D-14. Matrix4::Multiply*

```
void Matrix4::Multiply(const Matrix4& in, Matrix4& out) const
{
        assert(this != &in && this != &out && &in != &out);
        out.m_m[0]
                = (m_m[0] * in.m_m[0]) +
                  (m_m[1] * in.m_m[4]) +
                  (m_m[2] * in.m_m[8]) +
                  (m_m[3] * in.m_m[12]);

        out.m_m[1]
                = (m_m[0] * in.m_m[1]) +
                  (m_m[1] * in.m_m[5]) +
                  (m_m[2] * in.m_m[9]) +
                  (m_m[3] * in.m_m[13]);

        out.m_m[2]
                = (m_m[0] * in.m_m[2]) +
                  (m_m[1] * in.m_m[6]) +
                  (m_m[2] * in.m_m[10]) +
                  (m_m[3] * in.m_m[14]);
```

```
out.m_m[3]
        = (m_m[0] * in.m_m[3]) +
          (m_m[1] * in.m_m[7]) +
          (m_m[2] * in.m_m[11]) +
          (m_m[3] * in.m_m[15]);

out.m_m[4]
        = (m_m[4] * in.m_m[0]) +
          (m_m[5] * in.m_m[4]) +
          (m_m[6] * in.m_m[8]) +
          (m_m[7] * in.m_m[12]);

out.m_m[5]
        = (m_m[4] * in.m_m[1]) +
          (m_m[5] * in.m_m[5]) +
          (m_m[6] * in.m_m[9]) +
          (m_m[7] * in.m_m[13]);

out.m_m[6]
        = (m_m[4] * in.m_m[2]) +
          (m_m[5] * in.m_m[6]) +
          (m_m[6] * in.m_m[10]) +
          (m_m[7] * in.m_m[14]);

out.m_m[7]
        = (m_m[4] * in.m_m[3]) +
          (m_m[5] * in.m_m[7]) +
          (m_m[6] * in.m_m[11]) +
          (m_m[7] * in.m_m[15]);

out.m_m[8]
        = (m_m[8] * in.m_m[0]) +
          (m_m[9] * in.m_m[4]) +
          (m_m[10] * in.m_m[8]) +
          (m_m[11] * in.m_m[12]);

out.m_m[9]
        = (m_m[8] * in.m_m[1]) +
          (m_m[9] * in.m_m[5]) +
          (m_m[10] * in.m_m[9]) +
          (m_m[11] * in.m_m[13]);

out.m_m[10]
        = (m_m[8] * in.m_m[2]) +
          (m_m[9] * in.m_m[6]) +
          (m_m[10] * in.m_m[10]) +
          (m_m[11] * in.m_m[14]);

out.m_m[11]
        = (m_m[8] * in.m_m[3]) +
          (m_m[9] * in.m_m[7]) +
          (m_m[10] * in.m_m[11]) +
          (m_m[11] * in.m_m[15]);
```

```
out.m_m[12]
        = (m_m[12] * in.m_m[0]) +
          (m_m[13] * in.m_m[4]) +
          (m_m[14] * in.m_m[8]) +
          (m_m[15] * in.m_m[12]);

out.m_m[13]
        = (m_m[12] * in.m_m[1]) +
          (m_m[13] * in.m_m[5]) +
          (m_m[14] * in.m_m[9]) +
          (m_m[15] * in.m_m[13]);

out.m_m[14]
        = (m_m[12] * in.m_m[2]) +
          (m_m[13] * in.m_m[6]) +
          (m_m[14] * in.m_m[10]) +
          (m_m[15] * in.m_m[14]);

out.m_m[15]
        = (m_m[12] * in.m_m[3]) +
          (m_m[13] * in.m_m[7]) +
          (m_m[14] * in.m_m[11]) +
          (m_m[15] * in.m_m[15]);
}
```

A matrix multiplication is an expensive process, as each row from the member's matrix and column from the input matrix which intersect at each element are used as vectors and the dot product is calculated at each position.

## Matrix Transpose

Another common operation in graphics programming is calculating the transpose of a matrix. This is done by switching a matrix's rows with its columns, and the method for this is shown in Listing D-15.

*Listing D-15. Matrix4::Transpose*

```
Matrix4 Matrix4::Transpose() const
{
        Matrix4 out;
        out.m_m[0]      = m_m[0];
        out.m_m[1]      = m_m[4];
        out.m_m[2]      = m_m[8];
        out.m_m[3]      = m_m[12];
        out.m_m[4]      = m_m[1];
        out.m_m[5]      = m_m[5];
        out.m_m[6]      = m_m[9];
        out.m_m[7]      = m_m[13];
        out.m_m[8]      = m_m[2];
        out.m_m[9]      = m_m[6];
        out.m_m[10]     = m_m[10];
        out.m_m[11]     = m_m[14];
```

```
    out.m_m[12]      = m_m[3];
    out.m_m[13]      = m_m[7];
    out.m_m[14]      = m_m[11];
    out.m_m[15]      = m_m[15];
}
```

The transpose of a matrix proves to be useful in graphics programming as the transpose of an orthogonal rotation matrix is also its inverse. Orthogonal matrices are covered in Chapter 6.

## Transforming Vectors

The last methods which make up the Matrix4 class are the Transform and TransformTranspose methods. These methods are used to multiply vectors by the matrix. Listing D-16 contains the code to achieve this.

*Listing D-16. Matrix4 Transform and TransformTranspose*

```
Vector3 Matrix4::Transform(const Vector3& in) const
{
    return Vector3((m_m[0] * in.m_x) + (m_m[1] * in.m_y) + (m_m[2] * in.m_z),
            (m_m[4] * in.m_x) + (m_m[5] * in.m_y) + (m_m[6] * in.m_z),
            (m_m[6] * in.m_x) + (m_m[7] * in.m_y) + (m_m[8] * in.m_z));
}

Vector3 Matrix4::TransformTranspose(const Vector3& in) const
{
    return Vector3((m_m[0] * in.m_x) + (m_m[3] * in.m_y) + (m_m[6] * in.m_z),
            (m_m[1] * in.m_x) + (m_m[4] * in.m_y) + (m_m[7] * in.m_z),
            (m_m[2] * in.m_x) + (m_m[5] * in.m_y) + (m_m[8] * in.m_z));
}
```

# Planes

Planes are used to separate space. They are flat and extend infinitely. Planes are useful for constructing shapes to determine if objects lie inside a space or outside. Planes are used in this book to implement view frustum culling in Chapter 8. Listing D-17 shows the class declaration of the Plane class.

*Listing D-17. The Plane Class Declaration*

```
class Plane
{
private:
    Vector3      m_normal;
    float        m_d;

public:
    Plane();
    Plane(const Vector3& point, const Vector3& normal);
    ~Plane();
```

```
        void BuildPlane(const Vector3& point, const Vector3& normal);

        bool IsInFront(const Vector4& point) const;
        bool IsInFront(const Vector3& point) const;
};
```

Our Plane class is very basic. We have need only for methods to build a plane and test if a point lies in front of the plane. We know if a point is behind the plane if it is not in front. The constructor which takes the Vector3 parameters simply calls BuildPlane, so we look at the code for BuildPlane in Listing D-18.

*Listing D-18. The Plane::BuildPlane Method*

```
void Plane::BuildPlane(const Vector3& point, const Vector3& normal)
{
        m_normal = normal;
        m_normal.Normalize();
        m_d      = m_normal.Dot(point);
}
```

BuildPlane uses trigonometry to calculate the plane constant d. The dot product is covered in detail Chapter 9. We know that the dot product's result is the length of the two vectors multiplied by the cosine of the angle between the vectors. In BuildPlane, we normalize the normal vector to ensure that the length of that vector is 1. This will mean that the result of our dot product is the length of the point vector multiplied by the cosine of the angle between the two. This gives us the length of the adjacent edge of the right-angled triangle between the line along the normal and the point vector. This length is the distance of the plane from the origin along the direction of the normal vector.

We can now use this to determine if other points are in front of or behind the plane. We do this in the IsInFront method, which we show in Listing D-19.

*Listing D-19. Plane::IsInFront*

```
bool Plane::IsInFront(const Vector4& point) const
{
        return IsInFront(Vector3(point.m_x, point.m_y, point.m_z));
}

bool Plane::IsInFront(const Vector3& point) const
{
        return m_normal.Dot(point) >= m_d;
}
```

The Vector4 version of IsInFront constructs a Vector3 from the m_x, m_y, and m_z fields of the Vector4 and calls the Vector3 version.

The Vector3 version of IsInFront simply calculates the dot product or the normal and the supplied point and determines if it is larger than the plane constant. If it is larger, then we know that this point lies in front of the plane.

# Index